The Stronghold

Miriam Haynie

The Stronghold

A Story of
Historic Northern Neck of Virginia
and Its People

By
MIRIAM HAYNIE

The Dietz Press, Incorporated
Richmond, Virginia
1959

Copyright by
MIRIAM HAYNIE
© 1959

Printed in the United States of America by
The Dietz Press, Incorporated

TO MY HUSBAND
WILLIAM HAROLD HAYNIE
AND
TO THE MEMORY OF MY MOTHER AND FATHER:
OLIVIA FRANCES JETT WILLIAMS, AND
THOMAS JACKSON WILLIAMS, OF
"PLEASANT GROVE"
NORTHUMBERLAND COUNTY,
VIRGINIA

Acknowledgements

References have been given for each chapter so that in this way the persons who so kindly gave personal interviews could be recognized specifically.

I wish to express my appreciation to the personnel of the Reference and Circulation Section, General Library Division, of the Virginia State Library, for their splendid service. Without the books from the Library it would have been impossible for me to have accumulated the material for this book.

I wish to thank the *Richmond Times-Dispatch*, the *Fredericksburg Free Lance-Star* and *Virginia* and *The Virginia County Magazine*, for their kind permission to use any material which might be needed from articles written by myself and previously published in those publications.

M. H.

Reedville, Virginia,
June, 1959.

CONTENTS

PART I—Seventeenth Century

	Page
Tidewater	3
"Ye Northerne Neck"	3
The People	4
Indians and Early Explorers	5
Captain John Smith	5
Powhatan's Empire	7
Captain Smith Visits the Neck	7
"A Plaine Wildernes"	8
"Wild Beastes"	10
"Birds to Vs Unknowne"	11
The Nominies	12
The Discoverers	13
The River of Swans	15
Mother of Waters	18
Quick-Rising-Water	20
Henry and Pocahontas	23
Henry and King Patowmeke	25
Henry's Relation	28
Betrayed	28
Kidnapped	31
The Indian Trader	33
A Petition	34
From North of the Potomac	35
The First Settler	37
Coan Hall	38
Neighbors	41
The "Kids"	42
Indian Servants	43
Money	44
A Paradise Discovered	45
A Visit to Jamestown	46
Frances	48
Forever Lost	51
Ursula	52
The Yard	54
Kittamaqund	55

CONTENTS—Cont.

	PAGE
The Gift	57
The Cavaliers	58
"Charlie-Over-The-Water"	59
The Legacy	60
The Indian Deed	61
A Summons to Jamestown	62
The Oath	64
County Officers	64
Epraphrodibus's Will	65
The Challenge	65
Trade	67
The Colonial Sailor	67
John Carter	68
Fleet's Point	69
George Mason	70
Mary Calvert	71
He Lived Bravely	72
Witchcraft	74
Seahorse of London	75
"Tenn Mulberry Trees"	76
Roads	77
Markets	78
The Old Dominion	79
The Proprietary	80
A First Lady of Jamestown	81
Land	83
Processioning	84
"The Banquetting House"	85
The Land Agent	87
Hanna and the Horseshoe	89
Muster	91
The Store	92
The Wolf-Drive	92
The Indians and Robert Hen	93
The Royal Cavalcade	95
The King of the Northern Neck	97
Kith and Kin	100
The Fieldings	101

CONTENTS—Cont.

	PAGE
Pirates	102
Christmas at Colonel Fitzhugh's	104
Indian Visitors	104
Horse Racing	105
Manufacture	106
The Potomac Rangers	107

PART II—EIGHTEENTH CENTURY

Murders in Stafford	111
Free Schools	112
The Home in the Forest	113
Cherry Point	114
Sandy Point	117
Augustine	118
Popes Creek	119
The War Path	120
Falmouth	121
Burnt House Field	122
Stratford Hall	124
George Washington	125
Epsewasson	127
Ferry Farm	129
Fredericksburg	130
School Days	131
The Indians	132
The Pow-Wow	133
Mount Vernon	137
Washington Washed Here—	138
The Ordinary	139
Nelly	140
Miss Betsy	141
The Proprietor of the Northern Neck	142
The Marshalls	146
The Leedstown Resolutions	147
Fithian	150
The School in the Wildwood	154
James and John	154
Captain Dobby	156

CONTENTS—Cont.

	Page
Pedlars	158
Seven Satin Petticoats	158
Phi Beta Kappa	159
Light-Horse Harry	159
A Band of Brothers	161
The Divine Matilda	162
Madam Washington	163
After the Revolution	165
Mantua	166

PART III—Nineteenth Century

Robert E. Lee	171
Smith Point Light	174
The Raiders	175
Steamboats	176
Hannah and the Falling Stars	178
Dear to His Heart	178
The Blockade	179
The Home Guard	181
The Mystery of Horse Pond	184
Schooner in a Mill-pond	185
War Bonnets	188
Amanda and the Yankees	188
The Horsehair Ring	191
Miracle at Ketchum's Camp	193
Desperate Passage	195
After the War	197
Speech	199
Shopping Trips	199
Menhaden	200
The Old Stone Pile	205
Keepers of the Light	205
The Headless Dog	207

PART IV—Conclusion

The Ancient Mansion Seats	213
Appendix	217
Sources	219

List of Illustrations

John Smith in the shallop exploring the waters of Northern Neck, Virginia	14
Henry Spelman living amongst the Indians	24
Pocahontas is traded for a copper kettle and becomes an hostage to Captain Argall	30
First settlers at Coan	36
"King" Carter attends Christ Church	96
Mary Ball at Yeocomico Church	116
The infant, George Washington at Wakefield, his birthplace	126
Young Washington helping in the handling of "seine" on the Potomac	128
Young George Washington becomes a friend of Lord Fairfax, Proprietor of Northern Neck	136
Young Robert E. Lee learning to ride	172
Skirmish between the Virginia Militia and the British during the War of 1812 at Farnham Church	176
"Yankee" foragers during the Civil War	182

Introduction

I HAVE read with a great deal of pleasure the book called *The Stronghold*, which relates the history of the Northern Neck of Virginia in story form and was written by my good friend, Miriam Haynie of Reedville, Virginia. Mrs. Haynie is a native of the Northern Neck of Virginia, her family on both sides having settled there in the seventeenth century, and her direct ancestors having remained there until this day. She is the author of a number of articles dealing with the history and traditions and customs of the peninsula between the Rappahannock and Potomac Rivers that have appeared in the *Richmond Times-Dispatch*, the Washington papers and national publications. She is devoted to this section of Virginia and has spent a large part of her life in accumulating an enormous fund of historical data of the region.

The Stronghold is a most interesting book, especially to Virginians and to natives and descendants of natives of the Northern Neck of Virginia. It is divided into three sections, the seventeenth century, the eighteenth century and the nineteenth century. It tells a great deal about the early history of the Colony and more especially of that portion of the Colony of Virginia, of which she is a native, from the days when the white man first came to the Potomac and Rappahannock Rivers down to the beginning of the twentieth century. She relates in a most pleasing language the first visits of Captain John Smith to the waters surrounding the Northern Neck, also the capture of Princess Pocahontas by the colonists, which occurred on the Potomac River or on one of its tributaries, and many other events connected with our early history that we are prone to overlook in the rush and whirl of these modern days. Her book will be particularly interesting to children as it is written in simple language and in story form so that a child in the fifth grade may read and understand it. It is a most entertaining and interesting work and will impress upon children the early history of our part of the Colony of Virginia and the hardships endured by our ancestors who came here to settle in the wilderness. In saying that it will be particularly interesting to children I do not mean to restrict interest in the book entirely to children for it will be both interesting and educational to all lovers of history regardless of age.

As is true in all works of this kind some of the historical statements she has made will be open to contention but in the main it

INTRODUCTION—Cont.

is a true and correct history of the Northermost Peninsula of the Old Dominion and pays proper attention to the distinguished men and women who first saw the light of day within its confines. It will be excellent parallel reading to be engaged in by every student of history in the high schools of the State. It is also interesting in that it discusses and makes a record of many traditions and customs peculiar to the region. It will be both interesting and valuable as a reference book for future historians of Virginia and will afford great pleasure to all of us who love to read about the history of our State.

Prior to the coming of good roads to Virginia and the building of the bridges across the Rappahannock and Potomac Rivers what is known as the Northern Neck, although actually a peninsula, was to those living in the eastern portion almost an island and it was but natural that marked peculiarities of the people of this section distinguished them not only from those who lived in other sections of the country but to a less extent from those living in other parts of Virginia. These distinct peculiarities appeared in pronunciation, in folk-lore and traditions. With the exception of the colored people at least ninety-five per cent of the ancestors of the present population of this section came from Great Britain and preserved with little change the speech, the culture and the habits of the British people and it is these things that distinguished them to some extent from people living in other parts of the country. In Colonial days a very high state of culture was in existence among the great plantations of the Northern Neck and their contributions to the development of this country have included several of the great heroes of the nation. To a considerable extent all these attributes have been handed down from generation to generation and every one in the Northern Neck well knows and is proud of the fact that George Washington and Robert E. Lee were natives of the section.

All these things are emphasized by Miriam Haynie in her most excellent and readable book, which will be a real contribution to the history of Virginia.

Robert O. Norris, Jr.

Lively, Virginia,
May 16, 1959.

PART I

Seventeenth Century

THE STRONGHOLD

TIDEWATER

THE COUNTRY surrounding the Chesapeake Bay, which is known as the Tidewater, has been compared to the Bible Lands, the Netherlands and Venice.

Captain John Smith, military leader of the expedition to Virginia in 1607, who explored and mapped the Chesapeake Bay and the Bay Country, described it thus:

"There is but one entrance by sea into this country, and that is at the mouth of a very goodly Bay, the widenesse whereof is 18 or 20 miles.

"Within is a country . . . heaven and earth never agreed better to frame a place for man's habitation . . . Here are . . . hils, plaines, valleys, rivers and brookes all running most pleasantly into a faire Bay compassed but for the mouth with fruitfull and delightsome land . . ."

"YE NORTHERNE NECK"

ON THE western shore of the Bay there are three peninsulas, or necks, carved out of Virginia's shoreline by the tidal rivers.

The third, and northernmost, of these peninsulas lies between the Rappahannock and the Potomac Rivers. It was probably referred to orally by the first white men who settled at Jamestown as "the northern neck." The name appeared in print certainly as early as 1677, when in an official document it was mentioned as "ye Northerne Neck."

This third peninsula north lies aloof, and long, between its broad rivers, as they flow into the Chesapeake Bay on the east.

From the Bay the narrow strip of land, only fifteen or twenty miles wide, runs inland between the rivers for almost a hundred miles, until it narrows near Fredericksburg so that the rivers almost join—not quite an island but more cut-off than the usual peninsula. In the old days when there were almost no roads, and no bridges, the Neck was to those living in the eastern portion more like an island than a peninsula. Only from the west could one travel in or out by land and that exit was rarely used.

Its geographical position made the Northern Neck for many years almost as inaccessible as an ancient stronghold surrounded by a moat.

THE PEOPLE

THE NORTHERN NECK could be compared with ancient Mesopotamia—a land between two rivers where a new civilization started.

The early settlers came to the wilderness in satins and velvets, they surrounded themselves with the niceties of living, as near like those they had left in England as was possible. They shopped in London as they had before and traded with the world directly from their own habitations.

But the conditions of their new wilderness home changed and moulded them and made them into something different—a new breed of men.

By the time unusual men were needed to shape an unusual type of government, descendants from this stock were ready for the undertaking.

In the Northern Neck there are still so many reminders of these remarkable people that it is not hard to imagine them as they might have been in their habitat several centuries ago—John Mottrom sailing into the Coan in his brightly-colored shallop; the Mottrom children playing their medieval games in the shadow of the primeval woods; Ursula twirling the venison roast on its hempen string before the fire; Hanna Neale passing the witchcraft test; young Jack Lee dashing down the forest aisles on his spirited mount; George Mason pulling the arrows from the "poor people"; Moore Fauntleroy measuring off his thirty arm's lengths of rhoanoke for the waiting Accopatough; King Carter rumbling down his avenue in his coach and six; Mary Ball on her dapple gray; James Monroe and John Marshall walking down the Parson's Lane with school books and muskets; Nelly Madison singing to her new baby; young George Washington riding down to see "Miss Betsy" on a fruitless mission, and little Robert E. Lee saying good-bye to the cherubs in the nursery fireplace. . . .

INDIANS AND EARLY EXPLORERS

WHAT MEN first knew this land between the Rappahannock and the Potomac Rivers?

It is believed that Indians lived along the shores of the Chesapeake Bay's tributaries three thousand years ago.

The Vikings may have entered the Bay and explored the nearby streams and lands in the eleventh century.

Cabot, an Italian seaman under commission from King Henry VII of England, may have entered the Chesapeake at the end of the fifteenth century.

Spaniards sailed into the Bay and explored some of the region in the sixteenth century.

European traditions tell of adventurers of other nations who may have visited this region.

Late in the year 1607, Captain John Smith traveled from Jamestown as far north as the Potomac when, as a captive of Opechancanough, he was paraded before the Indian tribes of the Tidewater region. He may have been the first white man to make a comprehensive tour of the Northern Neck of Virginia.

CAPTAIN JOHN SMITH

WHEN JOHN SMITH heard about the New World across the seas it sounded good to him—it was the sort of adventure that he had been waiting for all of his life.

He had been born in Lincolnshire, England, in 1579. Even as a small lad John Smith had been "set upon brave adventures." Tradition says that he sold his books and satchel and was preparing to run away to sea when he was stopped by the death of his father.

He was soon apprenticed to a merchant but he hated the counting-house. He longed to be free and go to sea. When he was about fifteen he could no longer stand being caged so he ran away. After a number of adventures he became a soldier in the Netherlands.

Some time later he went home on a visit to Lincolnshire, where he "lived a great deal in society." He soon tired of this way of life and retired to a wooded pasture where he built himself a shelter of boughs and became a hermit.

In the peace and solitude of the pasture he studied Machiavelli's *Arte of Warre* and the writings of Marcus Aurelius. He exercised with a good horse, a lance and a ring, and lived mostly on venison, which he took without worrying too much over the game laws. His other wants were supplied by a servant, his only contact with the world.

Because of his unusual mode of life news of John Smith traveled around the countryside but it did not worry him because "he provoked the wonder of the peasantry."

At length an Italian gentleman, who had become interested in what he had heard of John Smith, penetrated his forest hide-out and persuaded him to come into society once more. After many more adventures and hairbreadth escapes in foreign lands he returned to England in 1604, in time for another adventure. He was still a young man, about twenty-five, but he was matured and hardened far beyond his years.

When the little band of colonists set sail for America from Blackwall, England in December 1606, John Smith was with them.

The voyage was a stormy one in more ways than one. By the time the little "sea-wagons" arrived in the West Indies Smith, who had been put in irons, came very near being hanged, according to tradition.

It was April when the ships with their bedraggled passengers entered the Chesapeake Bay. The fragrance of "pyne" reached them from the virgin forest that covered the face of the land. It was a New World in every sense of the meaning—new, fresh, untouched.

When the sealed orders of the King were opened it was found that John Smith had been named a member of the Council. He demanded trial for the charges preferred against him: "that he plotted on arrival in Virginia to murder the Council and make himself the king there." He was tried and acquitted by the first jury to serve in America. Smith was released but was not yet admitted to the Council.

As it turned out John Smith was the only man among them who was prepared to build a new country. In the beginning he warned the colonists that "no man is entitled to a place in America, he must make his own."

POWHATAN'S EMPIRE

WHEN JOHN SMITH started exploring the region around the Chesapeake he found that it was inhabited by a number of small Indian tribes. These Indians were known as the Algonquians.

These tribes made up a confederation under the iron rule of a powerful "king" called Powhatan. At his command there were about twenty-five hundred warriors.

Smith made a map which shows a total of one hundred and sixty-one villages within Powhatan's "32 Kingdomes."

Indian villages were owned in common. The hunting grounds, and pieces of cleared land used for the cultivation of corn, tobacco and vegetables belonged to the tribe. A warrior owned nothing except his garments, tomahawks, bows and arrows.

The Algonquians had no written laws. Their customs were handed down through the old men around the campfires from generation to generation. These unwritten laws were well-defined and worked in a positive and forceful way.

The tribes between the Rappahannock and the Potomac Rivers belonged to the Powhatan confederacy. Their language was a variety of the Delaware Indian language.

CAPTAIN SMITH VISITS THE NECK

IT WAS bitterly cold, "with frost and snow," when Captain John Smith first saw the land between the Rappahannock and the Potomac Rivers.

Captain Smith's first visit to the Neck was not one of pleasure or exploration. He came as a captive of the Indian chief, Opechacanough.

It was in the winter of 1607-08. During that year Smith made "3. or 4. journies and discovered the people of Chickahamania." It was on the last of these "journies" that he was taken prisoner, and led about in triumph and exhibited to the tribes of the Tidewater region, from the James to the Potomac.

Smith was carried to Tophanocke, "a kingdome upon a River northward." This river was the Rappahannock. Here they stopped at the village of the Nantaughtacunds.

Smith and his captors may have sped swiftly and silently through the forest but when they approached a village a triumphal procession was formed which was marked by "a barbarous sort of pomp."

Captain Smith was guarded on either side by a savage who kept fast hold upon his wrist. Opechacanough moved in the middle of the column and the swords, guns and pistols which had been taken from Smith and his companions were borne before the Indian chief.

Their approach was heralded by the songs and shrieks and dances of the warriors. Their yells of death and victory brought out the women and children to behold their triumph over this strange-looking creature from another world, after which there was great feasting.

Smith was feasted, too. He was fed so well "with bread and venison that would have served 20 men" that he believed that he was being fattened to be eaten later on.

From the Rappahannock the procession pushed on across the Neck until it reached the village of the Nominies,* near the Potomac. Here the same procedure was again repeated.

After their stay near the Potomac the parade turned back from whence it had come. The destination, now, was Powhatan's favorite spot on the York River, where that great chief was waiting to settle the fate of Captain John Smith.

When at length Smith was brought before Powhatan, he was received with all the formal pomp and state known to the savage court. A long consultation was held by the council there assembled.

Captain Smith knew what the decision was when two large stones were brought in by the warriors. His end was not yet, however, for Powhatan's daughter, Pocahontas, according to Smith, saved the day by thrusting herself between him and the up-raised club.

By the time Captain Smith reached Jamestown again nearly seven weeks had elapsed since his capture. Though his tour of the Tidewater country had been under humiliating conditions he had gathered by observation and from the Indians a large amount of useful knowledge.

---

*Note: Variously spelled—Onawmanient, Onawma, etc.

"A PLAINE WILDERNES"

HOW DID the Northern Neck look to Captain John Smith on his first visit there?

Just like the rest of the Chesapeake Bay country—"all overgrowne with trees and . . . being a plaine wildernes as God first made it."

The size of the trees impressed him most, and the lack of undergrowth beneath them.

"So lofty and erect," he wrote, "were many of these trees and so great their diameter that their trunks afforded plank twenty yards in length and two and a half feet square."

Freedom from undergrowth he found was due to the annual burnings of the Indians in their efforts to capture whole herds of deer by surrounding them with a belt of fire. These firings made no impressions upon the giant trees.

The trees were so far apart, Smith says, ". . . that a man may gallop a horse amongst these woods any waie, but where the creeks or Rivers shall hinder." (Other early writers say that a coach could have been driven through the trees, and a person could be seen in the forest at a mile and a half.)

It was winter when Captain Smith first saw the Neck therefore he had a view unobstructed by foliage of the great tree trunks and spacious forest aisles, "bespred" with brown pine needles and ornamented with green vines and scarlet turkey berries.

Since it is impossible to travel far in the Neck without coming upon some stream of water, many of John Smith's forest vistas must have ended with a glimpse of a river or frozen pond. He wrote of the many "sweete and christall springs" that flowed through the woods on their way to the sea.

Many of the forest trees were white oaks, and some may have been a thousand or more years old. These groves were revered by the Indians. Indians were fond of the mulberry tree. Smith notes: "By the dwelling of the savages are some great Mulberry trees; and in some parts of the country, they are found growing naturally in prettie groves."

Besides pine, oak and mulberry, there were, Smith writes, ". . . goodliest Woods as Beech, Cedar, Cypresse, Walnuts, Sassfras, and other trees unknowne." Chinquapin was one of the "trees unknowne."

Locust and tulip poplar were plentiful. Sweet gum, live oak, holly and cedar flourished in low grounds. Bayberry grew in the swamps and near the edge of the water.

When Captain Smith first saw the Neck it was bitterly cold, with "frost and snow," so he may not have seen the pine needles and scarlet turkey berries. The forest aisles may have been deeply covered with snow.

"WILD BEASTES"

IF THE forest floor was covered with snow when Captain John Smith was led a captive across the Northern Neck in the winter of 1607, it is probable that he saw snowshoe rabbits scampering about between the big trees. Porcupines lived there too, and wildcats, pole-cats and a marten known as "black fox." The little animal he saw with the spotted coat, like the skin of a fawn, was a ground squirrel.

John Smith saw the flying squirrel and the opossum for he describes them: "A small beast they haue ... we call them flying squirrels, because spreading their legs, and so stretching the largeness of their skins, that they have bin seene to fly 30 or 40 yards. An opassom hath an head like a Swine, and a taile like a Rat, and is the bigness of a Cat."

Ordinary squirrels, rabbits, foxes and "Rackoones" were abundant. Captain John Smith no doubt saw beaver at work when they crossed the many streams. The Beaver," he wrote, "is as bigge as an ordinary water dogge ... His taile somewhat like ... a Racket, bare without haire."

The procession of Indians and the lone white man may have come upon a herd of heavy, slow-moving "Kine." (These were buffalo but are believed to have lacked the hump.) They were not as wild as the other animals of the wilderness. Perhaps Smith caught glimpses of the elk that roamed the forest.

At night John Smith heard the sounds of many wild beasts. The wolves were small but numerous and ravenous. In the evening they hunted like a pack of beagle hounds.

If the procession happened to be encamped near the head of a river he probably heard before morning the scream of a panther as he stalked his prey.

But of all the animals in the Tidewater region at that time, Smith says "Of beastes the chiefe are Deare."

The Northern Neck had been hunted less by the Indians than the lower peninsulas, and it was teeming with wildlife. The primeval forest furnished home and food for the "wild beastes."

"BIRDS TO VS UNKNOWNE"

WHEN JOHN SMITH traveled across the Northern Neck, from the Rappahannock to the Potomac, in the winter of 1607, he probably saw many birds, for this was their season.

"In winter," he wrote, "there are great plenty of Swans, Craynes gray and white with blacke wings, Herons, Geese, Brants, Ducke, Wigeon, Dotterell, Oxeies, Parrots, and Pigeons. Of all those sorts great abundance, and some other strange kinds, to vs unknowne by name. But in sommer not any, or a very few to be seene."

For ages wildfowl had been multiplying with little to hinder them. The Indians killed only what they needed and their weapons were too primitive to make an impression on the great flocks of waterfowl that came to the rivers and marshes to feed on the heavy growth of wild celery, oats and other aquatic plants.

In early winter when these fowl gathered in their annual migration from the North the sky, it was said, was darkened with them as they arose and descended from their feeding grounds in the marshes lying along shore.

John Smith probably heard the trumpet notes of the swans and saw the pattern of flight of the wild geese many times while on his "journie."

He may have at some time seen one of the flightless Great Auks, swimming along down the Bay on its way South for the winter. Or he may have espied a heath hen on the shores of the Chesapeake.

It is doubtful if he saw very many of the "Parrots" he mentioned. They were nocturnal creatures—small, swift, bright and beautiful. The passenger pigeons came in such flocks that their "weights brake down the limbs of large trees thereon they rested at night."

There were many red birds to brighten the somber forest aisles. A little bird with white breast and black wings and back was called "snow-bird" by the English because it arrived at the first fall of snow. Captain Smith probably saw these in the vicinity of the Indian villages as they stayed near habitations.

Turkeys were common in the reedy marshes. Flocks of four and five hundred were not unusual. These wild turkeys, early writers say, averaged forty pounds in weight.

Quail and other common varieties of birds were abundant.

THE NOMINIES

THE INDIANS reckoned their years by winters, or cohonks, as they called them, "which was a name taken from the note of the wild geese, intimating so many times of the wild geese coming to them, which was every winter."

There is no way of knowing whether it was the first or second moon of cohonks when John Smith and his captors arrived at the village of the Nominies, near the Potomac. It was so cold that Smith marveled at how some of the scantily clad warriors could endure it. He felt thankful that his own "gowne," which he had lost when he was captured, had been returned to him.

The village must have appeared bleak and primitive, with its fifteen or twenty arbor-like dwellings scattered among the sparse trees, its barren garden plots, its cornfields, marked by last season's dead stalks and some burned-out tree stumps.

As the procession approached there is little doubt that the scene came to life. The dogs were probably the first to join their howls with the death and victory yells of the warriors. These Indian dogs resembled a cross between a male wolf and an ordinary female dog. There were no other domestic animals, no beasts of burden, and no way to travel except by foot or canoe.

The women and children who emerged from the mat-covered doors of their houses were dressed in garments made of the skins of wild beasts with the hair left on for winter. Some wore long cloaks, made of skins embroidered with beads, others wore beautiful mantles of turkey feathers. Some wore feathered headgear, and jewelry fashioned of shells, beads and copper.

Smith wrote that the Indians gazed upon him "as he had beene a monster."

He was probably deposited in one of the houses, with a guard of six or eight warriors. These houses were built of flexible boughs, set in two parallel rows with floor space between, and lashed together at the top to form an arch-shaped roof. The entire framework was covered with bark or woven grass mats. "He who knoweth one such house," wrote Smith, "knoweth them all."

Inside the houses were "drie, warme, smokie." There was no chimney to conduct the smoke from the fire on the dirt floor to the vent in or near the roof. If the fire ever went out it was hard to start a new one—"their fire they kindle by chafing a dry pointed stike in a hole of a little peece of wood, that firing itselfe will so fire mosse, leaves, or anie such like drie thing that will quickly burne."

John Smith was no doubt glad to have a "warme," "drie" place to rest, even though "smokie." He could stretch out on one of the platforms running down each side of the building. There were no partitions in these houses. The platforms, about a foot high, served as beds, and were spread with "fyne white mattes" and skins. Whole families, from six to twenty persons, slept in these one-room dwellings, some on the platforms, some on the ground.

Captain Smith could probably hear the celebration going on outside. The Indians had a large plot which they used for feasts and a place where they made merry when the feasts were over.

With the abundance of wildfowl and game and the harvest of corn stored away, this was an ideal time for feasting. Oysters from the Potomac were probably included in the menu for the Indians were fond of roasted oysters.

Smith was not forgotten. He noted that they "fedde" him "bountifully," but would not eat with him. We can imagine him there at his solitary meal, supping on corn pone, "fish, fowle, and wild beastes, exceeding fat," by the light of "candells of the fattest splinters of the pine."

THE DISCOVERERS

WHEN CAPTAIN JOHN SMITH was in the Northern Neck he saw the Potomac and heard tales from the "Salvages" of a place where there was a mine of "glistering mettal." He made up his mind that if he got out of this predicament he would explore the river "Patowmeke," find the gold mine, and perhaps a passage "strait through to the South Sea."

When he finally did get back to Jamestown the colony was in a bad way. During the extreme cold of the winter of 1607-8, the heavy fires necessary for warmth had caused the thatch-roofed town to burn. This included the granary with all their provisions, and the "palisadoes."

By the time the town had been rebuilt, and other difficulties adjusted, it was summer. John Smith was impatient to begin his next adventure but he waited until the corn crop had been "laid by."

John Smith in the shallop exploring the waters of Northern Neck, Virginia.

He left the fort on the second of June, 1608, in an open barge of "less than three tons burthen." His only instrument was a compass. His companions were—a physician, six gentlemen and seven soldiers.

They crossed the Chesapeake Bay to the eastern shore, proceeding along the coast, "searching every inlet and bay fit for harbours and habitations." The Bay was easy to navigate, the greatest menace were the sudden thunder squalls.

Smith soon became disgusted with his crew. He wrote that they had not "a marriner or any that had skill to trim their sayles, use their oares, or any business belonging to the Barge, but 2 or 3. the rest being Gentlemen, or as ignorant in such toyle and labour."

For provisions they had "nothing but a little meale or oatmeale and water to feed them; and scarse halfe sufficient of that for halfe that time, but by the Savages and by the plentie of fish they found in all places, they made themselves provision as opportunitie served."

A thunder-storm took mast and sails and they were so "over-racked" by such "mightie waves," that it was with great difficulty that they kept the barge from sinking. They repaired the sails with their shirts. The crew begged to turn back to Jamestown but Captain Smith spoke to them in this manner:

"Gentlemen—

You cannot say but I have shared with you of the worst that is past; and for what is to come, of lodging, diet, or whatsoever, I am contented you allot the worst part to my selfe. As for your feares, that I will lose my selfe in these unknowne large waters, or be swallowed up in some stormie gust: abandon those childish fears, for worse then is past cannot happen, and there is as much danger to returne, as to proceed forward. Regaine therefore your old spirits: for returne I will not (if God assist me) til I have—found Patawomeck, or the head of this great water you conceit to be endlesse."

It was now the thirteenth of June.

THE RIVER OF SWANS

CAPTAIN JOHN SMITH headed the barge toward the western shore of the Bay. On the sixteenth of June "we fel with the river Patawomeck."

When John Smith had last seen this River of Swans, as the Indians had named it, water and sky were darkened by hordes of wildfowl. There had been the sound of the whirring of many wings and great clamour. Now all was quiet. There was nothing to remind him of that amazing congregation of fowl that he had seen during "cohonks" except the marshes, lying here and there along shore.

"Feare being gone and our men recovered, wee were all contented" as the barge sailed into the mouth "of this 9 myle broad river." On the south lay the Northern Neck, indented by numerous inlets that promised harbours, its eastern end extending into Chesapeake Bay. Its virgin forest was now decked out with leaf and flower which sent fragrance to the sea-weary voyagers.

For thirty miles they sailed without adventure. Then two Indians appeared and conducted them up a little creek towards Onawmanient—"where all the woods were laid with Ambuscadoes to the number of 3 or 400 Salvages; but so strangely painted, grimed, and disguised, shouting, yelling, and crying, as we rather supposed them so many divels."

Captain Smith thought it best to scare them a little, so he trained his guns so that the bullets would graze the water. This and the "eccho of the woods so amazed them, that down went their bowes and arrowes." Peace was made, hostages were exchanged and James Watkins, one of the company, was sent with them "6 myles up the woods to their king's habitation. Wee were kindly used by these Salvages: of whom we understand they were commanded to betray us by Powhatan."

Powhatan had his forces well organized. As they progressed up the river they found the Indians ready for them: "The like incounters were found at Patawomeck, Cecocawone, (Coan) and divers other places."

The only tribes that received them with friendliness were the Moyaones, Nacotchtants and Toags. There seems to be no further record of these tribes.

They went as far up the river as they could go in the barge, "140 myles"; this was above the site of the present city of Washington, and about ten miles above Georgetown. Captain Smith was stopped here by impassable falls. His disappointment must have been great that his search here did not yield an outlet to the "South Sea."

On the return trip they had the good fortune to meet a number of Indians in canoes loaded with slaughtered game—bears, deer and other "beasts." Smith and his party were given liberal portions of the fresh meat, which must have cheered them some.

In this part of the river there were great rocks on the shores towering above the trees, and the high banks gleamed in places like "a tinctured spangled skurfe, that made many places seeme as guilded." Dreams of gold were always in the minds of men at that time. Perhaps here was to be found the "glistering mettal" that John Smith had heard about from the Indians the winter before.

Most of the company clambered up the banks and burrowed in the earth among the cliffs. The ground was so sprinkled with gleaming spangles as to seem "halfe pin dust." Smith refrained from this made scramble and proceeded in a more organized way.

With Japazaws, King of Patowmeke, as guide, he ascended one of the tributaries of the river, called Quiyough, as far as the depth of water would allow. Here Captain Smith left the barge, taking with him six men. He was surrounded by Indians. Some of these he decorated with chains and told them that if they conducted him safely to the mine they could keep the ornaments.

When they arrived at the place of the treasure, nine or ten miles inland, the Englishmen saw that the Indians had been digging there with their shells and hatchets for a long time.

To their great disappointment the mine was not gold but antimony. The Indians, who had been in the habit of digging there, washed the element of its dross "in a fayre brooke of christel-like water" which "runneth hard by it" and put it in little bags and sold it all over the country. It was used to paint their idols and themselves. Smith noted that it made them look like "blackmoores dusted over with silver."

No minerals were discovered in this search either. They were rewarded in a slight degree by some furs of mink, beaver, otter, bear and marten, which they obtained mostly from the Indians of Cascarawaoke. This was a merchant tribe that did much of the manufacturing and trading of this country. The Potomac must have been used as a highway for trade as the word Patow-meke is said to mean "to bring again," or, in a freer rendering, "traveling traders, or pedlars."

Smith's party found "plentie" of fish, "lying so thicke, with their heads above the water, as for want of nets (our barge driving amongst them) we attempted to catch them with a frying pan; but we found it a bad instrument to catch fish with."

Smith now continued toward the mouth of the Potomac and the Chesapeake. He had little of tangible value to show for the trip up the river but he had added greatly to his store of knowledge and could now add the Potomac to his map of the Chesapeake and surrounding country.

He notes that the Potomac was "inhabited on both sides. First on the South side at the very entrance is Wighcocomoco (Little Wicomico) and hath some 130 men, beyond them Sekacawone (Coan) with 30. The Onawmanient with 100. And the Patawomekes more than 200."

A point of land at the mouth of the Potomac, on the south side, he named for himself, Smith's Point.*

---

*Smith's Point is also called Smith Point.

MOTHER OF WATERS

WHEN CAPTAIN JOHN SMITH and his bargeload of adventurers left the Potomac they passed the tip of Smith's Point and headed south. They were now on the Chesapeake Bay.

Indians had long used this great inland sea as their waterway. Their word, Chesapeake, has been translated in a number of ways, among them—country on a great river and great salt bay.

The Spaniards, who visited the Bay in the sixteenth century, had documented it as Bahia de Santa Maria (St. Mary's Bay). Later, they called it Bahia del Xacan (Axacan Bay), and a very old Spanish map calls it, Madre de Aguas, meaning Mother of Waters.

Captain Smith describes it simply as "a goodly bay." He wrote: "This Bay lyeth North and South, in which the water floweth neare 200-myles, and hath a channell for 140 myles, of depth betwixt 6 and 15 fadome, holding in breadth for the most part 10 or 14 myles."

Two of Smith's company recorded the fact that "Neither better fish, more plenty or variety, had any of us seene in any place, swimming in the water, then in the bay of Chesapeake."

The Indians well knew the riches of their great Bay. They caught the fat fish in weirs, with nets and lines for their angles made by their women from thread spun from "the barkes of trees, Deeres Sinews, or a Kind of Grass." They ate the sea-crabs that were said to be so large that four Englishmen could feast on one of them. They roasted the oysters reported to have been thirteen inches long at the time of the coming of the white man. The shells were not wasted by the Indians—they were used for medicine, ornaments, and wampum was made from the purple edges of the clams. Even the lowly periwinkle was eaten.

As the first English ships entered Chesapeake Bay the crews were startled to see whales and schools of tumbling porpoises. The early colonists were soon to learn that there were so many porpoises in the Bay that canoes were sometimes overturned by them.

When the Jamestown colony was starving they lived on the bounties of the Bay—they caught the sea-crabs and sturgeons and sheepshead; the latter they likened to the broth of their English mutton. And these same strangers "groped in the deep for oysters which lay in places thick as stones," according to an early writer.

There were many oddities in the Bay which intrigued the Europeans—a small fish that resembled St. George's Dragon, with legs and wings omitted, the stinging nettle, and "the Todefish which will swell till it be like to brust, when it commeth into the aire."

As Captain John Smith and his crew proceeded down the Bay in the barge they passed the end of the Northern Neck and came to the mouth of the Rappahannock River. It was the intention of Smith to explore this river and visit the acquaintances he had made "upon the river of Toppahannock" during his captivity the preceding winter. But they were stopped by the ebb-tide. The following account of what happened at the mouth of the Rappahannock was written by members of the company, Dr. Walter Russell and Anas Todkill.

"But our boate (by reason of the ebbe) chansing to ground upon many shoules lying in the entrance, we spied many fishes lurking amongst the weedes on the sands. Our captaine sporting himselfe to catch them by nailing them to the ground with his sword, set us all a fishing in that manner. By this devise, we tooke more in an houre then we all could eat.

But it chanced, the captaine taking a fish from his sword (not knowing her condition) being much of the fashion of a Thornebacke with a long taile whereon is a most poysoned sting of 2 or 3 inches long, which shee strooke an inch and (a) halfe into the wrist of his arme. The which, in 4 houres, had so extremely swolne his hand, arme, shoulder and part of his body, as we al with much sorrow concluded (anticipated) his funerall, and prepared his grave in an Ile hard by (as himselfe appointed); which then wee called Stingeray Ile, after the name of the fish. Yet by the helpe of a precious oile, Doctor Russell applyed, ere night his tormenting paine was so wel asswaged that he eate the fish to his supper: which gave no lesse joy and content to us, then ease to himselfe.

Having neither Surgeon nor surgerie but that preservative oile, we presently set saile for James Towne."

QUICK-RISING-WATER

IT WAS not until August of 1608 that Captain John Smith had the opportunity to explore the Rappahannock River. With him in the barge were twelve men—"nearly the same persons as before"—and an Indian guide named Mosco, "a lusty Salvage of Wighcocomoco."

Unlike the other Indians, Mosco had a fine black bushy beard, of which he was proud. Because of this peculiarity he ranked himself with the Englishmen. Smith believed him to have been the son of a Frenchman.

It was probably due to Mosco's influence that Smith's party was kindly received and entertained by the Moraughtacunds. Mosco hurried about, bringing wood and water, and guiding them throughout the neighborhood. When Smith decided that it was time to push on Mosco warned him not to visit the Rappahannock Indians. He described them as hostile to the Moraughtacunds, and would be to the English too, because of their friendly visit.

Captain Smith believed that Mosco was using this argument to keep all their trade for his friends. He headed the barge across the river toward the forbidden territory.

All seemed well as they neared the shore. A dozen or more Indians were on hand to direct them to a good landing in a creek, where three or four canoes filled with corn and other commodities for barter, were already lined up.

When in doubt Smith's custom was to exchange hostages. He made this known but the Indians were reluctant to comply. After consultation among themselves four or five of them ran out in the creek bringing with them their hostage.

Still distrustful, Smith sent one of his men, Anas Todkill, ashore to look around. Within a stone's throw of the landing Anas discovered two or three hundred Indians in ambush among the trees. Todkill attempted to return to the barge but was intercepted by the Rappahannocks. At the same time the Indian hostage jumped from the barge but was instantly killed in the water by the English. A volley of shot from the barge scattered the Indians and Todkill managed to escape. Several Indians were wounded and killed but the English were unharmed.

In this short while many arrows were shot but the barge was protected by Indian shields, or targets, woven so firmly of sticks

A Story of the Historic Northern Neck of Virginia

and grass that no arrow could penetrate them. These Smith had gotten from the Massawomeks.

Captain Smith and his comrades carried the captured canoes and arrows across the river as gifts to Mosco and his friends. The return of the English "was hailed with a trumpet."

When the barge started up the river the next day Mosco was one of the company. As they passed through a narrow place in the river, arrows that seemed to fly from unseen hands began to hit the shields around the boat. At the first arrow Mosco fell flat, hiding his head against the bottom of the barge, but he directed his friends where to look in the marsh, at the little bushes growing amongst the grass. The guns were trained accordingly and at the first volley the bushes fell down and the ambush disappeared. After the barge had moved about half a mile away the Englishmen looked back and saw the thirty or forty Rappahannocks of the ambuscade "dancing and singing very merrily."

As the barge progressed up the river the explorers were kindly treated by the several tribes that they encountered. But the company was saddened, and lessened, by the death of Richard Featherstone, whose body had weakened under the excessive heat and humidity of this unaccustomed climate.

The body of the young Englishman was laid to rest on the shores of a little bay. His comrades honored him as best they could by firing a volley of shot, and naming the bay for him—Featherstone Bay. Smith marked it on his map and it is believed by some to have been near the site of the present city of Fredericksburg.*

The next day they sailed as high up the river as the barge would float. Smith went ashore and set up crosses of wood and brass and cut their names upon trees to signify that possession had been taken of the country by English authority.

While Smith was thus occupied the sentinel was surprised by an arrow that fell beside him. The white men found that they were surrounded by Indians who were hiding behind trees. After a half-hour skirmish the Indians disappeared as suddenly as they had appeared. Mosco was the hero of the battle—he emptied his quiver, ran to the barge for fresh supplies and pursued the fugitives. Coming upon a wounded enemy Mosco would have beaten his brains out except for the English.

After the physician, Anthony Bagnalle, had dressed the prisoner's wounds, he recovered enough to answer Smith's questions. He be-

---

*The exact place of burial seems to be a controversial subject.

longed, he told them, to the nation of the Mannahocks and was the brother of a chief. He had heard that the English were a people come from under the world to take their world from them. When asked what was beyond the mountains, he answered, "The sun." This Indian's name was Amoroleck.

Mosco was not in sympathy with these proceedings. He told the English that the Mannahocks were a "naughty" race, as bad as the Rappahannocks, and that they had better be on their way.

Smith did not take Mosco's advice. It was night when the party finally embarked and started back down the river. Before long the arrows started rattling against the shields and dropping into the barge. The stream was narrow here, with high banks on one side. Amoroleck called to his people, but in vain; he could not be heard above the shrieks of the warriors. Every now and then Smith discharged a musket in the direction of the most noise. The Indians were persistent and followed the barge for about twelve miles. The darkness was probably all that saved the Englishmen.

At daybreak the barge emerged into a wide place, where the weary adventurers dropped anchor out of arrow-shot, and ate breakfast. They were so tired and hungry that they paid no attention to the four or five hundred warriors crowded along the banks, until after breakfast. Then they took down the shields and showed themselves, with Amoroleck in plain view amongst them. After a consultation the Indians hung their bows and arrows upon trees and two Indians, with bows and quivers on their heads, swam out to the barge and presented these in token of friendship.

Captain Smith now went ashore and told the Indians to send for their kings. Four kings, or chiefs, soon appeared. Smith gave them back Amoroleck. The Indians were happy over this and gave the English bows, arrows, pipes and pouches, but in return they asked for the pistols which the English carried. Smith satisfied them with less dangerous trinkets, and left them dancing and singing and making merry.

The barge continued its journey downstream until the neighborhood of the Moraughtacunds was reached. They stopped here to tell these friends of Mosco of their victory over the Mannahocks. The Moraughtacunds were a feeble race, and small in stature. They begged Smith to subdue the Rappahannocks also.

Smith decided to help this weak tribe, as he would be at the same time helping the English. He summoned the kings of the Rappahannocks to a conference. When they had assembled Captain Smith threatened to burn their villages, destroy their canoes and corn and prove himself a bad enemy. Among the things that Smith demanded was the son of a "king," named Rappahannock, as a hostage. The chief objected to this—he had only one son and he could not live without him—but he would give up certain of his women who had been stolen by the Moraughtacunds. Smith found that this was the cause of the recent wars.

Captain Smith returned to the Moraughtacunds* and had the three women brought before him. He had a chain of beads put around the neck of each. He then sent for the King Rappahannock to come, and bade him choose the one he most desired. The second choice was given to the "king" of the Moraughtacunds. Then Smith generously presented Mosco with the third woman. All parties seemed to be satisfied with this distribution.

The next day six or seven hundred Indians of both tribes assembled to celebrate the peace that had been thus established. No weapons were to be seen, friendship was pledged with the English, and the Indians volunteered to plant corn for them. In return John Smith promised hatchets, beads and copper.

Mosco was so pleased that at the height of the celebration he renounced his name in favor of one meaning "stranger" and voluntarily became a subject of the English King, James the First.

After the celebration Captain Smith sailed again into the Chesapeake, leaving behind this river that the Indians called Quick-Rising-Water.

---

*The name "Moraughtacund" was corrupted to the present "Morattico."

HENRY AND POCAHONTAS

IN 1609 an English boy landed at Jamestown. He was probably about fourteen years old at that time since records show that he had been baptized in England in 1595.

In a short while Henry Spelman was to find himself in a virgin forest among painted savages and wild beasts. What a change for this young son of a British nobleman!

Harry had no doubt been accustomed to a quiet and bookish atmosphere at his home at Congham, Norfolk. His father, Sir Henry, was interested in history and antiques, and in fact was noted for his studies along those lines.

And why did Sir Henry permit a boy so young to set out upon such a dangerous expedition? Was it because Harry was a third son

Henry Spelman living amongst the Indians.

and could therefore expect little in the way of lands and riches? Since Sir Henry was one of the Council for New England, and treasurer of the Guiana Company, he may have had his eyes on broader horizons.

It was August when Henry arrived in Virginia. It was the hot, muggy season when mosquitoes were plentiful. Shortly after his arrival Captain John Smith took him on a little journey to visit Powhatan. How excited Henry must have been at the prospect of seeing the great chieftain! How little did he suspect what Captain Smith had planned to do with him. Henry later wrote the following account:

"I was carried by Capt. Smith, our President, to ye litell Powhatan where unknowne to me he sould (sold) me to him for a towne called Powhatan (site of present Richmond city) and leavinge me with him, he made knowne to Capt. Weste, (Francis, brother of Lord Delaware how he had bought a towne for them to dwell in . . ."

Soon after Captain Smith left Henry with the Indians a massacre ensued in the Indian village. According to early writers of Jamestown, Henry's life was saved by Powhatan's daughter Pocahontas.

At this time the King of Patowmeke was visiting his emperor, probably to pay his tribute, and to save the white boy from the "furie of Powhatan" he took him home with him when he returned to the land between the Rappahannock and the Potomac.

This arrangement was probably made by Pocahontas. Before very long she too would be hiding out in the Northern Neck as a guest of the King and Queen of Patowmeke. It is believed by some that Pocahontas and Henry fled with the King of Patowmeke to his village on the Potomac at the same time.

HENRY AND KING PATOWMEKE

HENRY PROBABLY adjusted himself quickly to the way of life in the village of the Potomac Indian tribe. He was probably soon wearing a skin belt and a cord as a breechclout like the Indian boys of his age.

Henry doubtless played a game with them that was like football for he later described this game and indicated that it was played by both boys and women but with different rules: "They use football play which wemen and young boyes doe much play at. The men never. They make their gooles as ours only they never fight nor pull one another doune.

"The men play with a litel balle lettinge it fall out of ther hand and striketh it with the tope of his foot, and he that can strike the ball furthest winns that they play for."

We can visualize Henry learning to shoot the bow and arrow, and learning to follow a trail through the forest. The Indian boys probably taught him to snare beaver, otter and other small animals, and to fish with hooks of bone or stone, and to catch crabs with dip-nets made of silk grass.

We know that Henry watched the women gather corn in hand baskets and dump it into larger baskets for he later recorded these facts. He no doubt learned quickly to like the Indian food—the corn pones that came brown-crusted and smoking from the ashes, the fish and meat broiled on hurdles over the fire or turned on a spit. He doubtless tasted the broth and bread made from chestnuts and chinquapins and reserved for the chief men at the greatest feasts, and opossum and beaver, stews of fish and vegetables, and doves and partridges baked in wet clay, and dined on venison, turkey and oysters.

Henry had chores to do too. He wrote that one of his duties was "stilling the king's young child, for none could quiet him so well as myselfe." This undoubtedly makes Henry Spelman the Neck's first white baby-sitter.

He perhaps had his turn with the Indian boys to sit in a little hut on a platform in the field and scare crows away from the newly planted corn.

We can be certain that Henry avoided the hideous priests and their temples and the houses where the bodies of the dead kings and statues of their god Okee were kept. These places were considered too holy for ordinary people to enter. Indians passed these houses quickly, and even when going up or down the river they would throw "some peece of copper, white beads or pocones into the river for feare their Okee should be offended and revenged of them."

Henry attended funerals of the common people where he saw the body wrapped in mats and placed on a scaffold ten or twelve feet high. The relatives mourned greatly and threw beads among the poor. After the funeral the relatives entertained with feasting, music and dancing.

The corpse stayed on the scaffold until the flesh had disappeared and then it was wrapped in a new mat and later buried.

In the Potomac country punishment for crime was swift and

often final. Henry was an eye-witness to such punishment: "Then cam the officer to thos that should dye, and with a shell cutt off ther long locke, which they weare on the left side of ther heade, and hangeth that on a bowe before the kings house. Then thos for murther weare beaten with staves till ther bonns weare broken and beinge alive weare flounge into the fier, the other for robbinge was knockt on the heade and beinge deade his bodye was burnt."

The white boy saw many moons come and go there in the wilderness—the moon of stags, the corn moon, the first and second moon of cohonks. He was there at the budding of the spring, the earing of the corn, the highest sun, the fall of the leaf, and then again—cohonks.

He witnessed the solemn celebrations of the plentiful coming of the wild fowl to the river, the return of the hunting season and the ripening of certain fruits. He saw the greatest annual festival at the time of the corn gathering with its war dances, heroic songs, the music rattles and drums, and then the feasting.

One day news came to the village of a boat with sails that was moving up the river and stopping at the Indian settlements in quest of corn. The white men sent from Jamestown by Lord De la Ware were ready to barter copper, beads and other "trucke" for corn. While Henry had been dining so well with the Indians his own people at Jamestown were starving.

As the boat neared the village of the Potomac Indians a messenger came to the chief with word from the captain. Captain Samuel Argall had heard that in the village there was an "English boy named Harry" and he desired to "hear further of him."

King Patowmeke sent the boy to the ship where he conversed with Captain Argall and then returned to the village with an invitation to the chief to visit the ship. The chief accompanied the boy back to the ship.

The visit was pleasant and a deal was made between the chief and the captain—the vessel was "fraughted with corne" and Henry was exchanged for some copper.

Henry had lived with the Indians for "a year and more." Captain Argall found him healthy and apparently contented. He returned to Jamestown and stayed there until the following spring at which time he sailed for England in company with Lord De la Ware.

How different Henry must have seemed to his family! And he was different for he had become almost more like an Indian than a white boy.

HENRY'S RELATION

WHILE ON his return visit to England Henry Spelman wrote a manuscript, entitled "Relation of Virginia," in which he described the country between the Rappahannock and the Potomac. It is probably the first recorded specific description of the Northern Neck:

"The cuntry is full of wood in sum partes, and water they have plentifull, they have marish (marsh) ground and smale fields, for corn, and other grounds wher on their Deare, goates, and stages feadeth, ther be in this cuntry Lions, Beares, Wolves, foxes, muske catts, Hares, a fleinge squirel, and other squirls beinge all graye like conyes, a great store of foule, only Peacockes and common hens wanting: fish in aboundance wher on they (Indians) live most part of the Summer time. They have a kind of wheat cald locataunce and Pease and Beanes, Great store of walnuts growing in every place. They have no orchard frutes, only tow kind of plumbes, the one a sweet and lussius plumbe, long and thicke in forme and liknes of A Nutt Palme, the other resemblinge a medler." (Persimmon)

BETRAYED

IN 1616 Henry Spelman returned to Virginia and was employed as interpreter to the colony. In 1618 he was again in England but returned to Virginia on board the *Treasurer* in that same year. By now he "knew most of the kings of Virginia and spake their languages very understandingly."

In August, 1619, Spelman was tried by the House of Burgesses for speaking disparagingly of Governor Yeardley to Opechancanough. These charges were preferred by Robert Poole, interpreter. Poole said that he had been present at the court of Opechancanough when Spelman had talked "unreverently and maliciously" against the colony government.

Spelman denied most of the charges but admitted that he "hade informed Opechancanough that within a yeare there would come a governor greater then this that nowe is in place."

For this misdemeanor Spelman lost his title of Captain and was sentenced to serve the colony seven years in the nature of interpreter to the Governor. Many thought that he had been "badly rewarded for much good service" that he had done.

When the sentence was read to Spelman it was reported that he showed no signs of remorse for his offenses and muttered to himself and acted more like a "Savage than a Christian."

It was not long before Henry was again in good standing in the colony. He was put in command of a small bark called *Elizabeth*, and was trading with the Indians along the Potomac at the time of the massacre in March, 1622. At Chicacoan (Coan) an Indian stole aboard his boat and told of the massacre and that Opechancanough had "plotted with his King and countrey to betray them also, which they refused; but them of Wighcocomoco (Little Wicomico) at the mouth of the river, had undertaken it." When Spelman heard this he went to Wicomico but the Indians seeing his men were so well armed appeared friendly and loaded his boat with corn.

In March, 1623, an expedition of twenty-six men, in the *Tiger* under the command of Captain Spelman, went to trade for beaver and corn with the Anacostan and other Indian tribes between Potomac Creek and the falls of the Potomac (probably near the present site of Washington, D. C.).

Captain Spelman, Henry Fleet and twenty of their companions went ashore, believing the Indians to be their friends. Spelman was "a warie man, well acquainted with the savage nature" but evidently he was not aware how bitterly these Indians had been antagonized a short time before by a party under the command of Captain Isaac Matthews.

While Spelman and his men were ashore the pinnace with only five men left on board was surrounded by Indians in canoes, some of whom climbed up on the deck. The sailors were thus surprised and one of them fired a cannon at random. The savages were so frightened that they jumped overboard and swam ashore leaving their canoes drifting.

The sailors then heard an uproar on shore. It sounded as if a fight was in progress. Suddenly they saw a man's head thrown down the bank. They recognized it as the head of Henry Spelman.

The Anacostan Indians had proved themselves to be too "subtile" for Henry Spelman. But "how he was surprised or slaine is uncertaine." The sailors hastily weighed anchor and set sail for Jamestown.

This ends the true story of the "English boy named Harry" who was betrayed twice in the wilds of Virginia—first by his own people and then by his adopted people.

Pocahontas is traded for a copper kettle and becomes an hostage to Captain Argall.

Henry Spelman was about twenty-eight years old when he was killed. He had contributed in many ways to the building of a new country. He left to posterity his valuable recorded observations so that others could profit by his courage and industry.

KIDNAPPED

IN THE autumn of 1609, Captain John Smith was disabled when his powder-bag was accidentally fired. He sailed for England and never returned to Virginia.

After Captain Smith left, Pocahontas came no more to Jamestown. But she did visit elsewhere. In the spring of 1613 she was visiting in the Northern Neck with her relatives and friends along the Potomac.

The sympathy which Pocahontas had shown for the colonists had caused an estrangement between her and her father, Powhatan. She lived with him no longer and was staying in some secrecy with her relations, the King and Queen of Patowmeke.

For the trip Pocahontas probably wore her robe of deer skins, which was lined with pigeons' down, and her royal jewels of shell, and the white feather in her hair which signified that she was a princess. Though slight of stature, she was doubtless impressive when dressed in her regalia.

In April, Captain Samuel Argall was sent to the Potomac to trade for corn. There, he became acquainted with Chief Japazaws, an old friend of Captain Smith, and learned from him that Pocahontas was his guest.

This knowledge gave Captain Argall an idea. Since Captain Smith had left the colony at Jamestown the Indians had again become troublesome. If, thought Captain Argall, Powhatan's favorite daughter could be captured and held as a hostage peace might be made. The idea grew, and he plotted to steal the little Indian princess.

Captain Argall bargained with Japazaws—a copper kettle in exchange for his guest. The chief agreed, but how could he get Pocahontas aboard the English ship?

Japazaws turned the details of the plot over to his wife. It was up to her to lure the princess into the hands of Captain Argall.

The chief's wife told Pocatontas that she had a great desire to see an English ship and that her husband had promised to take her aboard if the princess would go with her. Although she had no idea that her identity was known to Captain Argall, Pocahontas refused to go. She had seen "great canoes" before and did not care to see this one.

Japazaws threatened to beat his wife unless she could persuade Pocahontas to go aboard the ship. In tears the chief's wife again begged Pocahontas to go with her. The kind-hearted girl finally consented.

Captain Argall welcomed his three guests and ushered them into the ship's cabin where a feast had been spread for them. While the banquet was in progress, Japazaws stepped often on the Captain's foot, under the table, to remind him that his part had been done.

At an opportune time the Captain persuaded Pocahontas to go into the gun-room, pretending to have something to talk over in private with Japazaws. Presently, he sent for her and told her, before her friends, that she must go with him and "compound peace betwixt her countrie" and the English before she should ever see her father again.

Pocahontas began to weep and Japazaws and his wife joined in, howling and crying louder than the girl they had betrayed. Soon the chief and his wife, with the copper kettle, went "merrily on shore."

A messenger was sent to Powhatan by Captain Argall, to tell him that he must ransom his beloved daughter with the "men, swords, peeces, tools, &c. hee trecherously had stolne."

Powhatan did not respond to these demands as Captain Argall had planned. His stand against the invaders was more important to him than his own daughter.

In the meantime, fate took a hand—at Jamestown, Pocahontas and "Master John Rolfe, an honest gentleman," fell in love and were married. In this way peace was established, for a time, between the Indians and the colonists.

As "Lady Rebecca," wife of John Rolfe, Pocahontas traveled to England and had other adventures, but her last happy days as a free Indian maiden were spent in the land between the Rappahannock and the Potomac, later known as the Northern Neck. An Indian village called "Petomek," near the mouth of Potomac Creek, was the scene of her kidnapping.

Potomac Creek is located in Stafford County, three miles north of Falmouth. Some believe that Captain Argall found Henry Spelman and Pocahontas at the village of the Potomacs at the same time.

THE INDIAN TRADER

HENRY FLEET was one of the expedition of twenty-six men aboard the *Tiger* who under Captain Spelman in March, 1623, went to trade for beaver skins and corn with the Anacostan and other Indian tribes near the head of the Potomac.

Fleet was with Spelman when he went ashore. After Spelman was killed and his head tossed over the river bank, Fleet was taken prisoner and carried to the village of the Anacostans. This is believed to have been located not far from the present monument of Washington, in Washington, D. C.

Fleet was about twenty-five years old and had but recently arrived in Virginia. His father was William Fleet of the London Virginia Company, which may have been the reason that Henry came to the New World. Henry was adventurous, quick-witted and intelligent. He made good use of his stay in the wilderness of the Northern Neck by studying his new environment. Later he wrote down some of these observations:

"It aboundeth in all manner of fish. The Indians in one night will commonly catch thirty sturgeons in a place where the river is not above three fathom broad. And as for deer, buffaloes, bears, turkeys, the woods do swarm with them, and the soil is exceedingly fertile." He also wrote that he had seen "plenty of black fox, which of all others is the richest fur." This animal was a large marten, so fierce that it was the match for any forest animal up to the size of a deer.

Henry was kept in captivity for four years, when his friends managed to ransom him. Small vessels were then trading with the Indians of the Potomac and news of him was probably carried to Jamestown in this way.

During the year 1627 the London Merchants were surprised by the arrival of Henry Fleet from Virginia. Startling tales of his adventures spread abroad. It was said that he had lived with the Indians so long that he had forgotten his own language, that he had often seen the South Sea; that he had seen Indians "besprinkle their paintings with powder of gold."

These stories impressed William Cloberry, a merchant adventurer, and chief man in the Guinea trade. Clobery believed that Fleet could be useful to him as a trader among the Indians.

On September 6, 1627, the ship *Paramour* of London, one hundred tons burden, was licensed to clear with Henry Fleet as master. William Clobery and Company were the owners.

Captain Fleet was well suited by nature and experience to be an Indian trader. For years he traded with the Indians along the Potomac—bartering "beads, bells, hatchets, knives, coats, shirts, Scottish stockings and broadcloth" and other "trucke," for beaver fur, tobacco and corn. Some of the Indian tribes traveled "seven, 8 and 10 days journey" to trade with him. He was the most regular and dependable trader the Indians knew.

By 1632 Captain Fleet was operating several boats in the Indian trade, and in that year he built a shallop and a "Barque" of sixteen tons for his own use. He also opened a trade between the Massachusetts settlement and the Potomac River. Sometimes he carried as much as eight hundred bushels of corn at one time from the Potomac to New England.

One day, while trading for beaver with the Anacostans, Captain Fleet ran into trouble. He met the pinnace of a rival trader, and on board was John Utie of the Virginia Council. The latter arrested him by order of the Council for trading with the Indians without license. Fleet had to stop his activities and set sail for Jamestown, where he was tried, but soon given his liberty.

Captain Fleet became a powerful man in Indian affairs. After the massacre of 1644 he was commissioned to negotiate a peace, at his own expense should he fail. He was successful in arranging a treaty with Necotowance, successor of Opechancanough, "in terms that showed a marked advance of civilization; Necotowance must do homage for his land to the King of England, in token whereof he was fined 20 beaver skins at the going away of the Geese yearly."

When bargaining with Necotowance Captain Fleet had been authorized to build a fort on the Rappahannock, "an important station."

Fleet remained in the region of the Potomac long enough to see the first settlers come to the Northern Neck. He was their friend and interpreter and helped them with their Indian troubles.

A PETITION

IN JULY, 1639, owing to the increase of population in Bermuda, the Proprietors of the Island, in London, petitioned for the region "scituate betwixt the two Rivers of Rapahanock, and

Patowmack wch by good Informacon your petit'iors finde to be both healthful and otherwise—not yet Inhabited." (Lefroy's *Bermudas*, Vol. I, p. 558.)

FROM NORTH OF THE POTOMAC

THE FIRST settlers did not come to the Northern Neck from the direction of Jamestown, which would have been the natural direction. Nor did they come for the natural reason—new lands.

Instead, they came from north of the Potomac. In order to understand the reason for the migration of these pioneers from the north side of the Potomac to its south side, it is necessary to go back a few years and study the situation in the upper Chesapeake Bay region.

Before 1640 the activity of white men in the Chesapeake Bay centered about a trading post at Kent Island, situated far up the Bay. The trade there was with the Indian tribes in "fur, skins and Indian baskets."

Captain Henry Fleet, William Claiborne, a Virginian, and Lord Baltimore and his brother were chief among those who were making history in this region at that time.

Claiborne and a number of Virginians had established a colony on Kent Island under a charter secured before Lord Baltimore had settled his colony on the north side of the Potomac in a region that he called Maryland.

When Lord Baltimore was granted a charter to settle in this area, his charter included Kent Island. The charter, however, had said that he should have authority only over uninhabited lands.

Claiborne considered that Kent Island was inhabited and was not, therefore, a part of Maryland.

In 1634, the second Lord Baltimore sent about one hundred settlers, under the leadership of his brother, Leonard Calvert, to a point of land across the Potomac from the Northern Neck, and a settlement was established there, known as the "Citie of St. Mary's."

A year after this colony had been planted the settlers were instructed by their Governor, Leonard Calvert, to seize Kent Island.

Claiborne appealed to the Crown but the decision was in favor of Lord Baltimore's claim.

Claiborne did not give up so easily. With the help of Puritan

First settlers at Coan.

rebels he seized Kent Island, captured the "Citie of St. Mary's" and drove Calvert from the colony.

But Calvert was also tenacious. He returned a year later, regained control of his Maryland possessions and forced Claiborne to give up Kent Island. Later, the English government decided, once and for all, in favor of Lord Baltimore's claim.

At this time there was much religious dissension in England and in Virginia. Lord Baltimore, a Catholic himself, had hoped to establish a colony where religious freedom could be had by all. Many Puritans left the lower Tidewater Virginia and joined the Maryland settlers.

But Lord Baltimore's plan for a harmonious mingling of all religions did not work out. The Puritans seized the reins of government and there followed years of intolerance and persecution in the "Citie of St. Mary's."

Many Protestants and Royalists in the Maryland colony decided to look for a new home where they could live as they pleased.

Across the Potomac there was a long peninsula inhabited only by Indians. What better place was there to find peace?

It was in this way that the first settlers came to the Northern Neck from north of the Potomac.

THE FIRST SETTLER

IT WAS probably about the year 1640 when the Indians of Chicacoan* saw a white man's boat turning from the Potomac into their inlet, Sekacawone.

The boat was of the type called a shallop, built and used by Indian traders. This one may have been of fifteen or twenty tons burden, with two masts, and square sails that were higher than they were wide. The wood may have been turpentined, or painted in a gay combination of colors, such as red, blue, green or yellow. If oars were used as well as sails they were probably painted red.

The white men on board the shallop were doubtless dressed in the manner of seamen of their day—loose breeches and jerkins of canvas, hose of coarse wool and boots of leather. They may have

---

*Indian words had various spellings. Chicacoan, for example, was spelled Chickawane, Chickcoun, Chuckahann, Chickhan, Chiccoun, Accoan, Sekacawane, Secone, Chickoun, Chickacoon, Sekacawone, Chickacoan, Chicokolne, Chicokolue, Chicacoun, etc.

worn woolen stocking caps or felt hats, depending upon the season.

The owner of the vessel was an Englishman, not over thirty years of age. His clothes were probably of a finer weave and cut than those of his men. Unless he was different from other men of his time and station, he wore his natural hair long and flowing about his shoulders. He may have worn a sword at his side. This young gentleman's name was John Mottrom, formerly of Maryland, but more recently from the vicinity of the York River.

If the inhabitants of Chicacoan thought that the shallop held "trucke" to barter for their corn, they were mistaken. Far better for them had this been so.

John Mottrom was not looking for trade but for a new home, and he liked what he saw here—a wilderness peninsula, shut-away from the government at Jamestown by miles of water and forest, protected from Maryland by the Potomac, but close enough to keep in touch with his friends in the "Citie of St. Mary's."

He could see, too, that this wilderness held promises of future riches. He had done well as a merchant, trading with Maryland, around the Potomac and up the Bay at Kent Island, but now the fur trade was on the wane and tobacco was taking the place of beaver skins as currency.

Here, in this peninsula of northern Virginia, new lands could be had for the taking—fields for tobacco. This inlet of the Potomac that the Indians called Sekacawone was a sheltered harbor but deep enough for big ships to come in and take the tobacco away to foreign markets. The adjacent lands had been cleared by the natives; the forest would furnish materials for homes and boats.

There are no records to tell what kind of bargain Mottrom made with the Chicacoans for their land, but apparently the relations between the white men and the Indians were friendly. Marshvwap, King of the Chicacoan and Wicocomoco Indians, became a friend of his new neighbor, John Mottrom.

COAN HALL

WHEN JOHN MOTTROM came to the Indian district of Chicacoan to live, it must have been like the Garden of Eden. The river was there; the trees that were pleasant to the sight, and good for food; the beast of the field and the fowl of the air. Except for the Indian clearings along the margin of the river it was new, untouched and as it was in the beginning.

Mottrom chose a site for his house on the east bank of the Coan, and like all early Virginia settlers he knew how to select the spot. Springs were numerous in this region so that it was not necessary to dig a well.

And how did he go about building a house in this wilderness, so far from any place where skilled labor, tools and bricks, glass and nails could be obtained? No records to answer this question have been uncovered to this date. Perhaps, he brought indentured servants and a few crude tools with him in the shallop.

What kind of a house did he build? It is fairly certain that he did not build a log cabin, even for a temporary shelter.

In the seventeenth century the English settlers in Virginia built log forts, log prisons and log garrison houses but they were of "logs hewn square," and they were built in the traditional Old World manner.

These early settlers mentioned living in cottages, huts and frame cabins but, so far as is known, they never said that they lived in log cabins. The American-type log cabin is believed to have developed later and in another part of the country.

Mottrom and his men may have erected temporary shelters of saplings, boughs and bark, similar to the Indian houses.

If wood was cut from the forest for his permanent home, time was needed. Locust for sills, oak for framing, heart pine and cedar were at hand, but green lumber had to be seasoned.

Mottrom may have made several trips to Jamestown or Maryland for artisans and building supplies before his new home was completed. Meanwhile, he may have brought his family to live in one of the temporary shelters.

There are no buildings surviving in Virginia that were known to have been built before 1650, therefore, no true picture of the Mottrom home can be presented.

However, there are enough facts known of the period to enable one to reconstruct a reasonably accurate picture of the first house on the Coan.

First of all—the house had to be strong, for life itself might depend upon the house. Its style was, no doubt, patterned after the architecture of England but modified by circumstances in the New World.

A framed building, one storey and a half high, with brick underpinning, and brick chimneys at either end, was the typical dwelling of Virginia about the middle of the seventeenth century. Its size would have been about forty by twenty feet, with down-stairs ceilings about nine feet high.

We can visualize those workmen at Coan "riving" out the weather boards for the first known house in the Northern Neck. One of the men would be holding a rough-squared length of timber on a "frow" horse, while another would be pounding, with a wooden mallet, a wedge-shaped knife into the wood. Presently a board would fall off. With the same tools shingles for the roof would be split from cedar.

John Mottrom may have bought English bricks from some ship bound homeward with a load of tobacco and eager to get rid of the ballast of bricks at any price. It is more likely that his bricks were burned in a kiln at Coan, made with clay dug from the riverbank.

Nails were so hard to get that settlers when they were leaving to settle elsewhere burned their homes in order to get the nails to start a new house. Mottrom probably brought some nails from his former home and supplemented them with wooden pegs.

Rarely before 1720 were "windows sasht with crystal glass." Casements were used. Glass-making had ended at Jamestown in 1624. Mottrom's windows may have been diamond-shaped panes of oiled paper with solid wooden shutters, or merely sliding panels of wood. But it was possible to get imported glass and he may have had some glass, drawn lead and solder from England. The window openings were a structural part of the framing, not just holes cut in the sheathing. Sometimes the windows did not open, as they were mainly intended to let in light. In this case the leaded glass was permanently set in the frames in diamond-shaped panes.

Mottrom's front door may have had hinges made in the shapes of the letters H and L, to stand for Holy Lord, for it was believed then that such hinges would drive ghosts away from the door. The door may have had panels in the form of a cross to keep out the witches. Or, the door may have been made of oak battens, heavy enough to keep out wolves, Indians and "hurry-canes." In either case, it was fastened with a latch and string, with possibly an oaken bar inside for added strength.

The chimneys of Virginia houses were much larger than those in England, and the fireplaces were at least seven feet across, for the hearth was the heart of the home.

From these various facts of the time, we assume that the first house in the Northern Neck which John Mottrom named Coan Hall was strong, simple, functional, and its character was medieval.

NEIGHBORS

IN SPITE of its isolation Coan Hall was probably not a lonely place. Besides John Mottrom and his wife there were two children, and probably several indentured servants. There were at least a few domestic animals. The Indians were near, the forest was alive and rustling and "nimble" with wild beasts, the sky was darkened and animated by the various birds in their season. The shallop lay at anchor not far away and was a reminder that it was possible to reach some civilization beyond the woods and water.

And Coan Hall was hardly established before guests began to arrive. They came by boat, and perhaps after dark. These Protestant friends and refugees were from Lord Baltimore's "Citie of St. Mary's."

It was whispered in that unhappy "citie" north of the Potomac that treason was being plotted at Coan Hall.

John Mottrom's new home must have been filled to capacity in those days. Although the rooms were few we can be sure that there was no lack of beds or chairs. Rooms then, with the exception of the kitchen, had no distinct character. Beds were in every room, even in the hall where meals were taken.

On a winter's night we can imagine John Mottrom dispensing hospitality at Coan Hall—food, drink and roaring fires. Great plotting and planning must have gone on before the hearths, while the passing tankards of metheglin cheered and warmed the indignant gentlemen from Maryland.

Perhaps John Mottrom's guests were charmed with his new home and decided that it was easier just to settle at Chicacoan. At any rate we hear no more of treason. Instead, settlers begin to arrive in the Northern Neck.

William Presley and his English wife were among the first to arrive at Chicacoan. They built at the head of a creek not far from Coan Hall.

Richard Thompson and his family probably arrived early too. Richard was a young man, about twenty-seven, when he came to live at Chicacoan. He was a native of Norwich, Norfolk County, England. As a boy he had come to Virginia as an indentured servant and had served William Claiborne on Kent Island for three years.

When at twenty-one Richard became a free man, he went into

business for himself, trading with the Indians for beaver. He must have been a good trader for he acquired a considerable estate. He also worked as an agent for William Claiborne, which in the end brought about his downfall. When Claiborne was proclaimed an enemy by the Maryland Council, Thompson was denounced also. He was in this way forced to flee to Chicacoan.

Before long a settlement had sprung up along the Coan. John Mottrom became the unofficial leader of this first white settlement in the Northern Neck. Although he did not know it, there was one among them who was to play an important part in his life—her name was Ursula, wife of Richard Thompson.

THE "KIDS"

AS SOON as their homes were built the settlers at Chicacoan began to remove the forest and clear the ground for tobacco fields.

The sound of axes was no doubt heard from sunrise until sunset. Then the stumps had to be dug up, and the soil had to be broken up with hoes. This hard labor was probably done by white indentured servants.

These British servants were commercially known as "kids," probably because most of them were young, their ages ranging from thirteen to thirty as a rule.

An early English writer described the manner in which these "kids" were obtained to send to Virginia—"very many children . . . were violently taken away or cheatingly duckoyed without the consent or knowledge of their Parents by . . . persons . . . called Spirits . . . into private places or ships, and there sold to be transported, and then resold there to be servants to those that will give most for them."

A letter written in England in 1610 says that—"there are many ships going to Virginia with them 14 or 15 hundred children w'ch they have gathered up in divers places."

The shipmaster who brought the children over could sell the indentures for whatever he could get for them. If he could not find a purchaser, he could sell the children to persons known as "soul drivers" who would "buy a parcel of servants" to fill his wagon and drive through the country until he could sell them at a cash profit.

Other indentured servants were brought over by planters as "headrights," which meant that the planter paid for their transportation and received fifty acres of land as a reward for transporting an immigrant to Virginia.

The indenture was a simple bargain between master and servant with protection by law for each. The treatment of the servant depended upon the nature of his master.

The boys who had long terms to serve became restless and often ran away across the Potomac to Maryland or to an Indian village. They were usually caught and punished and put back to work. In Virginia the punishment was sometimes thirty lashes and the letter R branded on the cheek, forehead or shoulder. The hair was sometimes cropped, and the leg shackled with irons, even during working hours. There is no evidence that the settlers of the Northern Neck did anything more severe than to whip their "kids."

Food, clothing and shelter was provided by the master. The shelter was usually in "a house set apart for him." The list of clothing might include a coat of frieze, a pair of leather breeches, a black hat, or cap of fur, a pair of "wooden heel shoes," and underclothes of dowlas and lockram.

The indentured girl servants did not work in the fields unless they were slattern and offensive. Their work was to bake and brew, clean, milk, churn, wash and sew.

Due to the scarcity of women in Virginia the girl servants usually married within the first three months. If their reputation was good, they often married into a higher station.

INDIAN SERVANTS

THE SETTLERS at Chicacoan may have had some Indian servants. Tradition says that William Presley of Coan employed Indians to care for his "roaming stock."

It was customary in Virginia to take Indian children as apprentices to learn a trade, and to learn to read and write. This was with the consent of the parents that the child should be instructed in the Christian religion.

The children were usually taken at thirteen or fourteen years of age and the apprenticeships lasted until they were twenty-one.

The value of the Indian servant was about the same as that of the English indentured servant. The relationship between the Indian boy and his master was the same as that between the master and the English servant. Food, clothing and shelter was furnished by the master. Records of the clothing lists included leather breeches, cotton waistcoats, shoes and stockings.

MONEY

THE INDIAN word wampum meant "shells." Wampum and copper were the Indians' substitute for gold and silver. The early settlers also used the Indian wampum as a medium of exchange.

Wampum, in Virginia, was usually made from the oyster shell. The dark wampum, which was made from the black or purple part of the shell, had twice the value of the white. For instance, three of the dark beads or six of the white beads equalled one English penny.

The beads were cylindrical in shape about an eighth of an inch in diameter and one-fourth of an inch long. They were rubbed against stones until they were polished smooth. A hole was bored through the center of each bead with a flint instrument so that it could be strung on thread. Much of this wampum was made by tribes who manufactured and carried on commerce.

The most common wampum, made of white shell, was called rhoanoke. In old records wampum was sometimes referred to as "a chain of pearl." In a Northumberland County record there is listed among the items in the estate of "James Claughton, dec'd: Mr. Richard Thompson per order 20 arms length of Rhoanoke." Another early settler of the Northern Neck, Moore Fauntleroy, paid the Indians for his land "ten fathoms of peake" and "thirty arms length of Rhoanoke."

The English went so far as to import imitation wampum of white porcelain for sale to the Indians.

The early settlers also used beaver skins as currency. Northern Neck records about 1656 show that Colonel Nathaniel Pope offered to go security for John Washington "in beaver skins." Even hens were used for currency.

Tobacco soon became the most important currency in the colony. The words of the old song—"Where money grows on white oak trees," was almost true in Virginia for there tobacco was money and tobacco grew everywhere. Instead of gold and silver the colonial had his "tobacco note." The chief reason that metallic coin was scarce throughout the whole colonial period in Virginia was the fact that tobacco was currency.

It seems that there was always a small stock of coin in the colony, but it was either used in trade with other countries or it was hoarded by the colonists. A Virginia county record of 1700 says that: "Spanish money may not be exported out of this colony, but that it may pass currently from man to man and that all pieces of eight pass for five shillings specie."

The most convenient metallic money in Virginia (1722-1835) was a Portuguese gold coin called a johannes. A full johannes was called a "half-joe," and a double johannes was called a "joe."

As banking institutions were non-existent in the colony in the early days, and as robbers sometimes lay in wait in the woods for a lone horseman, travelers used to carry gold coins sewed under the lining of their waistcoats or quilted into their coats.

A PARADISE DISCOVERED

FOR SEVERAL years the settlers at Chicacoan lived in a dream-like paradise—ungoverned and untaxed.

But this state of freedom could not last. News of the thriving young settlement in the Northern Neck was probably carried to Jamestown by the stream of travellers who plied back and forth along the waterways between that city and St. Mary's in Maryland.

How great the consternation must have been at Chicacoan when one day a boat arrived from Jamestown. There may have been soldiers on board or other representatives of the government. They brought a startling message.

The message was in the form of an Act passed by the House of Burgesses at an Assembly in 1644. It said:

"Whereas, the inhabitants of Chicawane, alias Northumberland, being members of this colony, have not hitherto contributed toward the charges of the war (with the Indians) it is now thought fit that the said inhabitants do make payment of the levy according to such rates as are by this present Assembly assessed."

The rates were "for every 100 acres of land, 15 pounds tobacco; for every cow above 3 years old, 15 pounds tobacco."

But the real shock came at the end of the message: "And in case the said inhabitants shall refuse or deny payment of the said levy, as above expressed, that upon report thereof to the next Assembly, speedy course shall be adopted to call them off the said Plantation."

The settlers were no doubt infuriated at this command. They ignored it, and continued to live in their independent way.

John Mottrom, however, must have thought it high time to look into the situation. In the fall of 1645 he sailed for Jamestown.

A VISIT TO JAMESTOWN

ALTHOUGH A TRIP to Jamestown would have been an exciting change after years of wilderness living, there is reason to believe that Mrs. Mottrom did not accompany her husband to the capital city. She probably supervised the preparation of food for the voyage, and packed his clothes.

John Mottrom's clothes were no doubt as fashionable as the English tailors could furnish. Rich fabrics and bright colors were worn by Virginia gentlemen of the seventeenth century, and they never seemed to think that their "citified" garments looked out of place in the primitive setting of the New World.

Among the clothes that Mrs. Mottrom may have packed, there might have been "a sea-green scarf edged with gold lace," a scarlet coat with silver buttons, a camlet coat with sleeves ending in lace ruffles, a pair of red slippers, a Turkey-worked waistcoat, a whole suit of olive-color plush, silk stockings, a beaver hat, neckcloths of finest holland and muslin, shoes with shining silver buckles, delicately scented handkerchiefs of silk and lace, and a gold belt for her husband's sword.

The Mottrom household was probably on the bank of the Coan to wave good-byes when the anchor was weighed and the sails of the shallop were hoisted.

Out of the Coan sailed the shallop, and into the Potomac. Out of the Potomac into the Chesapeake. Then it was straight sailing down the Bay, past the mouths of the Rappahannock and York, and finally, into the James. It usually took four average sailing days to travel from the Northern Neck to Jamestown.

As the boat neared Jamestown Island John Mottrom could doubtless see the orange-tiled roofs and tall red chimneys of the "citie," which had long ago burst from its palisades and was now stretched for half a mile along the river front, as well as backward into the swamps and meadows.

He could no doubt see the tower of the new brick church, and east of it the State House, which looked so "London-like" with its three steep gable ends facing the river.

Captain John Smith had written that the water here was deep "so neare the shoare that they moored to the trees in six fathom water," but the Mottrom boat may have tied up at Friggett Landing in the rear of the Island. There were probably other vessels already tied up there, and others still arriving for the Assembly.

Mottrom may have seen a barge coming down from the upper James, loaded with gaily dressed men and women—a Burgess or Councillor and his family and retinue, perhaps.

Once ashore John Mottrom probably took a walk to stretch his legs and see what changes had taken place since he had last visited "James Citie." He may have passed the new church, which was still unfinished, and strolled along some of the narrow lanes. Outside the town there were some "cart paths," and over some of the swamps there were bridges. Back of the Island lay the forested Indian district of the "Passbyhaes."

"New Towne" was the most thickly settled part of "James Citie." Most of the houses were a story-and-a-half of "framed timber" with steeply-pointed roofs of tile, and a few of slate. Each had its garden and was enclosed with palings. The road along the river bank was edged with mulberry trees.

The State House, situated near the river and down stream from the church, was probably the most imposing building in the town. It was really three brick houses joined together in a row to form a block, like the medieval gabled houses in London. Its windows were casements with lattices of lead and diamond-shaped panes of greenish colored glass. The place had a garden, fruit trees and vines, all enclosed by palings.

This State House was the focal point of the government and the center of social life at Jamestown. John Mottrom probably stayed there during his visit for the governor, Sir William Berkeley, who lived in the building on the western end, acted as host to all important visitors.

The Assemblies, courts and councils were held in the "middle-most" of the three houses. The Assembly would soon convene and the visitor from the Northern Neck had come a long way to be present at that meeting of November 20, 1645.

We can imagine him there on that important day, sitting with that dignified group of men, dressed in their rich bright garments, all with their hats on in imitation of the House of Commons in far away England.

Little is known of what took place in that meeting that concerned Chicacoan except that John Mottrom was accepted and recognized in this Assembly as a Burgess from the "Plantation of Northumberland." It seems that an English name was preferred instead of the Indian name for that land between the Rappahannock and the Potomac.

FRANCES

MRS. MOTTROM probably did not accompany her husband to Jamestown because in that same year a baby was born at Coan Hall.

What a time that must have been in the wilderness household—the little indentured English maids scurrying about with wooden pails of steaming water, perhaps, and the curtains all drawn about the great bed, and John Mottrom pacing the floor no doubt like any modern father-to-be!

Frances Mottrom, for thus she was christened, may have been the first white baby to have been born in the Northern Neck.

The neighbors doubtless came to Coan Hall for a christening for it is a matter of record that Colonel William Presley's wife was named as the child's godmother. There must have been great cheer at the manor on that occasion, and many toasts drunk from the same tankard. Maybe a whole horn of metheglin was passed around in true medieval fashion to "speed the parting guests."

Frances probably lay in a wooden cradle with high paneled sides to keep out draughts. Its logical place was near the fireplace where she would be warm. She was doubtless clothed in white linen exquisitely embroidered and made. Perhaps her six-year-old sister Anne rocked the cradle now and then as she played around the floor, and little John Mottrom may have peered into its shadows to look at her face.

Among the first sounds that Frances knew were no doubt the ringing of the axes in the forest from sunrise until sunset in winter, and at night the howling of the wolves in the forest. The first light that she remembered was probably the firelight and the light from pine-knot or candle, or daylight filtered through diamond-paned windows of greenish glass or oiled paper.

One of the first familiar faces may have been that of her father's friend, Marshvwap, King of Chickacoan.

Frances must have been a sturdy baby to have survived the cold, heat, fevers, and all the other hazards to child-life in the seventeenth century.

When Frances was old enough to toddle about, Anne and John may have played a game with her called "honey-pots," in which they carried her about in a "chair" made by crossing hands, while they chanted:

"Carry your honey-pot safe and sound
Or it will fall upon the ground."

A little later they may have jumped a hop-scotch, but if so, they called it "scotch-hoppers." They probably played tag, ball, prisoner's base, asked riddles and blew soap-bubbles, as these simple amusements dated from medieval days.

Children of the seventeenth century played games but had few toys. There may have been a top to spin, and John probably played Indian with bow and arrow and club. Anne, who had been born in England, may have brought with her to the New World a stiff little puppet-like doll with a wooden face and painted hair. Frances may have had a doll made of corn-shucks, rags, corn-cobs or nuts. Or she may have had a doll like those of the Indian children, made of rawhide, feathers and wood.

The Mottrom children may have had wild animals for pets—a deer, a squirrel, or a raccoon, perhaps. The children could not venture far into the forest to play because of the dangers that lurked in its depths, but they could stand at its edge and look down the aisles between the trees, some of them "twenty feet round and Ninety high." In spring and summer the forest floor was "bespred with divers flowers" and wild strawberries. In winter they might glimpse a snowshoe rabbit flying over the snow, or a herd of deer. We can imagine them there—three little figures dressed in long clothes, exactly like those of their parents, looking into the forest and pondering upon its mysteries.

When Frances was nine years old, Colonel William Presley presented her with "one cow calfe . . . she being my wife's God daughter." This was great potential wealth for a little girl! A cow over three years old was at that time worth exactly the same as one hundred acres of land. Frances probably thought of the "cow calfe" only in terms of milk and butter and future cakes that might be baked. She may have named the calf Pansy, Daisy, Cinnamon or Nutmeg, as such names were then popular for cows.

As Frances grew older there was little time for play. The

Mottrom household was doubtless astir by daybreak. We can picture the sleepy child pushing aside the heavy red or green curtains of linsey-woolsey that surrounded her bed, or if it was summer, the hangings of "muskitoe" net.

Her toilet equipment was no doubt simple—a basin and ewer, and a "pot de chambre," all of pewter. She may have owned a gilded hand looking-glass and a comb of ivory or horn. She washed her face with home-made soap which may have been soft or, more likely, a hard green soap made from the berries of "sweet myrtle."

Frances' clothes were probably kept in a "case of drawers." Her everyday dress was perhaps of blue holland, but for special occasions she wore silk or brocade. In either case the skirt was full and long. Over this she wore a white linen apron with bib, and on her head a close-fitting cap of white linen. The latter was always worn by little children at that time, and sometimes the cap was beautifully embroidered. When Frances went out-of-doors she probably wore a loose silken hood over the cap.

Her hair, if she was fashionable, was cut in bangs across her forehead with long flowing locks in front dropping forward on her chest. Her back hair was stuffed out of sight in the cap.

After she had dressed Frances probably ate a simple breakfast of porridge from a wooden bowl with a pewter spoon. Anne and John probably ate their breakfasts from the same bowl with their pewter spoons.

Lessons may have come next. Education was simple then, especially for girls—"bookes to bee learned of children" were "abcies" and primers, then the Psalms in metre, then the Testament. Frances' teacher may have been her mother or an indentured servant.

Little girls were taught to knit as soon as they could hold the needles. Frances probably knitted stockings and mittens when she was four or five years old. Children also made quilt-pieces. Girls did household chores and learned early the duties of a housewife.

Anne was old enough now to embroider the family coat-of-arms, or to paint it on glass in rich colors. Young girls in the families of seventeenth century gentlefolk spent much time in the study of heraldry.

Frances may have been taught to play a musical instrument— the hand lyre, hautboy or virginal. The latter was most commonly used by young girls, from which its name was derived. It was a small rectangular spinet without legs.

John may have played the flute. We can imagine him earnestly playing for guests at Coan Hall, dressed in his best, which probably would have been a dark suit with a white square collar, the pants ending in light-colored ruffles that fell over his boottops. From under his wide-brimmed hat, which he would wear indoors on such occasions, his hair probably fell to his shoulders, with bangs on his forehead.

It is safe in assuming that the Mottrom children looked forward to guests for they doubtless liked to listen to the talk around the fireplace. Here the men discussed taxes, the colonial government, the English King and his followers who were called Cavaliers. They talked of witchcraft, ghosts, wolves, Indians and the Assembly at "James Citie."

Did all this talk make little Frances long to visit Jamestown and see the fine ladies who came from their plantations with their husbands at the time of the Assemblies? If so, her dream was one day to come true. She would not only visit Jamestown and see the ladies in their silks and satins but she would be one of them. For Frances Mottrom was destined to leave her wilderness home some day and become the first lady not only of Jamestown, but of the whole Colony of Virginia.

FOREVER LOST

ALTHOUGH JOHN MOTTROM was recognized at Jamestown in the Assembly of November 20, 1645 as a Burgess from the "Plantation of Northumberland," Chicacoan was not established as a county and the order concerning taxes was not changed. The settlers continued to ignore the order and went on living as usual in their independent way.

In 1647, the Assembly passed another act for the "reducing of the inhabitants of Chicacoan and the other parts of the Neck of Land between the Rappahannock and the Potomack River."

This must have been an unhappy and unsettled time at Chicacoan, but in some way a compromise was reached the following year. In 1648, the Assembly repealed the act for "reducing the inhabitants of Chicacoan," and enacted instead that "the said tract of land be hereafter called and knowne by the name of the Countie of Northumberland and from henceforth they have power of electing Burgesses for the said county."

The settlers of the Northern Neck had now gained representation in the colonial government but the price they were forced to pay for it was dear—their tax-free paradise was forever lost.

URSULA

JOHN MOTTROM'S wife may ever remain a mystery. There seems to be no clue to her personality, no facts that would make her into a flesh and blood woman. Even her name is unknown. She was John Mottrom's wife and the mother of his three children, Anne, John and Frances. The records disclose not even a crumb more.

Between the years 1645 and 1655 Mrs. Mottrom passed away. She may have died in childbirth when Frances was born, or shortly thereafter. It was after her death that Ursula came into the life of John Mottrom.

Ursula Bish Thompson had been among the refugees who fled to Coan from the "Citie of St. Mary's." Her husband, Richard Thompson, was now dead. A young widow's position in a frontier community was dangerous and insecure and quick remarriages were a practical necessity. John Mottrom, the widower, was in urgent need of someone to look after his children and home. Ursula and John were married.

Ursula probably brought the Thompson children with her to live at Coan Hall. Colonial households more often than not included several groups of children by former marriages.

Ursula's name reveals the fact that she was British, named perhaps for the martyred princess, St. Ursula. The facts of her later career assure us that she was a healthy and attractive woman.

As the wife of a prominent man of the colony it was Ursula's duty to hold to the high standard of living that had been transferred from England to this wilderness, and to maintain this standard it was necessary for all to work from morning until night.

Ursula doubtless loved the gay rich clothes that were so fashionable at this period. Her wardrobe may have included a pair of scarlet sleeves, a petticoat of flowered tabby and several pairs of green stockings.

We can imagine Ursula hustling about at Coan Hall, her clothes a blur of brightness, as she supervised the servants, disciplined the children, twirled the roast of venison on the spit in passing, or lowered her candle or betty-lamp into the cooking pot to see if the stew was ready.

The rooms of Coan Hall were probably part "waynscot" and part "daubed and whitelimed," the latter plaster being made from the plentiful oyster shells. The woodwork may have been painted "deep blued olive green" or "dragon's blood."

The rooms of seventeenth century houses were usually identified by names, such as "the outward," "the lodging," "the chamber," and so on.

The kitchen and pantry were probably detached or in a wing. This was the busiest and coziest spot in all early homes, and the hearth was its glowing heart. There were the fire-dogs holding the big logs and the little andirons used with them called "creepers." On pothooks and trammels hung the brass and copper kettles, some with a fifteen gallon capacity, and that most beloved pot of iron, which sometimes weighed as much as forty pounds. In summer when a large part of the cooking was done out-of-doors this iron kettle was the main utensil used.

A boiler of copper and brass may have been imbedded in brick and mortar and heated from beneath for the purpose of brewing the ale that was so necessary to a transplanted Englishman.

When the chimney was built there was usually a brick oven on one side. This oven was as a rule heated once a week. Convenient to the oven was a long-handled shovel called a peel, which was used for placing the dough in the oven, or for tossing it on cabbage or oak leaves which were often used instead of pans.

The simplest way of roasting a fowl or joint of meat was to suspend it in front of the fire by a hempen string.

The laundry was allowed to accumulate into great monthly washings. This seems to have been the custom for a hundred years after the colony was first settled. Soft soap was made by the barrel from refuse grease and wood ashes. This soap was used for the laundry but a toilet soap was made from the bayberry, or "sweet myrtle," as it was called in Virginia. Candles were also made from the myrtle berries, and from tallow. The myrtle berry candles were prettier and more fragrant.

The brick-floored milkhouse at these early plantations was a separate building. Besides the milk pails, bowls, skimmers and churn, this house was a storage place for pewter that needed repairing, powdering tubs for salting meat, rum casks, spinning-wheels, chamber pots, fish kettles, stillyards, hides, tanned leather and so on.

Brooms were made at home, and turkey wings were saved for brushing the hearth.

Perhaps another duty of Ursula and her indentured maids was the picking of the tame geese. Their feathers were more valuable to the colonists than their meat. Goose feathers were prized for beds and pillows, which were handed down as heirlooms. The feathers were stripped from the live geese three or four times a year, but the quills, which were used for pens, were never pulled but once. Ursula probably dreaded goose-picking because it was a hard and cruel work. Feathers from wildfowl were also carefully saved for beds and pillows.

Probably the last chore on a winter's night was the warming of the beds. The brass or copper warming pan with its long handle hung by the fireplace where it reflected the firelight. At bedtime, which was early, the pan was filled with hot coals and thrust within the beds and moved rapidly back and forth so as to warm the bed but not burn the linen. Sometimes a large chafing-dish was used in the bed-chambers for "knocking the chill off" the ice-cold room.

And so at last, after the last chore had been attended to, Ursula could crawl between the warm sheets, pull up her quilt, or leather coverlet, and fall into a well-earned sleep.

THE YARD

THE SURROUNDINGS of a seventeenth century planter's house, such as Coan Hall, were simple, lacking in ornament of any kind.

Near the back door was a garden in which vegetables and a few simple flowers grew side by side. Real flower gardens were not developed until the next century.

Some flax and hemp were probably included in the garden at Coan. And herbs, such as thyme, rosemary and majoram were considered almost a necessity at that time.

There was usually an orchard, containing a few apple, pear, cherry and peach trees.

There may have been a dovecote at Coan Hall. There must certainly have been a tall pole in the yard with a bee-martin's house on top, for these birds notified the settler and his household of the approach of hawks and other enemies of the poultry. They were the watch-dogs of the yard. There may have been a few birdhouses made Indian fashion of gourds.

The planter's dwelling, even though it was little and plain, sometimes no larger than 24 x 24, was referred to as the "manor house," "great house" or "mansion," in order to distinguish it from its dependencies, the kitchen, milkhouse, smokehouse, henhouse, stable, barn and cabins for servants.

According to an early order by the Assembly, all dwelling houses throughout the Colony of Virginia must be palisaded. This order was still in effect when Coan Hall was built, but as the Indians were friendly in this region and there was no one at Chicacoan to enforce the law, the yard may have been surrounded by a stout fence of locust instead, or by palings to keep out hogs and cattle which wandered without restraint.

Needless to say, a bubbling spring was somewhere close by the dwelling, and perhaps a gourd dipper.

KITTAMAQUND

POCAHONTAS WAS NOT the only Indian girl of royal blood who once lived in the Northern Neck. Kittamaqund, too, lived for awhile, died and, it is believed, was buried in the land between the Rappahannock and the Potomac.

Kittamaqund was the only child of the Tayac, or Emperor, of the Piscataway Indians. Their village was located on Piscataway Creek on the Maryland side of the Potomac. At this point the Potomac, which separated the Province of Maryland from the Colony of Virginia, was less than a mile wide.

In the winter of 1640 Father Andrew White, a Catholic missionary, came to "Piscatoe" to baptize the Indians. Among those whom Father White baptized were the Emperor and his wife.

Shortly after the missionary's visit, the Emperor brought his seven-year-old daughter, Kittamaqund, to St. Mary's "Citie," Maryland, and put her in the care of Father White. He loved his daughter very dearly and he wanted her to be educated and "when she shall well understand the Christian mysteries, to be washed in the sacred font of baptism."

The "little Empress," as she was called by the settlers, was adopted by Mistress Margaret Brent of St. Mary's. By 1642 Kittamaqund had become "proficient in the English language" and she was baptized by Father White at that time and given the Christian name Mary.

Before long romance took a hand in the situation. Mistress Margaret had a brother, Giles Brent, who had left England with her on the ship *Elizabeth* in 1638, and they had arrived together at St.

Mary's. Giles had been born in Gloucestershire, England, about 1600.

Giles and the little Indian "Empress" were married when she was about twelve years old. Giles had a home on Kent Island where they lived for part of the year and the rest of the year they stayed with Margaret at her home "in St. Maries, where he had certain goods &C"—"divers cattle and other commodities . . . linen, shoes, stockings, sugar . . . and also a little cabbonett containing Jewels &C."

About 1646 Giles took his Indian bride and crossed the Potomac to the Northern Neck of Virginia. He settled on the north shore of Aquia Creek and there built a house which he called Peace. This name seems to indicate that he may have had troubles, probably religious persecution, in Maryland. He had also failed in his attempt to claim Kittamaqund's royal domain, which was most of Maryland.

The home of Giles and Kittamaqund in the Northern Neck was in the midst of the wilderness. They were the northernmost English residents in Virginia. When in 1651 settlers pushed northward to patent land above the Brent home they all stopped at Peace for refreshments and information. It was the point of departure into the unknown.

Giles built another home in the same region which he called Retirement. Their second son, Giles, was born there.

Giles traded with the Indians and continued to keep open house for the settlers from the southern region. He also patented thousands of acres of land in Westmoreland and Northumberland.

Kittamaqund, the little wilderness flower, wilted and died before she scarcely had time to blossom. She left three children, Richard, Giles and Mary. Before she died Kittamaqund made a deed of gift to her daughter of her inheritance in Maryland, since she herself had no brother or sister to inherit it.

Giles again laid claim to most of Maryland in his daughter's name, but the Indians opposed the claim as being contrary to their tribal customs. They chose a king of their own instead.

Thus Kittamaqund lost her royal heritage. According to traditions she was buried somewhere in the upper Northern Neck.

Giles Brent became a great landowner in his own right. He was largely responsible for opening up the northern part of the "Chicakoun country" to the white settlers. His homes at Peace and later at Retirement were outposts of civilization.

THE GIFT

WHILE THE settlers of the Northern Neck of Virginia were hacking away at the forest, planting crops in the land thus cleared and building houses of the felled timber, events were taking place across the sea that would eventually change the history and culture of the land between the Rappahannock and the Potomac.

For some time a civil war had been in progress in England and early in the year of 1649 Charles I was beheaded by Oliver Cromwell's men. A new government, known as the Commonwealth, was immediately established in England, under the direction of Cromwell.

The late king's oldest son, Charles, had escaped from England and was now living in exile in France. His misfortune was shared there by some of his father's supporters, who now had plenty of time to brood over their lost estates back in England. These gentlemen with the flowing hair had little left except the clothes on their backs, plumed hats and buckled boots. Some of them were walking the streets of Paris in search of cheap board and lodging, for which they would pay with their jewels—pawned or sold. Some had already gotten into the clutches of money-lenders. Their only hope was that Charles would be restored some day to the throne of England.

Charles wished that he could in some way repay these noblemen, soldiers, diplomats and favorites of his parents who had proved their loyalty. But what, he may have wondered, did he have to give? Apparently nothing remained. Then he thought of land—other land to replace the estates his followers had lost. This was not a new idea of his own for the English government had at times awarded frontier lands to deserving soldiers.

But where could lands-to-give-away be found? It was then that Charles remembered the colony across the sea—Virginia. That was the answer—a slice of the Virginia wilderness as a grant to his courtiers!

Charles apparently knew little about Virginia, or about the size of the slice which he selected as a gift to his friends—"all that entire Tract, Territory, or porcon of Land situate, lying and beeing in America, and bounded by and within the heads of the Rivers of Rappahannock and Patawomecke," and "said Rivers."

A patent was written, dated September 18, 1649, at St. Germaine-en-Laye, France. It was written in close fine writing on both sides of a small piece of parchment and bore "Our Great Seale of

England." Charles signed it simply in the upper left-hand corner of the front page "Charles R." Thus the deed was done.

True, the grant was worthless unless Charles was restored to the throne of England, which event seemed improbable at the moment. However, he had paid off his obligations as best he could. The courtiers may have appreciated his gesture but some of them placed no value on their part of the patent.

Meanwhile, back in Virginia the colonists went on as usual for news was slow in crossing the ocean. The pioneers of the Northern Neck had their own problems—fevers and bloody flux, Indians, wolves, witches, and taxes to be paid to the Colonial Government at Jamestown. It would be a long time before they would know that their land had been given away lock, stock and barrel, for Charles had given his followers not only the land and the rivers, but all rights pertaining to them, even to the "wild beasts and fowle," the fish and the "wrecks of the Sea."

And should the grant ever become valid, future generations in the Northern Neck would have landlords over them and pay rent for the land that their forefathers had believed to be their own.

THE CAVALIERS

A MAN STOOD on the deck of the *Virginia Merchant*, a leaky English vessel bound for Jamestown. He had once been a fine gentleman, clothed in satin and velvet and gold lace. His beard had been trimmed to a peak, with small upturned mustaches, and his shoulder length hair had been curled and perfumed. "Love-locks" his curls were called.

Now the velvet was stained and the lace tarnished and his silver buckles looked more like pewter. The plumes on his hat dangled against his salt-matted hair. The ship was loaded with men just like him. In England they were called Cavaliers because they had been loyal followers of the King. A writer of that time described these Cavaliers as "of the best material in England"—the nobility, the clergy, the landed gentry and officers in the King's army.

Tradition says that there were three hundred and thirty Cavaliers on board the *Virginia Merchant*. This number included the wives and children, and probably the ship's company.

The voyage had been a nightmare. Rats lived in the dark cabins with the people, and when the cabin doors were opened a stench rushed out. Some lay ill from the ship's diet of "pease-porridge" and salt beef. Worms wriggled in the cheese and hard bread that was called ship's biscuits. And there was not even enough of this food to last the trip.

Desperation had driven these people to make this voyage, and they were lucky to have the six pounds to pay their passage. Their England was no longer good for them. It was a place to "fly from ... as from a place infected with the plague." Some of their comrades were now rotting in English prisons, their estates confiscated and sold to members of Cromwell's party.

Virginia seemed to be the only "city of refuge" left in his Majesty's dominions. When the *Virginia Merchant* at last arrived at Jamestown the Cavaliers were received with open arms by the colonists, whose sympathy was predominantly with the royalist cause. Still other Cavaliers reached Virginia from time to time during Cromwell's reign in England.

The *Virginia Merchant* had sailed from the Old World about the middle of September 1649. This was almost exactly the same time that the exile in France was affixing his signature to a bit of parchment. Both incidents were destined to change the pattern of life in the Northern Neck of Virginia.

A number of the Cavaliers settled in the Neck, bringing with them into the wilderness the grace and manners of the English Court and the way of life of the English country gentleman.

"CHARLIE-OVER-THE-WATER"

IN THE SPRING of 1650 a small Dutch vessel, according to one tradition, was bucking her way across the Atlantic. On board was a young man named Richard Lee. Richard had arranged this trip and "freighted" the vessel himself, it was said, and he was now on his way to visit England's royal exile who was at this time living in Brussels.

In Richard's pocket, the story goes, was Sir William "Barcklaie's" commission for the government of Virginia, which hadn't been worth a shilling since the execution of England's late King. But Sir William and Richard, who was his Secretary of State, were determined to hold the colony firm in its allegiance to "Charlie-Over-The-Water."

Richard arrived safely in Breda and made himself known to

Charles. Thereafter, it is said, a little comedy ensued which we can imagine.

The gentleman from Virginia, dressed in his finest trappings, kneels before the exiled prince and surrenders the Governor's commission. He then in flowery words extends a warm invitation to Charles to return with him to the New World and become "King of Virginia."

Charles is pleased, but he has other plans. Bigger plans. He thanks Richard and graciously presents him with a new commission for Governor Berkeley, which isn't worth the paper on which it is written.

After this little farce was attended to, Richard Lee, tradition says, returned to Jamestown to deliver the commission to Governor Berkeley. Richard was probably disappointed with the unsatisfactory outcome of his mission.

How different the history of the New World would have been if Richard Lee had brought Charles back with him to be crowned "King of Virginia!"

THE LEGACY

IT WAS a place especially dear to the Indians. They were still in the region when Richard Lee built his simple home in the wilderness.

He chose for his home site a neck of land in the southeastern part of Northumberland County. A creek flowed in here from the Chesapeake and divided into two parts. The neck was between these two branches of the creek. Richard called the estuary, Dividing Creek, and he named his home, Cobbs Hall.

It was wild and beautiful at Dividing Creek. The primeval forest with its savages and "beastes" was so close, and out in front the Creek led directly into the Bay—a highway to any place in the world. The Creek was deep so that foreign ships could come right up to his wharf and take away the loads of tobacco that this fertile soil would grow.

Richard knew that in this New World land was wealth, so he began to acquire land by purchase of headrights. He acquired land along the Potomac from its mouth to the site that later became Washington. He had laid the foundation for the future Lees of Virginia.

Richard Lee represented Northumberland in the House of Burgesses at Jamestown in 1651, which establishes the fact that he was living in the Northern Neck at that early date. He was also a justice, a member of the King's Council and Secretary of the Colony.

Richard had business interests abroad and he lived there part of the time. He owned partnerships in several ships, he was a tobacco merchant in London with his own warehouse and counting-house. He crossed and re-crossed the Atlantic almost as often as a modern American tycoon.

A London merchant at that time held a high social rating. In England he owned a country estate three miles from London. Whether Richard had inherited the estate or purchased it himself is not known. This was the property that caused him to sign his will, "lately of Stratford-Langton in the County of Essex, Esquire." The "Esquire" signified that he was the proprietor of land with tenants of his own.

Each morning Richard's coach appeared at his door and he emerged "silver-buckled and knee-breeched" and rumbled away along the road called "Strat-by-ford" toward London and his counting-house. And back again each evening, just like a modern American business man shuttling between his city office and his suburban home. But Richard finally sold his home and furnishings in England and returned to his home at Dividing Creek.

Richard Lee was the largest landowner in Virginia at the time of his death in 1664. He left his family firmly established with probably more than thirteen thousand acres of virgin tobacco land. He left his son, Hancock, land near Cobbs Hall. This son established his home there, called Ditchley.

Richard Lee stated in his will that he desired his family to live in Virginia. Perhaps after all that was his greatest legacy to his family. It turned out to be an important legacy not only to the Northern Neck, but to the American nation.

THE INDIAN DEED

PERHAPS ONE of the strangest deeds on record is the one signed by Accopatough, King of the Rappahannock Indians.

An Englishman named Moore Fauntleroy came to the Northern Neck about 1650, settling on the Rappahannock, rather far up from its mouth. He must have been very exact in his business dealings, because when he purchased a tract of land from the Indians it was conveyed to him by a written deed, dated April 4, 1651, and signed by:

"Accopatough, the true and right Born King of the Indians of Rappahannoc Town and Towns."

For the land, it is said, Fauntleroy paid the Indians "ten fathoms of peake and thirty arms lengths of Rhoanoke." The tract is said to have been a vast domain which extended from the Rappahannock to the Potomac and some distance along both rivers.

Later, after the Northern Neck became a proprietary, Moore Fauntleroy had his Indian deed confirmed at Jamestown:

"Act I, the grande assemblie at James Cittie, Va., the 23rd March, 1660-1; Sir William Berkeley, his Majesties Governor, 13th year of Charles II."

Fauntleroy's "ancient mansion seat" was located on the Rappahannock, above Cat Point Creek, and it was known as Naylor's Hole. This section of the Neck was established as Richmond County in 1692.

Colonel Moore Fauntleroy was said to have been the great-great grandson of Edward Lord Stourton. He came to the Northern Neck during the Cavalier migration.

A SUMMONS TO JAMESTOWN

AFTER THE county of Northumberland was created from Chicacoan, John Mottrom had many extra duties. As a justice he held court at Coan Hall. A unit of militia had been formed and he had been named by Governor Berkeley as its chief officer—it was *Colonel* Mottrom, now!

On the river just above Coan Hall Colonel Mottrom had started the nucleus of what he hoped would be a future town. He had built there the first wharf and the first warehouse in the Northern Neck. He had plans for a "Brew-house" where "ye good ale of England" might be had.

His activities were interrupted in the spring of 1652 by a summons from the Governor to appear at a meeting of the House of Burgesses.

The grapevine said that danger threatened the colony. It said that Cromwell's government had sent "a powerful fleet" from England with "a considerable body of land forces on board" and that the vessels had already arrived and had cast anchor before Jamestown. It said that the Governor himself was saying that the strangers were pirates and robbers who had come to steal the lands of the colonists.

Colonel Mottrom may have had two other burgesses to keep him company on this trip—George Fletcher from Northumberland, and Francis Willis from the newly organized county of Lancaster.

When Colonel Mottrom arrived within sight of the Island, he could probably see that the royal standard was still flying above the town, even though the English warship *Guinea* and her armed fleet of merchantmen had weighed anchor and were moving in closer.

All was astir at Jamestown, especially in the State House. The "middlemost" of the "stack" of brick buildings was like a busy hive, with burgesses pouring in and out, and conversing in agitated groups, while they warmed themselves before the fireplaces in the two rooms.

Governor Berkeley was very much disturbed. Ever loyal to the Crown, he had boasted that Cromwell's forces would not risk an attack on the colony. But to be on the safe side, Sir William had, during the fall and winter, reinforced his defenses. The militia, which he had called up, was strengthened by the veteran Cavaliers from the King's army who had so recently come to the colony. He had the promise of help from five hundred Indian braves, and several armed Dutch ships which were lying in the river were pressed into service.

In spite of these plans for defensive measures the House of Burgesses showed no enthusiasm for going into active warfare. They reasoned that the loyalty of the Indian allies might be uncertain, and the presence of the enemy fleet in the James was but a reminder of England's sea power. The Governor was finally persuaded to disband his small army.

An agreement was signed on March 12, 1652, between the commissioners from the Commonwealth of England and the "Governor and counsel for a cessation of Arms."

This was probably the most stirring event ever associated with the first State House at Jamestown.

The agreement was favorable to Virginia, even though the colony was subdued. Most of the essential liberties of the colonials were retained. One of Cromwell's commissioners, Richard Bennett, was chosen as Governor by the Assembly.

Sir William had refused to serve under the Commonwealth. He retired to his estate, Green Spring, near Jamestown, where he could entertain Cavalier guests and drink toasts to King Charles as much as he pleased.

THE OATH

WHEN COLONEL MOTTROM and the other burgesses from the Northern Neck returned home from Jamestown after the treaty with Cromwell's commissioners had been made, they brought news that every "white male" in the colony would be required to take an oath of loyalty to this new government in England. If any should refuse to do so they would have to move away within a year.

As the news traveled into the creeks and coves to the homes of the planters on the fringes of the wilderness, we can visualize the reluctant men of Northumberland straggling along to "Cone"—in shallops, sloops, barges, canoes, and perhaps a few on horseback. A disgruntled lot no doubt.

But "within the year" of 1652, one hundred "white males" had signed a statement at Coan which said that they would be "true and faithful to the Commonwealth of England as it is established without King or House of Lords."

Under the treaty the people might toast the late King in private as much as they liked, but no public stand against the Commonwealth would be tolerated.

COUNTY OFFICERS

THE HIGHEST OFFICE in the county was that of county lieutenant. In early records he was called "Commander of Plantations." In England this office was usually held by a knight, and in Virginia it was always conferred on the class of "gentlemen," and they were chosen usually from the large landholders. He was appointed directly by the governor.

The county lieutenant commanded the militia, with the rank of colonel, and was entitled to a seat in the Council, and as such was a judge of the General Court. His powers were great in the civil and military control of the county. He presided over the county courts at the head of the justices.

The executive officer of the county court was the sheriff. The judges in this court were called justices of the peace. They were important men and had almost entire control of the affairs of the county. They were chosen from the gentlemen class of the community and received their commissions from the governor with the advice of the Council. They received no compensation for their services, the office being considered one of honor, not of profit. In this way a high standard of men were obtained for this important office.

EPRAPHRODIBUS'S WILL

IN 1640 a patent was granted to Epraphrodibus Lawson, in Tarrascoe Neck Chuckeytuck Parish, Nansemond County. Lawson must have migrated to the Northern Neck. His will was recorded there, in Lancaster County, in 1652. It is believed to be the oldest recorded will in the United States. The will follows:

"In the name of God, Amen, I Epraphrodibus Lawson, of Rappahannock, being sick of body, but of perfect memory, Glory be to God, do make this my last will and testament. I make and ordain, ye child of my wife . . . my heir . . . my wife . . . third . . . March 31st, 1652.

"Epraphrodibus Lawson.
"Witness:
"Elos Lors,
"Joan Lee,
"Wm. Harper,
"Recorded June, 1652.
"G. John Phillips."

THE CHALLENGE

YOUNG RICHARD DENHAM almost broke up the Lancaster County court when he burst into the room bearing a message that challenged Mr. Daniel Fox to a duel.

The court was being held in the home of one of the justices as no court-house had yet been built for the new county. Lancaster had been formed from Northumberland in 1651. The date of the present court was about 1653.

Richard bore the challenge from his father-in-law, Captain Thomas Hackett. It ran as follows:

"Mr. Fox, I wonder ye should so much degenerate from a gentleman as to cast such an aspersion on me in open Court, making nothinge appear but I knowe it to be out of malice and an evil disposition which remains in your hearte, therefore, I desire ye if ye have anything of a gentleman or of manhood in ye to meet me on Tuesday morninge at ye marked tree in ye valey which partes yr lande and mine, about eight of ye clocke, where I shall expect ye comeinge to give me satisfaction. My weapon is rapier, ye length I send ye by bearer; not yours present, but yours at ye time appointed. THOMAS HACKETT. Ye seconde bringe along with ye if ye please. I shall finde me of ye like."

This message could not have been delivered at a worse time or place, for Mr. Fox, a justice, was at the time sitting on the bench with his fellow justices. That dignified group, dressed in their velvets and gold lace, were shocked by the lad's audacity.

One of the justices, John Carter, sharply scolded Richard—"saying that he knew not how his father would acquit himself on an action of that nature which he said he would not be ye owner of for a world."

Richard answered in a slighting way "that his father would answer it well enough!"

When sternly questioned by the court, Richard admitted that he knew that the message he bore was a challenge. He then boldly demanded of Fox what answer he proposed to send back to Captain Hackett.

The court then made a quick and emphatic decision that Richard was "a partye with his father-in-law in ye crime," and that for bringing the challenge, whose character he well knew, and for delivering it while the justices were sitting, as well as for his contemptuous manner and bold words he was "adjudged"—"to receive six stripes on his bare shoulders with a whip," at the hands of the sheriff.

The sheriff was then directed to arrest Captain Hackett and have him "detained in safe custody without baile" until he should "answer for his crimes" at the next session of the General Court at Jamestown.

Thus a duel was averted, and Mr. Fox did not meet Captain Hackett "in ye valey." The valley was probably chosen by Captain Hackett so that the duel could take place without observation or interruption, and it was the dividing line between their estates.

Hackett was scrupulous to inform Fox of the length of the rapier he intended to use, but had he followed regulations exactly, he would have left the selection of the weapon to his opponent.

TRADE

IN THE early days the Northern Neck carried on trade with various places besides England. Lancaster County seems to have been especially active in this trade. From the following record it appears that tobacco and grain were not the only articles used in trading with the Barbadoes: "In 1686 the sloop Happy transported from Lancaster County to that island, 2 firkins of butter, 2 barrels of pork, and 22 sides of tanned leather, in addition to 144 bushels of Indian corn." Trade to the West Indies was conducted in small Virginia-built sloops.

The Dutch brought to the Neck to exchange for tobacco such things as linen, coarse cloth, beer, brandy and "other distilled spirits." In 1653 Henry Mountford of Rotterdam appointed an agent in Lancaster. About the same time, Jacobis Vis had "important transactions in exchange of merchandise for tobacco in the counties of the Northern Neck." It was said by the Dutch that Virginians could beat them in a deal.

A letter from Captain James Barton of New England to a citizen of Lancaster indicates that there was commerce between these places. Barton stated in the letter that he wished to secure a cargo of tobacco, hides and pork for market in the Barbadoes. His ketch, with a cargo of rum, salt, sugar, cloth and salted cod and mackerel, would sail from Salem and exchange cargoes in Virginia and then continue to the West Indies. Boats from the West Indies sailed to Virginia and then on to New England.

THE COLONIAL SAILOR

A SAILOR was always a source of interest to the public in colonial days, whether he wore his tarry working clothes or his shore outfit. There was the aura of foreign lands about him—he brought stories of far places to the news-hungry colonists of the New World.

On shore the sailor was a glamorous figure in his flapping trousers, scarlet sash and cutlasses, or dressed "in a strange habitt with a four-cornered Capp instead of a hatt and his Breeches hung with Ribbons from Wast downward a great depth, one over the other like Shingles of a house." He wore his pigtail shoved into an eelskin, which was supposed to make his hair grow longer.

JOHN CARTER

ONE DAY in the year 1654 the frontier home of Thomas Meade on the Rappahannock, in Lancaster County, was the focal point toward which the men of the Northern Neck were converging. Some came galloping on horseback between the big forest trees and others probably came by sloop.

The Assembly at Jamestown had recently ordered that an armed force be raised in the Northern Neck: "100 men from Lancaster, 40 from Northumberland and 30 from Westmoreland." After meeting at Meade's house the force under John Carter was to proceed to the Rappahannock Indian town and demand satisfaction for injuries done the white settlers in that region, but they were to commit no acts of hostility unless attacked.

Swords and firearms were glinting that day, and no doubt the flagon was passed many times. Among the men assembled, there was Captain Henry Fleet, the old Indian trader. He and David Wheatliff were to act as interpreters.

There seems to be no record of the outcome of this expedition. With the assistance of Captain Fleet, who was well known as "a powerful man in Indian affairs," it probably turned out well.

After this affair John Carter was known as "Colonel Carter of Lancaster County."

Colonel Carter had but recently settled in the Northern Neck. He had sailed one day from the Chesapeake into the Rappahannock and there before him lay virgin territory—tobacco soil and a readymade highway where ships could sail to his dooryard and carry his tobacco straight to foreign markets.

He patented land and built his home on a neck cut out from the land by a creek and a river. He gave his home the Indian name of the river, Corotoman. The creek was called Carter's.

John Carter left England in 1649 when Cromwell seized the government. Little is known of his family in England. When he came to Virginia he settled first in Upper Norfolk and lived there five years. He probably came to Lancaster County because he saw more opportunity there.

John Carter prospered in the wilderness of the Northern Neck. He acquired many acres, considerable wealth and all the offices and honors that went with his position as a substantial landowner. He was even appointed to his Majesty's Council in Jamestown, which was a high honor.

His dwelling at Corotoman was no doubt a good house for that time. Inventories show that it had glass windows, and the basement was floored with paving stones which he had imported from England. The floors of the dependencies were probably of the same.

He wanted his children to have religious training. He built a church on his property so that his family could have a place to worship God.

Although women were scarce in this frontier country, Colonel Carter managed to find five wives within twenty years.

In 1669, Colonel Carter died at Corotoman and was laid to rest in the yard of his church.

Colonel John Carter of Lancaster County was the founder of the Carter family in Virginia. His son, Robert, was left to carry on the family traditions. He did so in a spectacular way.

FLEET'S POINT

WHEN A SAILING vessel left the Potomac and headed south toward Jamestown it traveled about six miles down the Chesapeake and then it came to the entrance of the Great Wicomico River.

On the north side of the mouth of the Great Wicomico there was a point. This point was called Fleet's Point because the plantation of Captain Henry Fleet, the Indian trader, was located there.

Between the year 1650 and 1655 Captain Fleet had patented large tracts of land in Northumberland and Lancaster. He apparently lived in Lancaster for awhile because he was a burgess from that county in 1652.

But Captain Fleet finally settled in Northumberland at Fleet's Point. In that region there had been an Indian village named Cinquack. It was thus marked on an early map. By the time Captain Fleet settled on the point the Indians may have moved inland, or to an island in the Chesapeake. Or Fleet may have bought the land from the Indians.

Weary voyagers on the Chesapeake, if evening was near, must have looked for the lights of Captain Fleet's dwelling on the point. Probably because of its location Fleet's Point became a stopping place for "persons passing from Maryland to Virginia."

Captain Fleet no doubt welcomed these guests, but he would stand for no misconduct at Fleet's Point, as is shown by a deposition that has been preserved:

"One Henry Carline, of Kent County, Maryland, in 1655, stopped at his house with a woman, and that he provided lodgings also for another woman, and a man. Fleet becoming indignant at Carline's loose behavior, turned him, and the woman who came with him, out of his house, and had them arraigned before the Rappahannock Court. Carline was fined for keeping the servant woman from her employer, and disowning his wife, and the woman was ordered to receive 30 lashes."

All records concerning Captain Fleet seem to end here. Did he ever return to England? Or was he killed by the Indians?

Perhaps he spent the rest of his life at Fleet's Point and was buried there.

GEORGE MASON

GEORGE MASON was another early settler in the upper wilderness of the Northern Neck.

The first George Mason came to Virginia during the Cavalier emigration. He "went up the Potomac River and settled at Accohick, near Pasbytanzy."

Apparently the first mention of this founder of the Mason family in Virginia occurs in the patent of land obtained by him in March, 1655: "Said land being due the said George Mason by and for the transportation of eighteen persons in to the colony." Mason was married but it is not known if his wife or family were among these persons transported as "head-rights."

The next mention of George Mason in the records is in 1658 when he sold five hundred acres of land to Mr. John Lease for "five cows with calves and two thousand five hundred pounds of tobacco." Westmoreland County at this time included land on the Virginia side of the Potomac from the northern boundary of Northumberland to the present site of Georgetown in the District of Columbia. With the land sold to Mr. Lease, Mason included "all privileges of hawking, fishing and fowling."

By this time George Mason was fairly well established in his wilderness home among the Indians, some of whom were friendly and some were not.

George Mason, Giles Brent and Gerrard Fowke were the "men

of the border" at this time. From time to time they were involved in troubles with the Indians.

Colonel Mason's death occurred probably in 1686. He was buried in the "Burying Place, at Accokeek." He was the great-grandfather of George Mason, the Revolutionary patriot and author of the Bill of Rights.

MARY CALVERT

"YE SAID MRS. CALVERT shall personally receive thirty stripes upon her bare shoulders for her offence." Thus the court of Northumberland decided in the case of Mary Calvert in the year of our Lord 1655.

This court was probably held at Coan Hall, the home of Colonel John Mottrom, as it is doubtful that a court-house had yet been built.

Court Day was a great event to the men of Virginia in colonial times. It created an opportunity for the discussion of politics, for trading livestock, bargaining for the sale of tobacco, catching up with the news, and last but not least, a free enjoyment of rough horse-play, accompanied by the passing of the jug.

Let us imagine this Court Day at Coan Hall. If the weather was warm enough the session may have been held out of doors under the trees. In the rear the virgin forest must have furnished an impressive background. In front flowed the river where the small sailing vessels, barges and log canoes belonging to the men who had come to court were tied or anchored. A few horses may have been tied in the barn-lot or tethered out to graze, but there were not many horses in the Neck at that time, probably not more than fifteen or twenty in the county.

In cold weather court was doubtless held inside before the blazing fire in the great hall. Colonel Mottrom, if he was presiding, was no doubt dressed in his best, as befitted the occasion and his position as justice. Ursula was probably in the kitchen supervising preparations for a feast for those among the gathering who would be their guests.

If the crowd overflowed outside there was perhaps an outdoor fire near the stables for warmth. And the passing flagon of ale no doubt helped to warm and cheer the crowd. Contests of strength and skill, such as westling, cudgeling, running, riding and shooting may have been going on there while the court was in progress inside the house.

Mary Calvert must have been embarrassed to have been the only woman in such a crowd of men, for as a rule women stayed out of sight on Court Days. The records reveal only enough information about Mary Calvert to arouse the curiosity. What sort of woman was she?

She was perhaps fairly young, as women of that day usually married early and died early. There is no clue as to her appearance but it is safe to assume that her clothes were bright because colonials wore gay colors, and that she wore a hood of some sort over her head, and if it was cold a mantle that covered her other garments.

What heinous crime had this woman committed that she deserved to be lashed thirty times across her bare shoulders?

Mary Calvert had been so bold as to speak in public against Oliver Cromwell and the Parliament of England. She had called them "rogues and rebells."

Now, Mrs. Calvert confessed in court that she had made this statement, but in her own defense she stated that she was in danger of being murdered by her husband and "spake those words" to bring about her arrest and thus be "secured from her husband."

Was Mary telling the truth? The true answer will never be known. But the ancient county records do reveal the fact that her husband either loved her and could not stand by and see her lashed, or that he wanted to save his own self-respect.

Whatever his reason may have been he did come forward and beg to pay a fine in order that Mary's sentence be revoked—

"Upon Mr. Calvert's petition in behalfe of his wife," the court ordered him to pay a thousand pounds of tobacco for commuting "of ye corporall punishment to be inflicted upon his said wife, with charges of court."

HE LIVED BRAVELY

COLONEL JOHN MOTTROM may not have presided at the county court of 1655 for he died about that time. He was but forty-five years old and he had not yet built his brew-house or seen his vision of the town at Coan come true.

The funeral was no doubt a big affair for Colonel Mottrom was a prominent man, and all funerals then were important occasions.

These early funerals were carried on in a reverent manner but there was a cheerful side too. Funerals could even be called festive. The reason for this was that a funeral brought about one of the few chances friends and neighbors had for a reunion, and for feasting and drinking together.

The guests had to travel a long way by boat or on horseback to attend a funeral and these funeral guests were regarded as even more "sacred" than ordinary guests. The unwritten laws of hospitality would have been broken if these guests had been allowed to return home without more than ample food and drink.

Thus the bereaved Mottrom household probably had to put their sorrows aside while they made preparations for the funeral.

Sometimes the minister and pall-bearers, who were usually the leading citizens of the county, were directed to wear certain special items, such as gloves, ribbons and a "love scarf." Mourning-rings and gloves were often gifts to chief mourners from the family of the deceased. Often the will of the deceased directed the family to make such gifts.

Colonel Mottrom may have desired to be "buryed . . . in the garden plote." It was the usual custom to be buried not too far away from the dwelling.

It could be truly written of this first settler of the Northern Neck, as it had been said of another early Virginian—"he lived bravely, kept a good house and was a true lover of Virginia."

After the body was laid to rest the memory of the deceased was usually honored by a furious fusillade. This may have been done more for the entertainment of those who came to bury the deceased than to honor the dead. Sometimes as much as ten pounds of powder were used. Many accidents occurred at funerals because of the wild firing of guns by persons who had been drinking.

The extravagant use of powder was nothing when compared to the amount of liquor, of all kinds, consumed at a funeral. At one funeral sixty gallons of cider, four gallons of rum, two gallons of brandy, five gallons of wine, and thirty pounds of sugar to sweeten the drinks were used.

Food for the occasion may have included geese, turkeys and other poultry, a pig, several bushels of flour and twenty pounds of butter. Sometimes a whole steer and several sheep were prepared for the crowd. A big funeral cost many pounds of tobacco.

Colonel Mottrom's inventory was valued at 33,896 pounds of tobacco, which was as large as any estate in the colony at that time.

His inventory was recorded in Northumberland County in 1657, and shows that he was a man of "wealth and literary pretensions."

He left his children "well-fixed" as to land. In Northumberland alone he had patented 3700 acres. Tradition says that he left the daughter of his associate, Nicholas Morris, "a riding mare." His will was referred to the governor "because of some ambiguities in the procurings of it." No copy of it can now be found.

Due to distances and lack of fast transportation the widow's hand was sometimes spoken for at the funeral of her husband by one of the guests who was afraid that he might lose out if he waited to make another visit. This was probably not true in Ursula's case, but she did remarry soon enough for her new husband to act as one of the executors of Colonel Mottrom's will.

Major George Colclough, Ursula's third husband, was a burgess in 1658. After his death Ursula Bish Thompson-Mottrom-Colclough married Colonel Isaac Allerton. Even after she had married this fourth time she continued to have trouble in settling Colonel Mottrom's estate, because of the "ambiguities" of his will.

Colonel and Mrs. Allerton lived at his home, The Narrows, which was located in the new county of Westmoreland, formed from Northumberland in 1653.

Colonel Allerton was the son of Isaac Allerton, who came to Plymouth on the *Mayflower* in 1620, and of Fear Brewster, only daughter of Governor William Brewster, of Plymouth. He was born in 1630 and was one of the early graduates of Harvard College. He came to Virginia and settled in the Northern Neck at The Narrows.

From Ursula and Isaac Allerton was descended President Zachary Taylor.

WITCHCRAFT

THE BELIEF in witchcraft was prevalent amongst the early settlers of the Northern Neck. The Neck at this time was beset with wolves and Indians and was a true type of a frontier colony.

To the witch was ascribed the power of inflicting strange and incurable diseases, of changing men into horses when they were asleep at night, and after bridling and saddling them, riding them at a gallop over the countryside to the places where the witches had their frolics. Horses too were thought to be ridden at night, unbridled and barebacked. In the morning these horses would be fagged-out and caked with sweat and mud and their manes plaited into "witches' stirrups."

That witches were taken seriously by settlers of the Neck in the seventeenth century is proven by the following abstract from the Northumberland County records:

"20 Nov., 1656.

Whereas, Articles were Exhibited against Wm. H—— by Mr. David Lindsaye (Minister) upon suspicion of witchcraft, sorcery, etc., And an able jury of Twenty-four men were empanelled to try the matter by verdict of which jury they found part of the Articles proved by several depositions. The Court doth therefore order yet ye said Wm. H—— shall forthwith receave ten stripes upon his bare back and forever to be Banished this County and yet hee depart within the space of two monethes. And also to pay all the charges of Court."

SEAHORSE OF LONDON

ON A COLD DAY in the late winter of 1657 some men were busily working in the Potomac near the mouth of Mattox Creek. They were trying to lift a foundered ketch, the *Seahorse* of London. Among the men was young John Washington, son of an English clergyman.

John had sailed for Virginia in the winter of 1656, as mate and voyage partner in the *Seahorse*. After arriving in the Potomac the ketch was loaded with a cargo of tobacco. On her way out of the river she ran aground. Before she could be floated a storm hit and sank her. The entire cargo of tobacco was ruined.

During the delay John made friends with a wealthy planter named Nathaniel Pope, who lived in the neighborhood.

The *Seahorse* was finally raised but by that time John did not wish to return to England. Perhaps Nathaniel's daughter, Anne, was the attraction in Virginia.

John prevailed on Edward Prescott, the master and part owner of the *Seahorse*, to release him from further service in order that he might remain in the Northern Neck of Virginia. He also demanded payment of his wages. Prescott countered that Washington owed him money and was partly responsible for the damage done to the vessel. He threatened to have John arrested and imprisoned.

John's new friend, Pope, offered to go his bond in beaver skins. If there was a suit the outcome is unknown. Prescott finally sailed away in the *Seahorse* and Washington remained in Virginia, but they parted on bad terms and this was not the last of their quarrel—but that is another story.

John soon married Anne Pope. As a wedding gift Nathaniel gave them a seven-hundred-acre tract of land near Mattox Creek, in Westmoreland County. In 1664 John and Anne moved to a new home four miles eastward on Bridges Creek.

John Washington was the first of that name to settle in the Northern Neck. In Westmoreland he led an active life as a planter and as a leader in county affairs. He had received "decent schooling" before he left England. John and Anne were the great-grandparents of that most famous Washington—George.

"TENN MULBERRY TREES"

IN THE FALL or early spring of 1656-57 the Virginians were planting trees.

Since the pioneers of the Northern Neck were living on the edges of a virgin forest and had been trying desperately to clear away enough of it to make fields for tobacco and corn, it seems strange that they would now be engaged in planting more trees.

But these trees were different—they had been imported from China. The Assembly at Jamestown had recently declared that "whereas by experience silke will be the most profitable commoditie for the country . . . that everie one hundred acres of land plant tenn mulberry trees."

When the colonists came to Virginia they noticed the abundance of mulberry trees. These native trees, such favorites of the Indians, had reddish-blue berries. The early colonists thought that "the climate and soil of middle America were . . . adapted to the culture of silke."

So, the first Assembly, in 1619, in the church at Jamestown, had adopted measures on the planting of mulberry trees:

"About the plantation of mulberry trees, be it enacted that every man as he is seatted upon his division, doe for seven years together, every yeare plante and maintaine in growte six Mulberry trees at the least, and as many more as he shall think conveniente."

But the silkworms would not cooperate—they refused to eat the leaves of the red mulberry tree. In 1621, the white mulberry was imported from China. But still the silk industry languished, this time it was said, for want of cheap labor.

In the beginning the care of the silkworms was held to be especially suitable work for children. The mulberry trees were kept like a low hedge so that children could pick the leaves to feed the worms. This is probably where the singing-game originated:

"Here we go 'round the mulberry bush, mulberry bush—."

Tradition said that two boys, "if their hands be not sleeping in their pockets, could care for six ounces of seed from hatching till within fourteen days of spinning." After that three or four helpers, "women and children being as proper as men," were needed to assist in feeding the worms, airing, drying, cleansing and "perfuming" them.

Now, under the Commonwealth, the silk industry was again being stimulated. But all was in vain—the colonists had their minds set on raising tobacco and they could not be diverted.

ROADS

AS A RULE the settlers of the Northern Neck built their homes on the banks of rivers and creeks. Since travel was by boat there was little need at first for roads through the forest.

The Indians traveled through the woods over narrow footpaths not much over twenty inches wide. These had been made originally by animals. Now they were traveled by both Indians and wild beasts. These paths usually ran along high ground or where there was little undergrowth and few streams to cross.

When it was necessary for settlers to penetrate the interior they used these Indian and animal paths, or cut new paths and blazed the trees so that the blazes stood out clear and white in the forest.

Northumberland County records mention a horse path "wch leadeth from Wicocomoco to Chickacoon buttin upon the north west side of an Indian field knowne by the name of Fairefield." There was a cart path near the Corotoman river "knowne by the name of Morratico & Wiccomcomico Path." Early land patents mention other paths, horse paths and Indian paths.

Rolling-roads were narrow roads cut through the woods over which hogsheads of tobacco fitted with axles could be rolled or drawn. In this way inland plantations could send their tobacco to wharves and warehouses on the waterfront for shipment overseas.

The parish church, court-houses, ferries and ordinaries became the focal points that led from crude interplantation lanes. In 1658 the General Assembly appointed surveyors whose responsibility it was to clear general ways from county to county. These roads were to be forty feet wide and the surveyors were to see that the citizens kept them up. This last order was hard to enforce because for a long time the planters had little interest in highways on land.

MARKETS

THE CUSTOM of Market Day, which was a form of the English fair, was brought to Virginia by the colonists. In 1649 it was decided to hold markets every week in Jamestown, on Wednesdays and Saturdays.

The Assembly decided in 1655 to establish one or more marketplaces in each county. These were to be located on a river or creek, and all the trade of the surrounding country was to be concentrated at these places. Imported articles were to be brought from certain ports to each market place. Here were to be built the court-house, prison, offices of the clerk and sheriff, ordinaries and churches. Nothing seems to have come of this attempt.

Again, about 1679, certain places were designated as public marts, to which all the Indians who were at peace with the white settlers were invited to come, one day in the spring and one day in autumn. A government clerk was to keep records of all the trading which took place at each mart.

One of these marts was situated in Lancaster County, and another in Stafford. In Northumberland, the Wicocomico Indians were to be permitted to trade with the English under special regulations adopted by the authorities in that county.

The purpose of these market places was to encourage the building of towns, but the attempts were all unsuccessful. The settlers preferred their independent way of life on the plantations.

THE OLD DOMINION

IN MAY, 1660, Charles II returned to England by invitation of a new Parliament. Cromwell was dead and his son and successor, "Tumbledown Dick," had abdicated.

Charles rode into London, where the streets were dressed with green boughs and the windows hung with tapestry in his honor. Since everyone was so glad to see him he wondered why he had stayed away so long.

When the Virginians heard the news they went wild with joy!

Sir William Berkeley already had control of the Virginia government again. The Assembly at Jamestown had foreseen the restoration of the king and they had called Sir William back from his self-imposed exile at his plantation, Green Spring, in March, 1660—two months before Charles was actually crowned King of England.

It took four months for the news of the restoration to reach Virginia. In September, Sir William issued a command that the news be proclaimed in every county in Virginia.

This was what the Virginians had been waiting for and they celebrated in their typical way—by drinking healths and by making every kind of noise that they could contrive to make.

Hundreds of pounds of tobacco were exchanged for barrels of gunpowder and kegs of cider. In some places "ye trumpeters" were paid as much as eight hundred pounds of tobacco for their music, and at least one minister was paid five hundred pounds of tobacco for a service of thanksgiving.

In recognition of Virginia's loyalty to him, Charles II caused her to be proclaimed an independent member of his Empire. He had it engraved on coins that the English Kingdom should henceforth consist of "England, Scotland, Ireland and Virginia." Virginia's coat-of-arms was added to those of the other three countries comprised in his dominions. Traditions say that Charles wore a robe of Virginia silk at his coronation.

It was in this way that Virginia acquired the title of "The Old Dominion."

THE PROPRIETARY

THE SETTLERS of the Northern Neck had hardly ended their celebrations in honor of England's new king when they received a great shock.

One of the first things that Charles II did, at the insistence of those courtiers who had shared his exile, was to have the Northern Neck patent, which he had issued while he was in France, recorded and put on the market to be leased for the benefit of those courtiers to whom he had given it. Thus in 1661, the Northern Neck became a proprietary—that is, it was owned now by the seven courtiers.

In 1662, several English merchants took a lease of the proprietary from the original courtiers who owned it. The merchants hoped to settle new "adventures" in the land between the Potomac and the Rappahannock. King Charles then wrote a letter to Governor Berkeley instructing him to assist these men who had leased the patent.

Even Sir William who had always been fanatical in his loyalty to the Crown was shocked. The royal order aroused the opposition of both the governor and the council to the proprietorship and to the lease of it. It was a threat to the colonial government and they were afraid that they would lose their power to defend themselves. They felt that the rights of the colonists should be protected.

Before 1661, a total of 576 grants of "headright" lands in the Northern Neck had been made in the King's name by the Colonial Governor. The meaning of "headright" was that any person who paid his own way to Virginia would receive 50 acres of land. He would also be assigned 50 acres for each person he transported "at his own cost."

Now titles to these lands previously taken would be clouded. Or the lands might be completely lost.

Instead of assisting the lessees of the patent the colonial government at Jamestown prepared an address to the Crown and sent one of their ablest citizens to England to act as an agent for Virginia.

The King ignored this protest, rebuked the colonial government and sent their representative back to Virginia with a renewed petition of the proprietors and orders to "protect his agents and encourage them."

Nevertheless, no more was heard of the English merchants. The colonials had scored their first victory in the war over the Northern Neck patent, but many troublesome years were still to follow.

A FIRST LADY OF JAMESTOWN

WHILE LIFE flowed on at Chicacone, what had become of little Frances Mottrom?

Frances had been growing up. She was now, in 1662, seventeen years old and about to become the bride of one of the most important men in Virginia.

Since her step-mother's marriage Frances had probably been living with her sister, Anne, who had been married for five or six years to Richard Wright, formerly a merchant of London. The Wrights lived part of the time at Coan Hall and part of the time at Cabin Point, in Westmoreland County. The latter estate had been left to Anne by her father, Colonel John Mottrom.

And how did Frances find a suitable bridegroom in the wilderness of the Northern Neck? Probably through her brother-in-law, Richard Wright. Her future husband, the Honorable Nicholas Spencer, Esq., had also been a London merchant who had taken up lands in the Neck. He was now a neighbor of the Wrights, in Westmoreland County.

And where was the wedding to take place? There are no records to tell us, but a deed made a few years after Frances' marriage refers to her as being "late of Chickacone." It is doubtful if a church had been built as yet, although the Parish of Chicacoan had been established in 1653, and the Reverend David Lindsaye, of the Established Church of England, had arrived in the Northern Neck as early as 1656.

Let us assume that Frances and Nicholas were married at Coan Hall by the new minister, who would have been dressed for the occasion in a white surplice with bands and a "close" cap of black velvet.

The ceremony would probably have taken place on a Wednesday morning between eight and noonday.

The bride was doubtless radiant in a low-cut gown of the latest London fashion. It may have been pink, yellow or some other pastel shade but we can be sure that it was not white. The gown, no doubt fell in soft folds to the ground, as hoops had not yet come into vogue. Her hair was probably arranged just as she wore it as a child, with a veil in place of the cap.

Coan Hall was no doubt "passing sweet trimmed up with divers flowers" or evergreens. All the kettles were doubtless a-bubble in the kitchen, and the silver, pewter, brass and copper gleamed in the fire-light.

There seem to be no surviving records of the festivities accompanying a seventeenth century wedding in Virginia, but we may be sure that there was "an open cellar, a full house and a sweating cook," three things dearly loved by these transplanted English people.

They also loved noise—the sound of guns and firecrackers, bells and music. They liked to sing the old ballads brought from "home," as they still called England.

The wedding guests may have brought small spiced buns to the wedding and piled them high in the center of the table. If the bride and groom succeeded in kissing each other over the mound, lifelong prosperity was assured.

Dancing and games were very likely to have followed the feasting. The wedding guests may have lingered on a week or more at Coan. It is possible that the wedding party followed the bride and groom to the groom's house in Westmoreland and continued the festivities for awhile there.

And how did Frances reach her new home? Most likely by sailing vessel, up the Potomac. If she traveled by land it was doubtless on horseback as there were few if any carriages then, nor any roads. She may have been seated on a pillion behind her new husband, holding on tight to his waist. If the wedding party traveled by land they must have made quite a clatter—riding at the reckless "planter's pace" between the big trees, shouting and singing and making the forest ring with happy sound.

Two wedding gifts that Frances may have brought to her new home were a "garnish of pewter," that is a full set of pewter platters, plates and dishes, and a bread "peel," which was significant of domestic utility, plenty, and was a symbol of good luck. These were favorite wedding gifts then. Glass and earthenware were scarce at that time because of breakage on the trip across the Atlantic. An inventory later on shows that Frances had only twelve glasses and not more than eighty-eight pieces of earthenware. Silver plate was abundant in the homes of the wealthy.

At the time of their marriage Frances' husband was a member of the House of Burgesses. Later (1679-89) he was Secretary of the Colony which made him, next to the Governor, probably the most powerful man in Virginia at that time. People started calling his home on Nomini River, Secretary's Point, by which name it was ever after known.

Colonel Spencer's neighbors named their parish "Cople" in honor of his ancestral parish in Bedfordshire, England.

About 1675 Colonel Spencer and John Washington procured a patent for five thousand acres of land on Little Hunting Creek, which later became famous as the Mount Vernon estate. This land descended to the heirs of Spencer and Washington.

Colonel Spencer became President of the Council, which was a position of great honor and dignity. As President of the Council in the absence of the Governor, his cousin Lord Culpeper, he became acting governor from 1683-84.

"Madam Spencer," as Frances was now respectfully addressed, had seen many changes since she had left her wilderness playground in the Northern Neck, to become for awhile the "First Lady of Jamestown." She had borne six children. One son went to England and remained there to claim the large estates which his father had inherited.

After Governor Spencer's death Frances married Reverend John Bolton.

LAND

"CLEAR TITLES" to their lands were extremely important to the landholders of the Northern Neck, probably because for many years due to the proprietary their land was not wholly their own.

To the natives of the Neck, land was an almost sacred possession. To acquire more and more of it was an obsession with some of them. Land was their wealth—without it tobacco could not be grown. The virgin soil lasted only about three years under tobacco cultivation. It was easier and cheaper to look for new lands than to enrich old acreage so the planter was always looking for new lands, in the fertile river margins or in the vast forests. It was a wasteful system.

Land made a man's social position then. For social rating purposes the amount of land he owned did not matter so much, but if he was to be "somebody" he must own some land. Common expressions in those days were—"he is a big landowner" or "he owns land." This manner of social rating persisted for many years in the Neck.

Land was a man's security—even if he could no longer make money on it "the land was still there." If he did not have wealth he still had land and a social position.

The landowner rarely sold his land. The bulk of it was left to the oldest son; other sons received smaller portions and the daughters received still smaller portions. The girls were supposed to marry into landed stock.

The importance of land to natives of the Northern Neck in bygone days can hardly be exaggerated.

PROCESSIONING

A MORNING in spring between Easter and Whitsuntide found all Virginians out-of-doors. This special day came once each year—it was the day of the "processioning."

On this day, required by law, the planters would ride and walk over their lands and inspect their property lines. We can visualize the scene—the planter and his older sons leading the way, servants following with axes and other implements, chattering women and girls, servant women bringing up the rear with lunch baskets, and children riding pillion, or in front of some older person, or when the procession halted, darting about chasing a butterfly or rabbit.

"Processioning" day was an important time, for in those days land surveys were not always true and the boundaries of each man's plantation were uncertain. At this time the various landmarks were impressed upon the minds of the older sons—"yonder is a corner pine," "the four red and the one white oak," "there is the grove of tulip poplars," "the dogwood corner," "the hickory corner," "the two gums and the white oak"—there was so much to remember!

Sometimes the lands were divided by ditches, for ditches would last a hundred years or more it was said. Landmarks were renewed at this time. Blazes were recut on trees and in the places where trees had fallen during the winter new ones were planted. Tradition says that pear trees were often planted as they were long-lived trees.

Here and there processions from neighboring plantations would meet at the boundaries where the lands joined. A sociable time then followed, and if it was at lunch time, perhaps a picnic. Disputed boundaries were decided upon at these times and announced to all persons present so that at the next "processioning" those who were still living would be able to testify as to the correct line.

"THE BANQUETTING HOUSE"

AMONG THE planters whose lands adjoined near Machodoc Creek, in Westmoreland County, were John Lee, Henry Corbin, Thomas Gerrard and Isaac Allerton.

John Lee was the oldest son of Richard, the immigrant, of Cobbs Hall in Northumberland. John was the first of the Lees to establish a seat on land acquired by his father on the Potomac. This first Lee home in Westmoreland was called Matholic. John had been educated at Oxford and had graduated at Queen's College, 1658, and then studied medicine. He had probably returned to Virginia with his father in 1664. Two years later he was seated at Matholic, and he immediately took his place among the leading planters in the county. Besides the usual offices that went with his station, he was on a committee appointed by the governor for the defense of the Northern Neck against Indians. Later he served on a commission with Colonel John Washington and others to "arrange the boundary line between Lancaster and Northumberland Counties." But what Jack really liked to do was to ride, shoot and fish. He liked the militia training and the celebrations that went with it. He was young, gay and a bachelor.

Henry Corbin had been born in Warwickshire, England, about 1629. His family was of high standing among the English gentry. Henry came to Virginia during the Cavalier emigration and took up an estate on the Potomac near Matholic. His home was named Pecatone for an Indian chief of the region, according to tradition. Pecatone was one of the great manors of Westmoreland. It was built of brick with a terrace and stone steps in front. The large rooms were wainscoted. The house was set in a grove of trees and the lawn sloped to the Potomac. The house had the massive look of a fort and it was plain to severity. Life at Pecatone was carried on in the grand manner.

Doctor Thomas Gerrard lived not far from Isaac Allerton on a plantation called Wilton. Gerrard had once owned lands and had been a prominent figure in the Province of Maryland, but because of religious persecution he had crossed the Potomac and found sanctuary in the Northern Neck. Wilton had originally been patented by Major William Hockaday in 1651. At that time the Indians were still living on the land and Hockaday had to wait to seat the place "until the Indians could be removed." Doctor Gerrard purchased Wilton from Hockaday in 1662.

Isaac Allerton was the grandson of that celebrated Puritan, Governor William Brewster of Plymouth. After Isaac graduated from Harvard College, in 1650, he left New England and settled in Westmoreland County, near the plantations of John Lee and Henry Corbin. Isaac called his home The Narrows. He became a leading planter of the county and was one of the men of Westmoreland "upon whom Governor Berkeley relied." In 1675 Allerton was second in command under Colonel John Washington to fight Indians. Allerton married Ursula, the widow of John Mottrom. From the union of Ursula and Isaac was descended President Zachary Taylor, as has been stated before.

These then were the four neighbors with such diverse backgrounds, whose plantations adjoined and who all came together each year at "processioning" time.

In March of 1670 these men decided to build a "banquetting house for the continuance of good Neighborhood."

The plan was that each neighbor, or his heirs, would take turns in preparing the banquet and entertainment "yearly, according to his due, to make an Honorable treatment fit to entertain the undertakers thereof, their wives, misters & friends yearly and every year, & to begin upon the 29th of May."

Thus the agreement was written, witnessed, and signed by Henry Corbin, John Lee, Thomas Gerrard and Isaac Allerton, on the 30th of March 1670. Jack Lee was assigned the responsibility of the building of the "banquetting house." There is documented proof that the house was built in "Pickatown field," and that the yearly celebrations were held.

At these celebrations Jack Lee, arriving on his spirited mount dressed in his "gray suit with silver buttons" and "gloves with silver tops," must have been a dashing figure.

We can imagine Ursula at "Pickatown field," escorted by her fourth husband, Colonel Allerton; Henry Corbin with his wife Alice and daughter, Laetitia; and the Gerrards—Thomas and Rose.

Since friends were to be invited, Colonel Nicholas Spencer of Secretary's Point may have been there with his wife, Frances Mottrom Spencer. The host would probably have been afraid to omit from the guest list Dick Cole of Salisbury Park, and his wife Anna.

Perhaps a little eight-year-old girl from Tucker Hill was dancing gaily at "Pickatown field" in the year 1671. In three more years "little Sarah Tucker" was to put away childish things to become the bride of Colonel William Fitzhugh, one of the wealthiest planters in the Neck. And in two more years the laughter of young Jack Lee would be stilled forever.

But in the springtime of 1671 there was probably no small cloud over "Pickatown field," and the "banquetting house" was filled with happy sound.

Here end all known records concerning the "banquetting house in Pickatown field"—America's first country club, circa 1671.

THE LAND AGENT

NOW, IN the year 1670, something new had been added to the Northern Neck—a land agent.

The grapevine must have been buzzing in those days—what is a land agent?—a man who represents the proprietary—what is a proprietary, anyway?—the people who have taken our land away from us—who is this land agent?—Thomas Kirton, from England—what will he do?—make us pay rent—rent our own land?—something like taxes—I won't do it—how can he make us?—what right have they—

The Northern Neckers had probably not fully realized that they no longer owned their own land until they came face to face with a land agent.

Thomas Kirton came to Virginia in 1670 and opened a land office in Northumberland County. He was to be assisted by Edward Dale, a prominent citizen of Lancaster.

Kirton came armed with credentials, a copy of the patent and power of attorney for himself and Dale. He presented these documents to the General Court at Jamestown, April 5, 1671. He was recognized and action was prompt ". . . the said letters, patent being read in court . . .," "obedience" and "submission" was given and recorded.

This complete acceptance of Kirton, and what he stood for, by the Colonial Government was another shock to the settlers of the Northern Neck. There had never been "anything to so move the grief and passion of the people as uncertainty whether they were to make a country for the King or for the Proprietors."

It had become a very real fact to the settlers now that they had landlords over them. They had been accustomed to the utmost freedom and independence and this was an almost unbearable blow.

A strange thing about the story of the proprietary is that the people who lived within it had very little understanding as to what it was all about. Most of them lived all of their lives without understanding the terms of the proprietary. This was partly due to the fact that everything was done in secret. Even the Colonial Government was kept in the dark as to the various changes and renewals, while the proprietors increased their authority over the domain of the Northern Neck.

Kirton's main duty was to collect quit-rents. The quit-rent was handed down from the feudal system of medieval times. In simple terms—it was the "bond between the lord and the land." The quit-rent was a monetary payment to relieve the tenant of obligations, such as laboring for the lord of a manor on a certain number of days a week, or paying him with a portion of the produce.

Under the system of the quit-rent the tenant still had complete control of his land although he did not own it. He was free to bequeath the land to his heirs.

Kirton had little success in collecting quit-rents although they were small, only two shillings per one hundred acres. The settlers had no intention of paying anything to the proprietors unless they were compelled to do so. As the years went on they acquiesced to a certain degree, but the quit-rents were never willingly paid.

However the settlers did not object to patenting new lands. These could be paid for in English coins, Spanish pieces of eight, or in tobacco, if metallic money was not to be had.

Kirton was ousted from his office, in 1673, because for some time he had failed to remit the quit-rents. Before this Kirton and Dale had quarreled and Dale had ceased to act as an agent.

Thomas Kirton probably had few friends in the Northern Neck. The fact that he married Anna, the widow of Dick Cole, tells quite a lot about him. She was despised and feared by her neighbors because of her slanderous tongue.

Kirton's home was in Westmoreland County, near the Northumberland boundary. He probably remained in the Northern Neck, for in 1686 he informed the Westmoreland court that its records were "somewhat delayed and the transfers through time and carelessness were scarcely legible." The court directed him to transcribe all the records in one book. For this he was paid 2,000 pounds of tobacco and cask, if he finished the work by 1688.

HANNA AND THE HORSESHOE

IN EARLY DAYS the horseshoe was believed to have a magic potency. When butter was slow in coming, a heated horseshoe was thrown into the churn. A horseshoe was also believed to keep off witches. Doubtless most of the early settlers of the Northern Neck had one nailed over the threshold.

An instance of the belief in the power of the horseshoe is found in the seventeenth century records of Northumberland County. From three sworn statements filed in that county, "April ye 11, 1671," let us reconstruct the strange happenings that were reported.

The story starts on board a vessel at sea, bound home to the Northern Neck from a trip to the Barbadoes. ("I Edw: Le Breton deposeth that being aboard of our ship & Mr. Edward Cole talking then and there of severall psons (persons) & among all ye rest of Mrs. Neall, Hanna Rodham, daughter of Matthew Rodham, and wife of Christopher Neall.")

We can imagine Le Breton and Cole in their ship's cabin relaxing a bit as they neared home—two mariners dressed in loose breeches and jerkins of canvas or frieze, with their warm Monmouth caps and outer garments swaying on the pegs where they hung and the swinging lanthorn casting crazy shadows over all. Perhaps a bottle of the West Indies rum had loosened the tongue of Edward Cole as he told of "a certyne time some yeares past" when "there grew difference" between himself and the family of Hanna Neall. "She then," continued Cole, "made a kind of prayer that he nor none of his family never prosper and shortly after his people fell sick & much of his cattle dyed."

When Edward Cole arrived home from the Barbadoes he found his wife ill and the "suspition of Doctor S——, & others was that his wife was under an ill tongue, & if it was soe he concluded yt (yet) it was Mrs. Neall by reason of imprecations made by her & yt indeed he thought soe," and "he did accuse Mrs. Neall of it alsoe."

Edward Cole was greatly troubled. If Hanna Neall could do this much, she could do worse things. He was almost "beside himself" with fear and worry when he remembered the horseshoe nailed over his threshold. It was there to keep off witches. If he could induce Hanna Neall to cross over the horseshoe he could find out once and for all if she was a woman or a witch.

And so it came about that Edward Cole at "a certyne time sent for Mrs. Neall to come to see his wife."

Witches are usually thought of as being old hags, but from portions of these statements it seems that Hanna was not an ordinary witch. She was at least a fairly young woman, and quite possibly an attractive one. Records of early land patents show that she and her father were landowners, which gave her certain social distinctions, and only a small number of persons of the best condition had the designation of Mr. and Mrs. prefixed to their names in the seventeenth century. The Northumberland records prove that she was fearless, for she answered Edward Cole's invitation by coming at once.

Did she live near enough to walk? Since individual landholdings were large then we do not think that she lived close enough to walk. Did she come riding on a pillion? Or did she come across the water in a barge rowed by her servants? These are questions for speculation.

We can assume that she was dressed in the usual outdoor costume of women of that time and place. In April the air is still sharp in the Northern Neck of Virginia so she probably wore a linsey-woolsey gown of blue with undersleeves of white kenting, a dark mantle of wool, a hood with a bright lining turned back around her face, and a white muslin apron. Perhaps she carried a basket with some delicacy for the sick woman—a pair of quail shot by her husband and roasted by herself on the spit in her fireplace.

What feelings of dread must Edward Cole have had as he watched the approach of Hanna Neall! We can see him slowly opening the door and standing far aside for her to enter.

We can picture Hanna, looking into the dark room where the candle in the tin lanthorn threw shadows across the strained faces, and a pomander ball gave off the sickening odors that were supposed to ward off infection. And there in the dimness of the bed with its heavy hangings lay the sick woman.

Was Hanna frightened when she looked into the face of her accuser? Was she angry? Or did she pity him? In any case, when she trod on the threshold, brushed the horseshoe with her skirts, and entered the room—nothing happened.

Hanna crossed to the sick woman, knelt beside the bed and "shee prayed so heartily for her" that Edward Cole believed in her sincerity.

It was in this way that Hanna Neall was saved from being banished from the county, or from lashes at the whipping post, or from the ducking "stoole" at Northumberland County court-house, down in Hull's Neck. Saved by a horseshoe and a prayer!

And Edward Cole straightened matters out with the following statement:

"I, Edward Cole, doe acknowledge yt ye words which I did speake concerning Mrs. Neall as tending to defame her with the aspersion of being a witch, were passionately spoken.

Edward Cole"

April ye 11, 1671

MUSTER

IN THE early days of the colony there was a unit of militia in each county. The governor, who was in command, appointed for each unit a colonel, lieutenant-colonel, and major, who had lesser officers under them. Every freeman between the ages of sixteen and sixty was subject to this military duty. Single troops and companies were mustered four times a year, and once a year there was a general muster.

Everyone looked forward to the general muster—on that day all roads led to the county seat. Some of the people came as far as they could by boat and then walked the rest of the way. Others came in carts and on horseback, with the women and girls riding pillion behind their husbands, fathers or brothers. Small children were probably perched up in front of the riders. All were dressed in their bravest clothes.

At the county seat there was excitement in the air—the British flags were all flying, swords were glinting, and there was the sound of the "brass Trumpetts w'th silver mouth pieces" and the roll of drums. There were "Troopes of horse & Companies of Foot . . . provided w'th Armes & Ammunition" and with their "coullours" flying. The officers wore handsome belts and "Bootes." The men carried "firelock musketts" and had "Pistolls & Houlsters."

After the parades and drills were over the people mingled and enjoyed being together. It was probably the second day before the crowd broke up and the people started homeward. Liquor was no doubt flowing freely among the men.

The citizens of Northumberland petitioned the House of Burgesses in 1696, "praying" that no musters should be allowed to take place on Saturday, "as it led to the profamation of Sunday."

THE STORE

THE STORE was one of the principal institutions in the colony in early days. Every important planter kept a store somewhere on his plantation. Sometimes it was in a room in the manor but usually it was in a detached building. Storehouses were small, often not more than sixteen by eighteen feet.

The contents of these stores included nearly every article used by Virginians. A plantation store of 1667, with contents valued at six hundred fourteen pounds sterling, carried merchandise such as: materials of all kinds, carpenters' tools, bellows, sickles, locks, nails, staples, cooking utensils, flesh forks, shovels and tongs, medicines, wool cards, compasses, needles, stirrups, looking-glasses, candlesticks, candles, raisins, brandy, wine, and many other items.

Most of the manufactured articles came from England. To be very salable merchandise had to bear an English label.

THE WOLF-DRIVE

FOR A CENTURY after the first settlers came to the Northern Neck the forest was still alive with wolves. In the evenings they could be heard hunting and they sounded "like a pack of beagles."

These wolves were small, not much larger than a fox, but so ravenous that if a traveler was forced to spend the night in the woods he could hardly keep his horse from being devoured even though tied close to him and to the light of the fire.

The scattered sheepfolds and grazing pastures had to be guarded. Wolves were such a nuisance to the planters that authorities sought ways to destroy them. Rewards were offered for any person killing a wolf "provided the said wolf shall not be so young that it is not of age to do mischief."

The planters caught the wolves in various ways—in wolf-pits, log-pens and log-traps. Several mackerel hooks were fastened together and then dipped in melted tallow which hardened and concealed them. These were fastened to a chain so that after the wolf had swallowed the hooks he could not wander away in the forest and his head be lost for bounty.

In 1674, John Mottrom, II of Coan was rewarded with fourteen hundred pounds of tobacco for "killing seven wolves in a pitt." The settlers often paid their public dues in the skins of wolves.

As late as 1691 the county court of Northumberland made public arrangements for an annual wolf-drive. The wolves were hunted on horseback with dogs, very much in the manner of fox-hunting. Early writers state that it was possible while going at full speed to run down a wolf.

The wolf-drive was somewhat like the old English "drift of the forest," where a ring of men and boys with guns surrounded a large tract of woods. The wolves scenting them would retreat to the center of the circle, where the hunters would close in on them. Many were killed in this way. "Wolf-driving" was considered great sport.

Wolf-Trap Light, in Chesapeake Bay, is said to have been named because ashore near there was a famous place for catching the last of the wolves.

THE INDIANS AND ROBERT HEN

IN THE YEAR 1675, strange things were happening in the Northern Neck.

Thomas Matthews, a planter, whose "dwelling was in Northumberland, the lowest county on Potomack River," recorded these strange events—there "appear'd three prodigies in that country, which from attending disasters were look'd upon as ominous presages.

"The one was a large comet every evening for a week, or more at Southwest; thirty-five degrees high streaming like a horse taile westwards, until it reach'd (almost) the horizon, and setting toward the North-west.

"Another was, fflights of pigeons in breadth nigh a quarter of the mid-hemisphere, and of their length was no visible end; whose weights brake down the limbs of large trees whereon these rested at nights, of which the ffowlers shot abundance and eat 'em; this sight put the old planters under the more portentous apprehensions, because the like was seen, (as they said), in the year 1644 when th' Indians committed the last massacre, . . .

"The third strange appearance was swarms of fflyes about an inch long, and big as the top of a man's little finger, rising out of spigot holes in the earth, which eat the new sprouted leaves from the tops of the trees without doing other harm, and in a month left us." (This insect was the seventeen-year locust.)

The events which followed these strange occurrences not only justified the apprehensions of the old planters but also changed the course of history in the New World.

Thomas Matthews, of Cherry Point in Northumberland, also had a plantation, servants and cattle in Stafford County. His overseer there had bargained with an Englishman, Robert Hen, to come "thither" and be herdsman of the Stafford flocks.

Robert Hen arrived in due course of time and made his habitation on the Stafford plantation.

On a Sunday morning in the summer of 1675, people on their way to church found Hen lying across his threshold, and an Indian lying in the dooryard—"both chopt on their heads, arms and other parts, as if done with Indian hatchetts, th' Indian was dead, but Hen when asked who did that? answered Doegs, Doegs, and soon died, and then a boy who came out from under a bed where he had hid himself, told them, Indians had come at break of day and done those murders."

"Ffrom this Englishman's bloud," wrote Matthews, "did (by degrees) arise Bacon's rebellion."

Matthews continues: "Of this horrid action Coll: Mason who commanded the militia regiment of ffoot & Capt. Brent* the troop of horse in that county . . . having speedy notice raised 30, or more men, & pursu'd those Indians 20 miles up & 4 miles over that river into Maryland, where landing at dawn of day, they found two small paths . . . each leader with his party took a separate path and in less than a furlong either found a cabin, which they (silently) surrounded. Capt. Brent went to the Doegs cabin (as it proved to be) who speaking the Indian tongue called to have a council . . . such being the usual manner with Indians . . . the king came trembling forth, and would have fled, when Capt. Brent, catching hold of his twisted lock (which was all the hair he wore) told him he was come for the murder of Rob't Hen, the king pleaded ignorance and slipt loos, whom Brent shot dead with his pistoll, th' Indians shot two or three guns out of the cabin, th' English shot into it, th' Indians throng'd out at the door and fled, the English shot as many as they could so that they killed ten . . . and brought away the kings son of about 8 years old . . . the noise of the shooting awaken'd the Indians in the cabin, which Coll: Mason had encompassed, who likewise rush'd out and fled, of whom his company (supposing from that noise of shooting Brent's party to be engaged) shot ffourteen

---

*This was the second Giles Brent, who was half-Indian.

before an Indian came, who with both hands shook him (friendly) by one arm saying Susquehanoughs netoughs, meaning Susquehanoughs friends and fled. Whereupon Col: Mason ran amongst his men crying out ffor the Lords sake shoot no more, these are our friends the Susquehanoughs."

This attack upon the friendly Susquehannocks was a very unfortunate and costly mistake. The incensed Indians took to the warpath and murders were committed in both Virginia and Maryland. A body of Virginia militia under the command of Colonel John Washington, Colonel George Mason and Major Allerton, all of the Northern Neck, crossed the Potomac after the Indians.

This warfare ended, after much bloodshed, with Bacon in command. The allied Indians were defeated and the once friendly Susquehannocks were anihilated. And it was in this way, with an army at his command, that Bacon established his power and became strong enough to fight Governor Berkeley.

Thus it was, according to Thomas Matthews, that Bacon's Rebellion started with the murder of Robert Hen in the Northern Neck.

THE ROYAL CAVALCADE

WHEN ROBERT CARTER of Corotoman, Lancaster County, dressed on Sunday mornings he had a choice of several dress swords and of several belts to hold them—there was the silken belt, the buff, and the one of tan leather which was both "genteel and strong." His coat was of velvet with lace choker and cuffs, and his satin shorts were fastened at the knees with silver buckles to match those on his shoes.

If he looked in the mirror, as a servant adjusted his wig, he saw a strong man of medium height with a plump clean-shaven face and dark eyes that observed everything but saw no humour in anything.

When Carter and his lady, equally as splendid, stepped outside their mansion, a coach was a-waiting them, with liveried servants to help them inside. The coach was a heavy, four-wheeled, enclosed vehicle with two seats facing each other, and it carried four or more passengers. Most likely it was painted in shades of yellow and green, or a subdued red, with the family crest or coat of arms painted on the doors.

The six matched horses which drew the coach were being held in check by the driver and the outriders. A chaise may have been waiting behind the coach for the older daughters and guests. The

"King" Carter attends Christ Church.

sons of the house, if they were old enough, were mounted and attended by servants on horseback, one for each gentleman. Other mounted servants with led horses may have brought up the rear, but it is doubtful, as the distance to be traveled was only three miles.

There must have been a great rumbling of wheels, creaking of saddle leather and clatter of hoofs when the cavalcade swung onto the road which led from Corotoman to Christ Church. The master had built the road high, drained by deep ditches, and bordered on both sides by closely set cedars. It was like a long formal alley.

When the churchyard came into view people could be seen waiting there. The procession came to a halt with noise and "a great to-do." The family alighted and the master led the way. At the church door he halted and drew a key from his vest pocket with which he unlocked the door. It was customary for gentlemen to remove their swords at the church door and place them in a rack provided for the purpose, but whether or not the head of the Carter family did so is not known.

The Carters entered the church and proceeded to their high boxed pews, where curtains on gilt rods screened them from the gaze of the congregation.

According to tradition, this bit of pageantry was put on by Robert (King) Carter every Sabbath, and the congregation, it was said, waited rain or shine in the churchyard until he came to unlock the door. If he chose to take a Sunday off, services were held in the churchyard, it was said.

Though it was the custom for the rector to sign the vestry minute book first and then the members in order of their rank, in Christ Church the Carters always signed first, tradition says.

King Carter was a vestryman at Christ Church. He wanted his children to belong to the Established Church—"As I am of the Church of England way so I desire they should be."

The first Christ Church had been built by John Carter, the immigrant, in 1669. The second Christ Church was built on the same site by King Carter in 1732.

THE KING OF THE NORTHERN NECK

ROBERT CARTER was born to be a king among men. His fellow countrymen called him "King" and his real name was eventually forgotten. Like King Midas, everything that King Carter touched turned to gold, but in the case of the latter there was no magic in it—he planned it that way and worked to make his plans succeed.

Robert Carter was the second son of John, the immigrant and Indian fighter. His mother was Sarah Ludlow Carter, his father's fourth wife.

Robert Carter was born in 1663, at his father's plantation, Corotoman, in Lancaster County. The foundation had already been laid there for his future success. The immigrant Carter had done well. His plantation was orderly and successful and he had accumulated considerable wealth.

John Carter died when Robert was six years old, and the elder son inherited the bulk of the estate, as was the custom then according to the law of primogeniture and entail.

But John Carter did not forget Robert. He left instructions that his younger son should be well educated, specifying that "during his minority" he should have a man or youth servant bought for him. This servant was "not only to teach him his books . . . but also to preserve him from harm and evil." He further specified that his son should learn both Latin and English. These instructions were followed and Robert's education was completed in England.

The elder brother soon died, without male heir, and the whole estate reverted to Robert. It was now up to him to carry on the family traditions.

Corotoman, a bee-hive of activity, was typical of the plantations of that day. It was like a village, which was dominated by the manor house. There were the cottages of the white indentured servants, the slaves' quarters, the barn and farm buildings, the spinning-house, the laundry-house, the milk-house. There were the shops of the artisans who manufactured and repaired the articles used on the plantation. There was a shop where boats were built. Corotoman had everything that it needed to make it a self-sustaining unit.

To the sloop-landing, near the mouth of Carter's Creek, ships came directly from foreign ports with cargoes of clothing, furniture and luxuries for the manor, and shoes and other necessities for the white serfs and negro slaves. These vessels went away loaded with tobacco and grain.

Robert Carter was aware of everything that went on at Corotoman and on his other plantations, not the smallest detail escaped him. He knew when a slave's shoes didn't fit, or when a servant's child needed medical attention. When his sons were in school in

England he followed their progress by remote control and never let them forget that he was holding the purse-strings—"Mind your book," he wrote his son, Landon. He wanted them to have a classical education, a thorough understanding of Latin and English. He also wanted them to have religious training.

Robert Carter was a politician as well as a planter. He held every high office in the county and colony, and even acted as governor for more than a year.

But most of all, the land fascinated Robert Carter. He loved the rich virgin soil that would grow tobacco. It was the same thing as growing money. But in about three years time tobacco had worn out the soil and new fields must always be on tap in this tobacco game.

Carter's big opportunity came in 1702 when he was appointed as a land agent of the Northern Neck proprietary. He set up a land office at Corotoman and began to acquire lands for himself as well as for others. He had accumulated 20,000 acres by 1711, at which time he lost the agency to Thomas Lee, of Westmoreland.

In 1719 Carter regained the agency and again became the representative of the Fairfax interests in the Northern Neck. In 1726 he took an even bolder step by leasing the entire Northern Neck from the proprietor for a fixed rental of 450 pounds a year. Now he had the income from the quit-rents for the entire region.

When King Carter died in 1732, he owned 330,000 acres of land, a thousand slaves and 10,000 pounds sterling. The latter fact was remarkable because there was such a small amount of metallic money in the colony. He also left more than a hundred head of horses, over two thousand cattle and swine and several hundred sheep. These slaves and stock were scattered over his various plantations. His estate also included indentured servants, ships and nautical equipment, crops, farming equipment, cabins and mansions, furnishings, personal effects and a library of 521 volumes.

King Carter had done well for himself, and well for the proprietor. He had also opened up the back lands of the Northern Neck to settlers, which automatically forced the Indians back.

King Carter was a builder. He had a large brick kiln at Corotoman, which doubtless furnished the bricks for some of his homes and the church. He built a breakwater at Corotoman to save the waterfront from being washed away by tide and storm. It was made of huge rocks, probably brought as ballast in some of the ships. He dug a well at Corotoman and had it lined with stone. It was a farcry from the early settlers' "spring near the door."

King Carter built a road from Corotoman to Lease-Land (Fredericksburg), a distance of almost a hundred miles. It was known as the King's Highway.

In everything that King Carter did he looked ahead. He was building for the future generations of his family. When he died he was the richest and most powerful man in Virginia. His given name had long since been forgotten. He was known to everyone in the Northern Neck as King Carter. He was laid to rest in the yard of Christ Church.

KITH AND KIN

THERE USED to be an old saying—"everybody in the Northern Neck is kith and kin." This was almost a fact.

It all came about because in the early days the families of wealth and ability assumed leadership locally and in the Colonial Government. It was the custom of these families to intermarry in order to keep the power of wealth and influence within their own circle.

By the end of the eighteenth century it was hardly possible to find a prominent Northern Necker who was not "kin" to some other outstanding Virginian. This rigid rule of "keeping up the bars," as they called it, resulted in an aristocracy similar in many ways to the nobility of the Old World. This system accounts for the high political intelligence for which Tidewater Virginia was noted.

The marriages of King Carter's children illustrate this characteristic of colonial life in the Northern Neck, and in Virginia. King Carter married only twice but he had twelve children.

By his first wife, Judith Armistead, King Carter had four children, John, Elizabeth, Judith and Anne.

Judith died in 1699, and he married Elizabeth Landon Willis, a widow and daughter of Thomas Landon of England. She died in 1719. The best known of her eight children are Robert, Charles, Landon, Mary and Lucy.

Elizabeth, the eldest daughter, was married to Nathaniel Burwell. King Carter gave her Carter's Grove. After Burwell died she married George Nicholas. Judith married Mann Page of Rosewell, in Gloucester County. Anne married Benjamin Harrison of Berkeley, on the James.

Mary married George Braxton of Newington, in King and Queen County. Lucy married Colonel Henry Fitzhugh of Eagle's Nest, in Stafford County, on the Potomac.

John became a barrister in the Middle Temple, London, and married Elizabeth Hill of Shirley, on the James. Robert settled on the plantation of Nomini, on the Potomac. He married Priscilla, the daughter of William Churchill, a member of the Council.

Charles married three times—Mary Walker, Anne, daughter of William Byrd of Westover, and Lucy Taliaferro. His home was Cleve on the Rappahannock.

Landon's home was Sabine Hall, on the Rappahannock. He married three times—an Armistead of Hesse, a Byrd of Westover and a Wormeley of Rosegill.

King Carter's direct descendants include: a signer of the Declaration of Independence (Carter Braxton), two Presidents of the United States (the Harrisons), and General Robert E. Lee.

Thus King Carter's children were well established. These Carters and the heads of other top-ranking families were sometimes known in the Northern Neck as the "river barons."

THE FIELDINGS

AMBROSE FIELDING was a justice of the peace for Northumberland County in 1670.

Ambrose's son, Edward, came to Virginia from England, about 1687-88, to take up his inheritance of three hundred twenty-five acres left him by his father in 1675. His Northern Neck holdings were increased in 1695 by the will of his "Uncle Edward" Fielding, a great merchant of Bristol, England, who left him "500 acres at Wiccomocco in the County of Northumberland, in the Country of Virginia beyond the seas." In the same year Edward, by grant from Lady Culpeper and Lord Fairfax, acquired four hundred twenty-five more acres on "Wicocomoco river . . . near ye Mill Dam of ye sd. Fielding, of Lee parish."

Edward owned a snuff box, marked with his initials, "E.F.," and the date "1716." The portrait of a young woman was painted on the lid. It is believed to have been his wife, or his daughter Sarah. The girl in the picture wears a dress of satin, with white skirt, green stomacher and plain colored bodice; the head-dress, which is like a scarf or loose hood, is of white and green, and the flower held in her hand is blue, as are the velvet cushions of the chair.

Edward's oldest son was born in 1689. Edward named him for his father, Ambrose.

When Ambrose was about twenty-one years old he married the daughter of a "chirugeon," Mark Attkins. After their marriage Ambrose and Catherine moved to Lancaster County and settled on a plantation known as Broad Neck Quarter.

The house of Ambrose Fielding II, was built like a small fort in the wilderness, probably for defense against Indians. It was built of brick with loop-holes in the walls. A brick wall surrounded the house, and it too was pierced with loop-holes.

This house is said to have been located near the seat of the Carters at Corotoman. This statement seems to have been borne out by the will of King Carter, 1728, in which he mentions a "Fielding's Place." In 1749 the King's grandson, Robert Carter III, of Nomini Hall, owned about two thousand acres in a tract in Northumberland called Fielding's Quarter.

PIRATES

IN THE TIME of King Carter of Corotoman, the Chesapeake was alive with pirates. He wrote that they were "very bold and roguish . . . miserable case, the Crown takes no more care of so vast a fleet of ships as uses this bay."

The pirates reaped a rich harvest from the unprotected ships that traveled to and from foreign ports. In one year four ships bound back to Virginia from England had been sunk.

There were three types of pirates—the "bloody pirate," who was simply a robber on the high seas; the privateers, who commanded armed private vessels commissioned to cruise against the commerce or war vessels of the enemy; and buccaneers, who were freeholders who preyed upon Spanish as well as American vessels and settlements.

With its many bays and rivers the coastline of Tidewater Virginia was hard to defend. Pirates could swoop down in their fast boats and rob vessels and plunder the plantations along the shore. It was easy to make a landing in the lower counties of the Neck where the land was low and there were wharves at the plantations.

In 1699, Captain Kidd, who tradition says wore a gold chain around his neck and picked his teeth with a toothpick of gold, entered the Chesapeake in his vessel *Alexander*. The militia of the maritime counties was called out but Captain Kidd, after plundering several ships, sailed away.

Louis Guittar entered the Bay in 1700 and plundered and destroyed five vessels while there. At some time during this period, a ship-load of pirates reached the waters of the upper Chesapeake, where they captured a large sloop. They anchored that evening not far from shore and, tradition says, "the pirates were heard beating their drums all night long."

The pirate, George Lowther, entered the Bay in 1722. Roger Makeele was another Bay pirate. He and his gang of thirteen men and four women preyed on small craft in the Bay channels. After a successful venture they celebrated by "drinking and feasting with Rumm or Brandy, mutton, Turkey &C." This gang was captured and brought to trial by the Governor of Virginia.

The Virginia government used several methods of defense: lookouts, militia, forts and guard-ships. There was a fort with twenty-four guns and one hundred fifty "available shot" at Corotoman, on the Rappahannock. At Yeocomico, on the Potomac, there was a fort with six guns. Since almost no maintenance was given to the forts in Virginia they were in a dilapidated condition by 1691. The guns were "spoiled in the sand with the water flowing over them at high tide." This form of defense proved to be ineffective. The colony had already turned to guard-ships as a means of protection.

These guard-ships were used to convoy merchant vessels to their destination, or to a safe "riding place." The designated "riding place" on the Rappahannock was above the fort at Corotoman. On the Wicomico and on the Potomac the "riding places" were "as high as they can go."

One of these guardships, *H.M.S. Deptford*, a ketch, under command of Captain Thomas Berry, was upset in a squall in the Potomac. Captain Berry, who was ill at the time, was drowned along with eight members of his crew.

In 1726, Joseph Parsons, mate of the ship *Tayloe* of Bristol, was tried in the court of Richmond County and convicted of piracy and the murder of Captain John Heard of the *Tayloe*. Parsons was sent to the "gaol" at Williamsburg. The Council in Williamsburg re-examined the case and discharged Parsons because of lack of sufficient evidence. The silver plate and other articles found in the possession of the crew were held by the authorities until the rightful owners could claim them. The crew said that they had taken the property from the *Tayloe* "for sustinance while journeying through the colony."

After Blackbeard was captured by Maynard, in 1718, piracy in the Tidewater declined. The last pirate reported in the Chesapeake was in 1807. Tales of pirates, piracy and buried treasure were told in the region for many years.

CHRISTMAS AT COLONEL FITZHUGH'S

AN ACCOUNT of a Christmas spent at Bedford plantation in the Northern Neck was written by Monsieur Durand, a Frenchman, who was journeying through Virginia in the holiday season of the year 1686. He wrote:

"We were now approaching the Christmas Festival . . . It was agreed that all should go to spend the night with Colonel Fitzhugh, whose house is on the shore of the great river Potomac. . . .

"By the time we reached Col. Fitzhugh's we made up a troop of 20 horse.

"The Colonel's accomodations were, however, so ample that this company gave him no trouble at all; we were all supplied with beds, though we had to double up. Col Fitzhugh showed us the largest hospitality. He had store of good wine and other things to drink, and a frolic ensued.

"He called in three fiddlers, a clown, a tight-rope dancer and an acrobatic tumbler, and gave us all the divertisement one would wish. It was very cold but no one thought of going near the fire because they never put less than the trunk of a tree upon it and so the entire room was kept warm."

William Fitzhugh, the owner of Bedford, came to Virginia in 1670. He secured a grant of land in the upper Neck, in what later became King George County. He married "little Sarah Tucker" of Tucker Hill when she was only eleven years old, and then sent her to England to be educated. Sarah and William reared a family of five sons. Colonel Fitzhugh became one of the largest landowners in the Northern Neck. At the time of his death in 1701 he owned 54,054 acres of land.

INDIAN VISITORS

WHEN THE French Huguenot, Monsieur Durand, was in Stafford County in 1686 he described the Indians who lived along the Rappahannock River as follows:

"As we were about to take horse all those savages, men, women & little children, came to return our visit. Those who had been able to procure jerkins from the Christians were wearing them, as also the women who wore some kind of petticoats, others wore some pieces of shabby cloth from which were made the blankets they had traded on some ships in exchange for deer skins. They had a hole in the center to put their heads through & fastened it around their body with deer-thongs. The women were wearing theirs as a mantilla, like the Egyptian women in Europe, & their children were entirely naked. They had taken to adorn themselves some kind of pure white fishbones, slipping a strand of hair through a bone, & so on all around their head. They also wore necklaces & bracelets of small grains which are found in the country."

HORSE RACING

HORSE RACING was the most popular form of amusement in Virginia in the seventeenth century. The lower counties of the Northern Neck were the center of horse racing in the colony at that time.

These races had many spectators, including women, but only gentlemen could participate. Racing was considered "a sport for gentlemen alone," and records show that if one not of that class presumed to enter his horse in a race he was heavily fined.

The races were taken seriously and conducted with fairness, even if it might be necessary to be assisted to this end by the courts. There are many records of contested decisions decided by jury.

Saturday was the customary day for the races. These occasions when a crowd was gathered together were used by the public authorities for making announcements to the people.

In 1696 citizens of Northumberland complained to the House of Burgesses that the races on Saturday often caused the Sabbath to be profaned. The races may have been carried over into Sunday, or they may have ended in drinking and fighting bouts which continued on that day.

There were three racing tracks in the lower Neck: Coan Race Course, Willoughby's Old Field, located in Richmond County, and a third course at Yeocomico. Of these the principal and the most popular was the Coan track. These race-tracks were kept in good condition. Early race-courses were not always oval. Some were over "race paths." The "quarter race" was the outcome of this—where two horses ran a straight quarter of a mile. The stretch was sometimes a quarter and a half-quarter of a mile.

Smoker, owned by Mr. Joseph Humphrey, was one of the most famous race-horses in the colony. He was later owned by Captain Rodham Kenner, who was High Sheriff of Northumberland. Prince, owned by Captain John Haynie, II, was another noted race-horse. In 1695 Smoker was run in a race against Prince on Coan Race Course. The stake was four thousand pounds of tobacco and forty shillings. The race was won by Smoker.

Betting was part of the pleasure of the races. The stakes ran high—they were usually made up of a large amount of tobacco with a small addition of metallic coin.

Another horse celebrated in the region was Young Fire, owned by John Gardiner. This horse was snow-white in color. Captain John Hartley owned a horse called Campbell. Folly was a mare owned by Mr. Peter Contanceau. The owners were sensitive as to the reputations of their horses and would go to great lengths to preserve them.

Other Northern Neck turfmen mentioned in seventeenth century records were: Mr. Yewell of Westmoreland, John Hartridge, Daniel Sullivant, Mr. Raleigh Travers, Mr. John Clemens, Captain William Barber and John Washington.

MANUFACTURE

EARLY ATTEMPTS at manufacture were begun in Virginia. The Assembly estimated that five children not over thirteen years of age could spin and weave enough to keep thirty persons clothed. In 1646 it was ordered that two houses be erected in Jamestown for spinning-schools.

These "Flax-Houses," as they were called in some records, were to be "one-storey, measuring eight feet from floor to ceiling, with a loft of sawn boards above." A "stack" of brick chimneys were to stand in the middle of each house, and suitable partitions were to be made.

Each county was to send to these schools two "poor children," about seven or eight years old, who were to work at carding, knitting and spinning. For their maintenance the county authorities were to supply each of their children when they were admitted with: "6 barrels of Indian corn, a pig, 2 hens, clothing, shoes, a bed, rug, blanket, 2 coverlets, a wooden tray, and 2 pewter dishes or cups."

This plan was not very successful and it probably failed before the counties of the Northern Neck had advanced far enough to send children to the spinning-schools.

To encourage manufacture in early Virginia, prizes in tobacco were given for every pound of flax raised, for every skein of yarn, and for every yard of linen produced.

In 1697, Tobias Hall of Lancaster County, claimed the reward for the production of linen. Inventories of Lancaster disclose woolen-wheels and wool cards. A loom was owned by Charles Kelly. Flannel, and even blankets, were manufactured on these looms.

Between 1660 and 1702 there were at least two tailors in Lancaster County. Daniel Harrison, of the same county, must have manufactured quite a lot of shoes, for the time and place. He employed three shoemakers, and his personal estate included: "122 sides of leather, 72 pairs of shoes, 37 awls, 26 paring knives, 12 dozen lasts and numerous curriers' and tanners' tools."

A reward of fifty pounds of tobacco was offered for any sea-going vessel built in Virginia. There was no lack of Virginia-built small vessels, such as barges, shallops and sloops.

Rural life was not favorable to manufacture, although each plantation manufactured those articles necessary to its needs. William Fitzhugh, a wealthy landowner of the upper Neck, wrote to his London agent in 1692 and requested him to send to his plantations several shoemakers, "with lasts, awls and knives, together with half a hundred shoemaker's thread, some 20 or 30 gallons of train oil and proper colorings for leather." He had set up a tan-house and wished to convert the product into shoes on his own plantation.

Later on, in the eighteenth century, Robert Carter of Nomini Hall, a grandson of King Carter, manufactured on quite a large scale.

THE POTOMAC RANGERS

THE POTOMAC RANGERS were appointed by the governor for frontier duty. The county lieutenant, in command of the county militia, was given the power to impress men who lived in the region for this service.

The outfit was composed of a commander and eleven men with horses, arms, and necessary equipment. The Rangers had orders from the Jamestown government to "seize any Indian or Indians whatsoever," and have him, or them, put in jail to remain there until "delivered by due process of law."

Indians were not the only public enemies in the frontier country. In 1698, the gentlemen of Stafford sent a letter of "grievances" to Jamestown asking that the "bloody villain, Squire Tom, a convict upon record," be demanded from the "Emperor of Piscataway," who was then protecting him from punishment.

The activities of the Potomac Rangers are described in a quaint journal kept by one of the Rangers in 1692:

"A Journiall of our Ranging. Given by me, David Strahan, Lieutenant of ye Rangers of Pottomack. June the 17th; We ranged over Ackoquane, and so we Ranged Round persi-Neck and ther we lay that night. And on ye 18th came to Pohike, and ther we heard that Capt. Mason's Servt-man was missing. Then we went to see if we could find him, and we followed his foot abut a mile, to a house that is deserted, and we took ye tract of a great many Indians and we followed it about 10 miles, and having no provisions we was forced to return. June 26th: We Ranged up to Jonathan Matthews hs. along with Capt. Masone, and ther we met with Capt. Houseley, and we sent over for the Emperor, but he would not come, and we went over to ye towne, and they held a Masocomacko and ordered 20 of their Indians to goe after ye Indians that carried away Capt. Masone's man, and so we returned. July the 3d . . . July 11th; We ranged up to Brenttowne and ther we lay. . . . The 19th we ranged up to Ackotink, and discovered nothing. . . . So we Ranged once in ye Neck till ye 20th Sept^{br}, then we mercht to Capt. Masone's and ther we met with Capt. Houseley and his men; so we draved out 12 of our best horses, and so we ranged up Ackotink and ther we lay that night. Sept 22^د . . . Sept. 23^د we marcht to the Suggar Land* . . . And the 24th we Ranged about to see if we could find ye tract of any Indians, but we could not see any fresh signe . . .; the 26th marcht to Capt. Masone's, and ther dismissed my men till ye next March."

---

*Suggar Land was named for the sugar maple trees that at that time grew in the region of what was later Fairfax and Loudoun counties.

PART II
Eighteenth Century

MURDERS IN STAFFORD

THOMAS BARTON, of Stafford County, asked a neighbor to stay with his children while he and his wife went away for a day. The obliging neighbor, his wife and three children, came to the Barton plantation on a Sunday, June 16, 1700.

There were three children in the Barton family, and an orphan boy. On that peaceful June day all must have been drowsy contentment at the wilderness plantation—six children at play in the house, and the neighbor and his wife trying perhaps to take a nap. Only the orphan boy was outside, playing alone.

Suddenly the peaceful Sunday afternoon was turned into a nightmare. A party of Indian warriors swooped down in a sudden attack on the Barton place. All was over in a few minutes no doubt. Only the orphan boy escaped and ran to a neighboring plantation.

Meanwhile Barton was on the way home. His wife had probably decided to stay overnight wherever they had visited for he was alone. He stopped by a mill where he had left some corn to be ground and picked up his bag of meal. When he was almost home about twenty Indians started up from the woods and closed in about him in a "half-moon." They were naked and unarmed.

Barton had a good mount but the meal was heavy. He finally got the bag loose and threw it off, and then at full speed he "broke through the woods and got safe to a neighbor's house."

Colonel George Mason II, who was probably at the head of the Stafford militia, was notified of the outrage. When he and a "small parcel of men" arrived at the Barton place they found plenty of work to do. They "pulled out of the people and a mare, sixty-nine arrows." They also found five "ugly wooden tomahawks." Mason and the men buried the "poor people." Arrows had made holes in the roof of the house as "big as swan shot."

From the tracks about the house Mason judged that there had been at least forty Indians in the party. He was of the opinion that most of them had gone back to Maryland.

After Mason returned to his home he wrote a long letter to the governor in which he described the murders as the "horriblest that ever was in Stafford." These two plantations would be deserted for the year, he wrote, and he was afraid that all the people would leave their plantations. "I am afraid," wrote Colonel Mason, "that we shall have a bad summer, but . . . if I can keep them upon their plantations, it will be some discouragement to the enemy . . . but God knows what I shall do now, for this has almost frighted our people out of their lives."

In another letter written in July, Colonel Mason seemed to have gotten the situation well in hand: "The Rangers continue their duties . . . they range . . . four days a week, which is as hard duty as can be performed. . . . The inhabitants still continue from their homes, but the abundance are better satisfied since part of the Rangers are constantly ranging among them." The Rangers had been re-enforced by the sons of the planters and other young men.

FREE SCHOOLS

IN 1652 the court of Northumberland County granted the petition of Richard Lee of Cobbs Hall "concerning a free school to be set up."

Francis Pritchard, 1675, Lancaster County, left a large estate for the establishment of a free school.

In 1700 William Horton endowed a free school in Westmoreland County.

In 1702 John Farneffold made provision in his will for a free school in Northumberland as early as August, 1672. In 1680 he was minister of St. Stephen's Parish, and remained such until his death in 1702. He was the son of Sir Thomas Farneffold of Sussex, England.

The provisions in John Farneffold's will concerning the free school were as follows:

"I give 100 acres where I now live for the maintenance of a free school, and to be called Winchester Schoole, for fower or five poore children belonging to ye parish and to be taught & to have their dyett, lodging & washing, & when they can read the Bible & write a legible hand, to dismiss them & take in more, such as my exors. shall think fitt, and for the benefit of the said school, I give five cows and a Bull, six ewes, and a ram, a carthorse & cart and two breeding sowes & that my two mulatto girles, Frances and Lucy Murrey, have a yeares schooling & be free when they arrive at the age of 22 years, to whom I give a sow shoat to each, & for further encouragement of a schoolmaster, I give dyett, lodging & washing & 500 pds. of tobacco & a horse, Bridle & Saddle to ride on during his stay, the place where the school house is to be directed, my will is to have it neare my dwelling house, some part of which may serve for a school house til another may more conveniently be built. Item what schoole books I have in my study, I leave for ye benefit of ye schoole. Then my will is that some of my estate be sold for the maintenance of the said schoole except what my exors. shall think fitt to select necessary for use as bedding, potts, & pewter. My will is that Mr. Tarpley, Mr. Leo Howson, Richard Nutt and Edward Cole carry me to the grave, three to have guineas, and Richard Nutt a gold ring. . . . If the school fail for want of maintenance, which I hope it will not, give that hundred acres & all the rest of my land to Farneffold Nutt, son of Richard Nutt; to the minister who preaches my funeral sermon, my Preaching gown & Cassocke."

Another school was provided for by Daniel Hornby, of Richmond County. In his will, proved April 2, 1750, he made provision that a Latin master should attend Travers Colston, a relative, at twenty pounds per year, and that he should be obliged to teach ten children.

In 1770-71 Colonel Landon Carter of Sabine Hall, Richmond County, was supporting a free school in that county. William Rigmaiden was the master of this school.

THE HOME IN THE FOREST

MARY BALL was born on a plantation "up in the forest," which was the way the Northern Neckers described any place that was not on the water.

In this Neck where one is never far from the water, river plantations were the rule in colonial days, and it is an unusual fact that Colonel Joseph Ball established his seat in the forest. Lancaster was still a frontier county and there were only horse paths through the woods, for the rivers were still used as highways.

Joseph Ball had inherited his forested lands from his father, William Ball, the founder of the Ball family in Virginia. William came to Virginia, probably as a merchant, in 1650, but he did not settle until about 1663, at which time he purchased land in Lancaster County and established his seat on the east side of the Corotoman River, where it empties into the Rappahannock. This location, which he called Millenbeck, became the county seat.

Joseph Ball followed in the footsteps of his father as a man of prominence in county affairs. He was Lieutenant-Colonel in the militia, and vestryman of St. Mary's White Chapel. This chapel was known as "the Balls' church" just as Christ Church was known as the "Carters' Church." Both churches were in Christ Church Parish.

Joseph Ball was married twice. Just before his second marriage he gave to the children of his first marriage certain portions of his estate, reserving the right of dower for his second wife.

Little is known of Joseph's second wife, Mary Johnson, except that she was a widow. When Mary Ball was born to Joseph and Mary, probably in the winter of 1708 or 1709, there was nothing to indicate that she was destined to become the most important woman of the Northern Neck. She was at that time just another baby born into the gentle, distinguished and religious Ball family.

Joseph Ball, who was no longer a young man, died when Mary was about two years old. In his will he left Mary four hundred acres of land near the head of the Rappahannock River, three slaves, fifteen cattle and "all the feathers in the kitchen loft to be put in a bed for her."

Within about one year, Mary Johnson Ball married again. Her third husband was a prominent merchant-planter, Captain Richard Hewes, who lived on his plantation Cherry Point in the upper part of Northumberland County, in the neck between Yeocomico and Coan Rivers.

When Mrs. Hewes went to Cherry Point to live she took her son by her first marriage, John Johnson, and Mary Ball with her. Thus Mary at three years of age had few, if any, memories of her birthplace "up in the forest" of Lancaster County.

Several generations later this Ball plantation became known as Epping Forest. It was named, it is believed, for a Ball estate in England.

CHERRY POINT

MARY BALL'S first memories were probably of the fields and rivers at Cherry Point. It was a pleasant place to remember. The responsibility of the plantation soon fell on Mary's mother, for Captain Hewes died in 1713.

There were few toys then. Mary may have had one of those wooden dolls with stiff joints and staring eyes. She probably played out-of-doors and had animals for pets.

There were no childrens' books then. A Mother Goose book was published in Boston in 1719, but that was too late for Mary. She probably had only a horn-book from which to learn her A B C's. Perhaps there was an indentured servant who could teach her a little.

On Sundays the family probably attended church at Upper St. Stephen's Parish*, where Captain Hewes had been one of the vestrymen. There may have been some sort of a road from the plantation to the church over which a coach could be pulled, but if so it certainly did not travel at the lively speed of King Carter's! More than likely they rode there on horseback—little Mary sitting up in front of some older person. She doubtless learned to ride at an early age.

Mary probably valued the feather bed left her by her father far more than she did the legacy of land. She had never even seen the land, but every night she could sink into the warmth and softness of the feather bed.

Mary's childhood days at Cherry Point ended in 1721. The child's half-brother, John Johnson, and her mother both died in that year.

Mary Ball was now an orphan, but her mother had planned it so that she would not be alone in the world. Mary Hewes had stipulated in her will that—"my said Daughter Mary Ball—be under Tutiledge and government of Captain George Eskridge during her minority." Colonel Eskridge was also named as executor of Mary's estate. She had received almost the whole of her mother's estate, consisting of lands, two horses and personal property. And she had received all of her half-brother's estate, consisting of land in Stafford County.

Mary Hewes had chosen wisely in selecting her "trusty and well beloved friend George Eskridge" as guardian of her youngest child. Colonel Eskridge was not only a lawyer of distinction, an experienced business man, a leading man in his community, but he was also a gentleman. And Colonel Eskridge was "connected by marriage" with Mary Ball's half-sister Elizabeth Johnson who had married Samuel Bonum. Mary was therefore equally welcome to make her home at her guardian's plantation or at the farm of the Bonum's.

---

*NOTE: This church is said to have been located near the present village of Lottsburg.

Mary Ball at Yeocomico Church.

SANDY POINT

BOTH THE Bonums and the Eskridges lived in lower Westmoreland County, just across the Yeocomico River from Cherry Point.

Colonel Eskridge's plantation, Sandy Point, was directly on the Potomac. Its name gave but a vague idea of the beauty of the beach and the sweep of river beyond. There was a feeling here of space. It was a place of restless sounds, made by the wind and waves. It was quite different here from the quieter waters and forest walls that Mary Ball had known.

Bonum's Creek Farm, the home of Mary's half-sister, Elizabeth, was east of Bonum's Creek. The "home-place" was situated on the bank of the Potomac, in sight of Pecatone, the manor home of the Corbin family.

Mary now had the choice of these two delightful places for her future home. She probably divided her time between the two. Perhaps Mary Hewes had this in mind when she left Mary a "good Pacing horse together with a good silk plush saddle," thus taking care of the problem of transportation.

Among the other things "bequeath unto" Mary by her mother were two gold rings, the "one being a large hoop and the other a stoned ring," a trunk and "all the rest of my wearing apparel." So when Mary went to her new homes she had a trunkful of clothes which would come in handy as she grew older, for it took a long time to receive an order from England, and ships were being taken by pirates during these years. It was lucky that fashions did not change much then, and that clothes were made to last.

Mary had a maid, who probably looked after her and her wardrobe. Mary had enough income for her needs, therefore she was more fortunate than most orphans of that time.

Sandy Point was doubtless the scene of many larks after Mary joined the Eskridge girls who lived there. In the evenings there was probably much talk around the fireplace—of pirates and witches and houses where mysterious lights flitted at night. And much giggling and chatter upstairs after the candles had been put out.

In 1726 Mary's life was again saddened, this time by the death of her brother-in-law, Samuel Bonum. In his will he left her "a young gray dapple horse."

While at Sandy Point Mary attended Yeocomico Church, where her guardian was a vestryman. She rode there on horseback, tradition says. In cold weather she probably wore a red cloak, and a hood or scarf to protect her head and face.

The simple church, cloistered in the virgin forest, invited worship, but the churchyard on Sundays was a festive place in those days. And it was a noisy place—there was the rattling of wheels, the cracking of whips, the neighing of horses and the chattering of the people, who were so glad to see each other. There were "rings of Beaux chatting" around the girls in their bright mantles.

It was cold inside the church in winter, sometimes too cold to have even the usual short sermon. The high-backed pews shielded their occupants from drafts, and some people had their servants bring in little stoves of perforated tin containing coals, or hot bricks to place under the feet.

After the service there was more "visiting together" in the churchyard, and the men had business transactions to make.

Near the church there was a spring, and a kiln where the bricks had been burned for the church when it was built in 1706.

Mary Ball lived among the gentle people of this region until she was married. There are no early portraits of Mary Ball, but tradition says that at the time of her marriage she was "a healthy orphan of moderate height, rounded figure and pleasant voice, aged 23."

AUGUSTINE

AUGUSTINE WASHINGTON was "connected by marriage" with Colonel Eskridge. He probably met Mary Ball on one of his visits to Sandy Point.

Sandy Point was an ideal place for romance but there is not even a traditional account of the courtship of Mary Ball. Even the scene of her marriage is not known, but it was probably at Sandy Point or at the Bonum home. Mary Ball and Augustine Washington were married by the Reverend Walter Jones, on March 6, 1731. Ministers at that time usually received "for marriage two shillings."

Mary's new husband was "blond, of fine proportion, great physical strength and stood six feet in his stockings, and had a kindly nature." He was called Gus by his friends.

Gus took his bride to his home on Popes Creek, in upper Westmoreland County. Mary was not the first mistress at Popes Creek, for Augustine had been married before, to Jane Butler, half-sister to Colonel Eskridge's second wife. Jane had been dead for about three years.

At Popes Creek now there were the servants and little Jane, who was about nine years old. Augustine's other two children were teen-age boys, Lawrence and Augustine, who were then at Appleby's School in England. Gus himself had been educated at that school.

Augustine Washington, while not a man of great wealth, owned land and buildings in at least three counties, and he was part owner of two iron furnaces. He was prominent in his community, having held at various times the positions of Justice of Westmoreland County court, Captain in the county militia, Sheriff of Westmoreland County, and he was a vestryman in the church. Although he was not one of the wealthiest planters in the Northern Neck, he was on an equal footing with them socially.

POPES CREEK

WHEN MARY came to Popes Creek to live she had some housefurnishings of her own to bring with her. There was the feather bed, and her mother had left her a bedstead to go with it, a quilt and a pair of blankets. She had also left Mary two table-cloths "marked M. B. with inck," two pewter dishes, two basins, one large iron "pott," one frying pan, one "Rugg" and "one suit of good curtains and fallens" (valance). It must have been with great joy that Mary arranged these things in her own home.

The house at Popes Creek was not a magnificent residence such as Stratford Hall or King Carter's manor at Corotoman. It is believed to have been "a simple abode," but it was comfortable and it had a quality that was lacking in the splendid mansions—it was homely. It was the kind of place where a planter could sit with his family in the evening and feel close to them and close to his earth.

The house was situated on the west side of Popes Creek, about three-quarters of a mile from the point where the creek emptied into the Potomac. About a mile to the northwest was the last habitation of John Washington, the immigrant, and near it was the family burying ground.

Augustine had bought his tract of one hundred and fifty acres of land on Popes Creek from Joseph Abbington in 1718. David Jones, a local builder and undertaker, had contracted to build the home for five thousand pounds of tobacco with extra amounts in cash for incidentals. He was probably assisted by Augustine's slaves and indentured servants. The house was completed and occupied by Augustine and his first wife about 1726, so it was still rather new when Mary came to live there.

Mary probably found it not too difficult to assume her duties as mistress of the plantation for the farm activities at Popes Creek were about the same as those she had known before her marriage on the plantations in lower Westmoreland.

Many years later the Popes Creek plantation became known as Wakefield.

THE WAR PATH

THE SHENANDOAH VALLEY was the historic war trail of the Six Nations of Indians of the north in their warfare with the southern Indian tribes. These wars had commenced before the settlement of Jamestown. There is no evidence to show that the Valley was inhabited to any extent by Indians immediately before the coming of the white man to the New World. Scattered burial mounds prove that Indians lived there at an early period but their history has been lost.

Governor Spotswood believed that this migration of Indian warriors from north to south would hold back the settlement of Virginia. He called a conference which was attended by the northern Indians and the governors of New York and Pennsylvania, and himself and other representatives from Virginia. At this conference the Indians were persuaded to limit their travel. In the Treaty of Albany, signed in 1722, the northern Indians promised to let the southern Indians live in peace, and agreed that their warriors would not cross Virginia without a passport. Disregard of this treaty was punishable with death or transportation to the West Indies and sale into slavery.

Governor Spotswood bound the bargain by dramatically handing the interpreter his "golden-horseshoe," which had been pinned at his breast, and bidding him to give it to the speaker and to tell him that "there was an inscription on it which signified that it would help him to pass over the mountains; and that when any of their people should come to Virginia with a pass, they should bring that with them."

A Story of the Historic Northern Neck of Virginia

After this treaty was signed the Northern Neck could be opened to settlers westward. And the planters could now patent immense tracts of land.

FALMOUTH

ABOUT THIS time there was considerable trade between the Northern Neck and both Ireland and Scotland. It has been said that Virginia tobacco helped Glasgow, Scotland, to prosperity. A street in that city was named for Virginia, and at one time Virginia merchants "thronged that street and were regarded with such respect that other men gave way that they might pass." Among these gentlemen were some of the planters from the Potomac. In 1720 George Mason III, was given the freedom of the city of Glasgow, in the form of a parchment "Burgess Ticket."

Falmouth, in Stafford County, was founded in 1727 by Scotch merchants. Boats from Scotland came directly to this trading village situated near the head of the Rappahannock River. Something of this once thriving trading center of the Neck is told in a letter written by a visitor by the name of Ellen Gray. The undated letter was written to her friend, Rose Douglas of Loch Lomond, Scotland. It says:

"Dear Rose:

Falmouth is on a river that empties into Chesapeake Bay. The houses are perched on declivities and hills. There are mills. I love water wheels when they glisten. . . . We saw scenery much wilder than any in Scotland. It consisted of islands in the Rappahannock, lying above Falmouth. We gazed on them from a long plank bridge. What a pity the Virginians will span their streams with plank instead of stone! A stone bridge overgrown with moss is a bewitching sight. Several Scotch families have lived in Falmouth, tho the place is called Fal from a river in England. Among its most successful merchants was Basil Gordon. He arrived a poor boy in Falmouth. He died a millionaire after a life of patient industry."

Basil Gordon is believed to have been one of America's first millionaires.

BURNT HOUSE FIELD

IT WAS a cold night in January, 1729. Thomas Lee was ready to go to bed. He had probably checked the doors and windows and all seemed well at Matholic.

His family were already asleep but perhaps Thomas lingered awhile, thinking about his new home, Stratford, which he was building on his own plantation twenty miles away. How good, he may have thought, it would be to have something of his own. For Matholic, this ancestral Lee estate in Westmoreland where he was now living, did not belong to Thomas. He was leasing it from his older brother, the third Richard Lee.

Thomas Lee was a younger son and therefore he had received little in the way of a heritage; even his education had been neglected. His older brothers had received the customary classical education, while Thomas learned only reading, spelling and ciphering, probably from an indentured servant. He had been ashamed of his lack of education. To pass in the elegant society to which his family were accustomed it was necessary to have a knowledge of Latin and Greek. After he was a mature man he studied long hours alone until he had mastered these subjects.

Thomas' father, the second Richard, had thrown at least one crumb in the direction of his younger son. When he was compelled by age to resign as naval officer of the Potomac, in 1710, the elder Lee persuaded Governor Alexander Spotswood to give this post to his son, Thomas. So, before he was twenty-one, Thomas was reporting on the maritime trade of his district, and collecting fees from the ships' captains.

Through his uncle, Edmund Jenings, Thomas had acquired the position of manager of the Northern Neck proprietary. His uncle, who was then in England, had a lease on the proprietary at that time. Thomas had opened a land office at Matholic. He also traveled on horseback all over the Northern Neck so that in this way he well knew the lands of that vast domain.

By the time Thomas was established, and thirty-two years old, his thoughts turned to marriage. He went "a-courting" down at Green Spring, near Jamestown, and won the hand of young Hannah Harrison Ludwell. When Hannah came as a bride to Matholic she added to the family fortune with her dowry of six hundred pounds sterling.

Things were going well with Thomas Lee. Now, on this winter's night, he probably went up to bed with a contented mind.

Sometime during the night Thomas awoke suddenly to find the house in flames around him. He shook Hannah and they grabbed up the children from their beds and started for the stairs only to find that it was too late to get down that way. The heat was hot on his back when he helped Hannah over the window sill and watched her fall to the ground—fifteen feet. He dropped his small children and then jumped himself. Just in time, too, for he was hardly on the ground before the roof caved in—too late to save the twelve-year-old white servant girl who was asleep in the house.

Shivering in their night clothes the family watched the barns and outbuildings burn to the ground, shocked into silence by the loss of the little servant.

Later the ashes of the house were searched for Hannah's silver. When not a trace of it was found the origin of the fire seemed evident—burglars had broken in, stolen the silver and other valuables, and then set fire to the house.

The villians who burned the house were never caught. There were at large a number of English convicts who had been transported to Westmoreland as indentured servants. They had joined together and formed a lawless gang—they frightened and robbed the citizens of the countryside. Thomas Lee in his line of duty as a local magistrate had no doubt at some time given them reason to want revenge. These convicts may have burned the house.

As naval officer of the Potomac, Thomas had to prevent smuggling. A year before Matholic was burned his life was threatened by the crew of the *Elizabeth*. No doubt some of his enemies made in the line of his duties were at the bottom of this outrage. At any rate the Lords of Trade in London thought so, for they sent him a bounty, three hundred pounds of which was from the privy purse of Queen Caroline. Tradition says that this bounty helped Thomas Lee to finish building his home, Stratford.

In the meantime he built another house on the Matholic estate at a spot removed from the original house. The new house was called Mt. Pleasant.

The site of the destroyed house was ever after known as Burnt House Field. It was used as a family burying ground.

STRATFORD HALL

LONG BEFORE Matholic burned Thomas Lee had started building his own home.

As a land agent for the Northern Neck proprietary he was well acquainted with its desirable lands, but the portion which he selected for his own belonged to the Pope family, and had been patented by Colonel Nathaniel Pope about 1650, before the proprietary came into being.

"I want to buy the Clifts," said Thomas Lee. This land was situated in Westmoreland County and bordered on the Potomac. Here the banks rose sharply above the River. We can imagine Thomas Lee standing at the edge of those bold cliffs, looking across the River while he dreamed of the manor house which he would some day build.

One day in 1716 a representative of the Pope family closed the deal by ceremoniously presenting Thomas Lee with a handful of earth and a twig—an ancient symbolic confirmation of the transference of the 1,450 acres of land called "the Clifts Plantation."

Thomas Lee built his home nearly a mile inland from the "clifts," where it would not be so open to an enemy attack from the River. Pirates were still roving the surrounding waters.

It took a long time to build the kind of house that Thomas Lee had in mind—a house with walls of brick two feet thick, that would stand for centuries. The thousands of bricks required for this undertaking had to be made there on the place.

Thomas Lee made a trip to England at the beginning of his project, some traditions say, and while he was there he doubtless visited the estate at Strat-by-the-Ford, once owned by his grandfather, Richard Lee, the immigrant. There could scarcely be any other reason why he would name his own home, Stratford.

Thomas Lee planned his house, it is said, after viewing the manor houses of England, and the result was that Stratford turned out to be a sort of medieval fortress. It was shaped like the letter H with pointed roofs. The crossbar of the H was the Great Hall, about thirty feet square.

On the roof of each wing arose a cluster of four great chimneys, which were joined together by arches of masonry. These clustered chimneys gave the appearance of two belfries, or towers. The space inside each group of chimneys was made into a summer-house. A member of the Lee family later described them thus:

"Eight chimneys formed the summer-house pillars,
From which were seen Potomac's sea-like billows. . . ."
In medieval times the use of the summer-house was functional, and so were these at Stratford—the activities of the plantation and on the Potomac could be seen from them.

At first glance Stratford appeared to be a one-story building, but its main floor was raised to the level of a second story. Thomas Lee had an idea of his own about architecture which was remarkably modern, that was to bring the beauty of nature inside. He did this by having long flights of steps leading directly from the lawn to the front and rear entrances of the Great Hall. Doorways and windows framed the fields, forest and lawn.

The manor occupied the center of a large square marked at the corners by four dependencies. A ha-ha wall ran across the front of the square, the purpose of which was to keep the cattle away from the house without obscuring the view.

Stratford Hall was built between 1725-30.

GEORGE WASHINGTON

IT WAS about ten o'clock of a February morning in the year 1732,* when a baby's cry was heard in the dwelling at Popes Creek. A son had just been born to Augustine and Mary Washington.

The baby was named George. It is believed that Mary's first born child was thus named in honor of her former guardian, Colonel George Eskridge.

Neighbors, godparents and the minister assembled, probably at Popes Creek, for the christening. A notation in Mary's Bible recorded the event: ". . . and was Baptised the 5th of April following." George's godmother was his aunt, Mrs. Mildred Washington Gregory.

George's first memories must have been happy ones—of woods, fields and water, and of animals, fowl and birds. His family loved him, and the dark faces were kindly.

George soon had a sister, Betty, to play with, and then Samuel. The first three and one-half years of George's life were spent at the Popes Creek plantation.

---

*George Washington was born "11th Day of February 1732, Old Style," or February 22, 1732, "New Style." The latter is the now accepted date.

The infant, George Washington at Wakefield, his birthplace.

EPSEWASSON

IN 1735, AUGUSTINE decided to move his family from Popes Creek to his farm about fifty miles up the Potomac.

This farm was part of the land acquired years before by John Washington, the immigrant, and Nicholas Spencer, husband of Frances Mottrom. Augustine had bought twenty-five hundred acres of it in 1726.

This property was located on Little Hunting Creek, which flowed into the Potomac. It was still called by the Indian name, Epsewasson.

Tradition says that the Washington family moved in March, as soon as "the ice cleared in the river." It was a new adventure for the children, but one of them was missing. Little thirteen-year-old Jane had passed away in January.

Epsewasson was still quite primitive; some of the land had never been under the plow. The Indians lived no longer in the forest, but the wild animals were still there.

At Epsewasson there was probably already a small dwelling, and Augustine had cabins built for the slaves and servants. And there had to be a mill—Augustine had one on Popes Creek and he built one here on Doeg Run.

Mary probably found life much harder at Epsewasson. The location was isolated, but she was never lonely for the children kept her company, and a fourth baby, John Augustine soon came to join his brothers and sister.

Thirty miles from Epsewasson was a place called Accokeek, where Augustine had interest in an iron-works. He seems to have been the only American actively interested in the iron enterprise, Principio Iron Furnaces. The rest of the company was owned by Englishmen.

Between Epsewasson and Accokeek there were several streams and marshes and Gus found that it was just as hard to get to as it had been from Popes Creek.

Little George may have gone to Accokeek with his father sometimes and watched the pig iron from the furnace being carried by cart to a landing six miles away on the Potomac. Augustine had men and oxen there for that purpose—"three hundred weight being a load for a cart drawn by 8 oxen."

1738 was an eventful year for the Washingtons. First, another baby, Charles, was born, and then, Lawrence returned from his

Young Washington helping in the handling of "seine" on the Potomac.

school in England. He was a grown man now, with grace and polish. He immediately became George's hero, and remained so forever.

Augustine now made a decision—they must move out of the wilderness so that the children could have schooling and so that he could be closer to the iron works.

A place near Fredericksburg seemed to fill these qualifications. It was within easy riding distance of the iron-works, it was near a school, and it was situated between the land bequeathed Mary by her father and the land left her by her half-brother, John Johnson.

Augustine bought the property, which was known as the "Strothers estate," in 1738. They left Epsewasson, on Little Hunting Creek, which was later to become well-known as Mount Vernon.

NOTE: Epsewasson was sometimes spelled Eppsewasson, Ipsewason, etc.

FERRY FARM

THE WASHINGTON family moved to their new home in December, 1738. The "Strothers estate," or Ferry Farm as it was called then or at some later date, was located in what was then King George County but later became Stafford County.

The house was of moderate size, with the necessary farm outbuildings nearby. There were open fields and some woodland. The property was on the Rappahannock and at this part of the River it had dwindled to a small stream. It was not much of a river here when compared with the Potomac which the Washingtons had just left. The ferry which was operated not very far from the house must have been of especial interest to the children.

Ferry Farm was by no means luxurious, but it was adequate for the needs of the Washingtons. Here they lived a simple farm life.

The meals were probably served in the hall, as the custom had been in the seventeenth century. The china and linen were ample but in keeping with farm-living. There were twenty-six silver spoons but no silver plate.

The family doubtless arose early, maybe at dawn. After grace was said a simple breakfast was served. The main meal was served in the middle of the day and it was called dinner. Game, fowl, fish or hot meat and greens, vegetables and hot breads were included in this meal. The hominy may have been made in the Indian fashion with a pestle and a hollowed-out tree stump. Supper was a light meal.

The objects which were probably of the most interest to George were his father's surveying instruments, rifle and axe.

Mary's chamber, it was said, was directly in the rear of the hall downstairs. There were two beds in it, the trunk, a chest of drawers, four rush-bottomed chairs, and a tea table before the fireplace. The two windows had hangings. It was probably in this room that another baby girl was born in June, 1739. She was the last child born to Mary and Augustine.

October, 1740, was a sad month for the Washingtons. The baby died that month, and Lawrence sailed from the Chesapeake to a far-off war in Cartagena.

FREDERICKSBURG

THE TOWN of Fredericksburg was just across the Rappahannock from Ferry Farm. To the Washington children, straight from the wilderness, it must have been a source of delight.

Sloops lay at the wharf there, close to the public warehouses which were built in the shape of a cross. Near the wharf there was a quarry of white stone, and there were several other quarries in the river bank. There was one building in the town that was built of the stone, and that was the prison. Most of the buildings were of wood with wooden chimneys. In a few years the wooden chimneys were to be outlawed by the Burgesses.

Fredericksburg was a new town, and it was "by far the most flourishing town in that part of Virginia." It was "pleasantly situated on the South Shore of Rappahannock River, about a Mile below the Falls." It had been established in 1727 on a fifty-acre tract of land known as the Lease-Land.

The preamble of the act which established the town stated its purpose: ". . . good houses are needed and greatly wanted upon some navigable part of said river, near the falls, for the reception and safe keeping of such commodities as are brought thither from remote places with carriages drawn by horses or oxen."

When Colonel William Byrd of Westover visited Fredericksburg in 1732, he stayed at the home of its "top man," Colonel Henry Willis, whose wife was George Washington's aunt, Mildred.

Colonel Byrd relates that after a breakfast of beefsteak, his host walked him about "his Town." He saw the stone prison, the shops of the tailor, the merchant, the smith, and an ordinary. There was also Mrs. Levistone—"Who acts here in the double capacity of a doctress and coffee woman. And were this a populous city, she is qualified to exercise two other callings."

"Mrs. Levistone," or Susanna Livingston, was for some years the only physician in Fredericksburg. The vestry of St. George's Church paid her for attending the poor who were sick in the parish: "To Mrs. Livingston, for salivating a poor woman, promising to cure her again if she should be sick again in twelve month, 1,000 pounds of tobacco." It was not unusual then for a woman to be a "doctress."

Probably the most interesting place in Fredericksburg to the Washington children was the shop of William Lynn who sold, along with other things, brown and white sugar candy.

The same year that the Washingtons came to live at Ferry Farm, a law was passed that "fairs should be held in Fredericksburg twice a year, for the sale of cattle, provisions, goods, wares, and all kinds of merchandise whatsoever," and "that all persons attending the Fair at Fredericksburg were immune from arrest and execution during the fairs and for two days before and after them."

SCHOOL DAYS

IT WAS EASTER, 1743. George Washington was visiting his relatives at Chotank, in King George County. His vacation was interrupted by a messenger from Ferry Farm who told him that he was to return home at once as his father was ill.

Augustine Washington died on April 12, 1743. He was buried in the old family burial ground, near the banks of Bridges Creek, not far from his old home on Popes Creek.

Both of George's older half-brothers were now home; Lawrence was back from Carthagena, and "Austin" had returned from his school in England in June, 1742.

Augustine left Lawrence, his eldest son, the largest part of his estate, including all the property on Little Hunting Creek. "Austin" inherited the Popes Creek Farm. George was left the Ferry Farm and three lots in Fredericksburg. He was to receive his inheritance when he was twenty-one.

There is no definite proof as to where George lived after his father's death, but it seems that he lived at various times, at Ferry

Farm with his mother, at Popes Creek with "Austin," and on Little Hunting Creek with Lawrence.

Tradition says that George had a convict-teacher named Hobby who taught him to read, write and "cipher," that he attended a school in Fredericksburg run by Reverend James Marye, and that while he was at Popes Creek with his brother Augustine, he attended Henry Williams's school near Oak Grove. These traditions have not been as yet verified.

It is known that "ciphering" was George's "absorbing interest." Tradition says that when he was attending school in Fredericksburg he usually worked at his figures while the other boys were playing bandy during recess, but one day he was "romping with one of the largest girls; this was so unusual that it excited no little comment among the other lads."

THE INDIANS

AT THE TIME of the founding of Jamestown in 1607 Powhatan had more than thirty Indian tribes under his rule. Eight of these tribes lived in the land between the Rappahannock and the Potomac Rivers:

Moraughtacund, on the bank of the Rappahannock River in the territory that was later Richmond and Lancaster Counties. Their main village was at the junction of the Rappahannock and the Morattico Rivers. Population about 300.

Onawmanient (Nominies), in the section later known as Westmoreland County, near Nominy Bay. Population about 375.

Pissaseck, on the bank of the Rappahannock River in the area that was later King George, Westmoreland and Richmond Counties. Its chief village or "Kings howse" was located just above the present Leedstown. A large number of surface artifacts found in late years indicate that it was a large village.

Patawomeke (Potomac), the principal village site, was in latter-day Stafford County at the mouth of Potomac Creek. (It was here that Pocahontas was kidnapped by Captain Argall in 1613.) Population about 750.

Rappahannock (Toppahanock), on the bank of the Rappahannock River, in Richmond County, from a short distance below Totuskey Creek to a point some distance above Rappahannock Creek (later known as Cat Point Creek). This was an important tribe with a rather large village at the mouth of Little Carter Creek. Population about 380.

Secacawoni (Cekacawon), in Northumberland County, along the Coan River near its entrance into the Potomac River. Population about 110.

Wicocomoco (Wighcocomoco), in Northumberland County on the Potomac River, near its entrance into the Chesapeake Bay. Their principal village was on Wicocomico River. Population about 490.

Cuttatawomen, one town by this name was located at the junction of the Corotoman and the Rappahannock Rivers, in what was later known as Lancaster County. Population about 115. The other town was on the Rappahannock at the mouth of Lamb Creek, in what was later King George County. Population about 75.

It is believed that the Yeocomico Indians moved to what is now Westmoreland County in 1634, after they sold their lands in Maryland to Calvert.

At the time of the settlement of the New World it is evident that there were more than two thousand Indians living in the land between the Rappahannock and Potomac Rivers. A century later the Indians were extinct along the Rappahannock. And in Northumberland in 1700, according to Beverley: "Wicomico has but few men living which yet keep up their kingdom and retain their fashion; yet live by themselves, separate from all Indians, and from the English."

By 1700, wars, white men's diseases, liquor and a general moral breakdown had caused the disappearance of most of the Indians east of the Blue Ridge. Some had moved westward or southwestward.

There was little left in the Northern Neck to mark the passing of the Indians except their ossuaries, an occasional tomahawk or arrowhead and the musical names of the waters.

THE POW-WOW

FRIENDS AND relatives had gathered at the Stratford Hall landing to watch the sloop *Margaret* start on a trip down the Potomac. It was a May morning, in 1744. The forest was "a-bloom" with dogwood and redbud and the "pyne" was sending its fragrance across the water, just as it had when Captain John Smith traveled this way so many years before.

On board the *Margaret*, "seven flaming fine gentlemen," headed by Thomas Lee, were about to take off on the first lap of a history-making mission. Indian war drums were sounding. Thomas Lee and William Beverley had been appointed commissioners from Virginia to meet the chiefs of the Six Nations of the Iroquois at Lancaster, Pennsylvania.

Amid shouts and laughter and the booming of cannon the sloop headed down the Potomac, in the direction of the Chesapeake.

The *Margaret* sailed up the Bay toward Maryland and before noon the next day Annapolis had been reached. Here for five days and nights, the party was wined and dined. Philip Ludwell Lee, eighteen-year-old son of Thomas, danced until one in the morning with the pretty girls of Annapolis.

The remainder of the journey was by land. After four more days of travel the party was refreshed near Chester by a big bowl of lemon punch. In Philadelphia they were highly entertained for three weeks. While in that city Lee and Beverley marched in a procession to the market place to hear an official proclamation of a war between England and France. They were solemn now, for their mission was more important than ever. The colonists needed the Indians on their side.

This excursion was turning out to be an important diplomatic mission for the colony. It was to be Britain's first serious answer to French encroachments.

It was late in June when Lee's party finally reached Lancaster, a new and still raw town. The conference convened in the courthouse, with Governor George Thomas, of Pennsylvania, presiding. On his right sat Lee and Beverley and on his left were the two commissioners from Maryland. The Indians occupied the space usually allotted to the audience, but the powerful chiefs, like Jonnhaty, Canasatego and Tocanuntie, met the white men as equals. A Pennsylvania Dutchman named Conrad Weiser, acted as interpreter. He was trusted by both sides.

The meeting was opened by the commissioners from Maryland, since they had issued the invitation to the meeting. This was in accordance with a rigid Iroquois custom.

The complaint of the Six Nations was that the white settlers were coming over the "Great Mountains" and moving into the Valley and trespassing on their ancestral lands. "You English have come settling on our lands like a flock of birds," said Canasatego.

A Story of the Historic Northern Neck of Virginia 135

The white men explained that when they entered the country west of the Blue Ridge it "was altogether deserted and free for any people to enter upon." To which the Indians replied: "We have the right of conquest, a right too dearly purchased and which cost us too much blood to give up without any reason at all. . . . All the world knows we conquered the several nations living on Susquehanna, Cohongaranta and at the back of the Great Mountains."

Thomas Lee, when his turn came to speak, answered this charge by saying that the King of England held Virginia by right of conquest and that the bounds of the conquered land extended west as far as the Great Sea. However, he continued, the "Great King" was willing to pay them for certain lands. He was speaking, he told the Indians, for Assarogoa, Virginia's governor. Coming to the point, Thomas Lee laid down the customary string of wampum and said:

"We have a chest of new goods and the key is in our pockets. You are our brethren; the Great King is our common father, and we will live with you as children ought to do in peace and love. We will brighten the chain and strengthen the Union between us, so that we shall never be divided but remain friends and brethren as long as the sun gives us light."

The Indian spokesman replied: "We are glad to hear that you have brought with you a big chest of new goods, and that you have the key in your pockets. We do not doubt that we shall have a good understanding on all points and come to an agreement with you."

Each oration was ended with belts of wampum and "Jo-hahs." The great Iroquois chieftains no doubt understood what was happening, but the wampum and rum, the gifts of camlet coats and gold-braided hats, the festivities and ceremonial dances which accompanied the conference, must have caused them to shut their eyes to the truth. Or maybe they already saw the handwriting on the wall.

We can visualize the scene—the handsome and elegant Thomas Lee, in his crimson suit and flowing white wig, and the grave and eloquent Indian spokesman, in his equally gorgeous regalia. And the silent Indians, listening and smoking their pipes.

For 200 pounds in cash, and 200 pounds in knives, hatchets, kettles, jew's harps, and other "trucke," the Six Nations, said to have been the fiercest and most courageous of all the Indian tribes, finally put their marks on a piece of parchment which said that the white men could have all the country of their ancestors west of the "Great Mountains"—all the land between the Blue Ridge and the Ohio.

Thus it was that the red men surrendered their heritage to the white men in the town of Lancaster, Pennsylvania, on July 2, 1744.

*Young George Washington becomes a friend of Lord Fairfax,
Proprietor of Northern Neck.*

MOUNT VERNON

GEORGE WASHINGTON probably liked visiting his brother Austin at Popes Creek, for there he was close to the Potomac where he could sail and fish and go ducking, as wild fowl were plentiful there. He no doubt rode and hunted and enjoyed the countryside just like any other Northern Neck boy.

Popes Creek was more luxurious than Ferry Farm. Austin kept a racing stud that he probably raced at the Fredericksburg fairs. His wife owned enough millinery and kid gloves to have been a "rather dashing figure at the races." She had been Anne Aylett, of Westmoreland, a young woman of birth and station.

Although George was not destined to receive an English education, as his father and brothers had, he learned, when he visited his brother Lawrence at Hunting Creek, to move in the society of polished gentlemen.

The old house at Epsewasson, where George had lived as a child, had either burned or Lawrence had torn it down. Lawrence had built a new home and he called it Mount Vernon, in honor of Admiral Vernon, under whom he had served as captain of marines at Cartagena.

Lawrence had married Anne Fairfax, daughter of Colonel William Fairfax, who was a cousin and agent of Lord Fairfax, the proprietor of the Northern Neck. Belvoir, not far from Mount Vernon, was the home of the Fairfax family.

While he was at Mount Vernon, George visited Belvoir and became friends with William Fairfax, the son of the house, who was seven years his senior. At Belvoir, in 1748, he also met Lord Fairfax. They became friends and hunting companions. Lord Fairfax remained at Belvoir, amusing himself with reading, fishing and foxhunting, until he moved to his own home, Greenway Court, in 1751.

In the spring of 1748 a party of gentlemen were about to start for the South Branch of the Potomac for the purpose of surveying lands for Lord Fairfax. George Washington, then sixteen, and a big lad for his age, was invited to accompany this party.

George was glad of this opportunity for the training it would afford him, and because he enjoyed being in the company of polished gentlemen. He did not go on this expedition as one of the surveyors.

George Washington was not a rich boy but he was accustomed to nice things. When he and his friend, "Mr. Fairfax" (George

William) set out upon this new adventure into the wilderness, he was dressed not as a frontiersman but in "some of the clothes of fashion," and he carried a watch.

WASHINGTON WASHED HERE—

WHEN GEORGE WASHINGTON came back from his trip with the surveying party, in June, 1748, he went down into the Northern Neck and visited his cousins at Chotank. He probably visited all of the neighbors near there and told them of his experiences in the wilderness—of the Indians and the frontier families. He probably stayed in the Neck for awhile.

About this time, while he was at Ferry Farm, he decided one day to "wash" in the Rappahannock. At that time in the Neck, and for many years after, to "wash" meant to bathe.

George undressed on the Fredericksburg side of the River. He probably picked a secluded spot and believed that he was alone, for he undressed and went in the water to "wash."

When George came out of the water and started to dress he found that his clothes had been robbed!

George reported the theft to the Sheriff, or Constable. As a result two women servants of Fredericksburg were arrested and locked in jail—

"Ann Carroll and Mary Mc Daniel, of Friedericksburg, being committed to the gaol of this county by William Hunter, Gent, on suspicion of felony and charged with robbing the cloaths of Mr. George Washington when he was washing in the river some time last summer, the court having heard several evidences are of the opinion that the said Ann Carroll be discharged, and admitted on evidence for Lord the King against the said Mary Mc Daniel, and upon considering the whole evidence and the prisoners defense, the court are of the opinion that the said Mary Mc Daniel is guilty of petty larcency, whereupon the said Mary desired immediate punishment for the said crime and relied on the mercy of the court, therefore it is ordered that the sheriff carry her to the whipping post and inflict fifteen lashes on her bare back, and then she be discharged."

The case was heard, December 3, 1751, and Ann had turned King's witness and testified against Mary. George was ignorant of the outcome of the trial for he was far away at the time. He had sailed in September to the Barbadoes with his brother Lawrence, who had not been well since his return from the war at Cartagena.

Whether George ever recovered his stolen money or valuables is not known.

THE ORDINARY

AT SOME TIME between 1750-55 George Fisher of London crossed the Northern Neck on his way from Williamsburg to Philadelphia by horseback. When he returned to England he wrote an account of his trip to America. The following excerpt from his narrative tells of the night he spent at Leedstown, Westmoreland County, a thriving tobacco port of the Rappahannock River. George Fisher writes as follows:

"So taking a feed of Corn with me into the Boat, which my Horse eat in his passage, I crossed the River Rappahannock. In going over the River about Two miles wide, I could see Leids Town on the other side, two or Three miles up the River, the Place I now intended to rest this night in . . . I did not arrive till Seven o'clock . . . I put up at one Mr. T——ts, esteemed the best Ordinary in Town, and indeed the House and Furniture has as elegant an appearance as any I have seen in the country, Mr. Finnays or Wetherburnes in Williamsburg not excepted. The chairs, Tables, &c of the Room I was conducted into, was all of Mahogany, & so stuft with fine large glaized copper Plate Prints; That I almost fancied myself in Jeffriess' or some other elegant Print Shops. I had the happiness, at my first Coming in of my Landlord's Company, who understanding I came from the Metroplis (and the Assembly now sitting) gaped after news; he was troubled with gout, for he came limping in upon a stick; When I had answered all his interrogatories, and he had picked what intelligence of me he was able, and I calling at First for a half Pint of wine only, he vanished and I could see him no more; tho' I sent twice (at supper and afterwards) to request the favor of his Company, in hopes of receiving in my turn some useful directions, in the ensuing Day's Journey. His excuse was, first, indisposition, and afterwards he was gone to Bed; tho' the Boy who lighted me to mine assured me he was sitting with his Housekeeper, and that not one Person had been in the House since my arrival. By what I could hear and preceive myself this Landlord who bears the name honest Mr. T——, like most of his Trade, proportions his regard to their extravagance, in which respect I was doubtless too contemptible for his notice. The Host—he could tell me nothing of the Rout I was to take, so that I was now quite destitute of intelligence.

"This House stands pleasantly upon the North side of the River, and a tolerable garden seemed to be in as decent order as most I have seen in America. The method of Single men having House-keepers is esteemed here very reputable and genteel. In the morning while my Breakfast and Horse was getting ready, I sought after some instruction for my journey, and as it happened, I found a Person up that kepped a store, who gave me a draught of the road to Hoes Ferry on Potomac River. I have since been informed of my true Route was from Southern on this Rappahannocke River to Lovels Ferry on Potomac River, it being not only a better Road, but I should have saved at least Ten or Twelve miles in the Riding of Thirty, the only objection being that at the Hoes the River is not more than five miles wide; but at Lovels to Cedar Point (in Md.) it is eight or ten, consequently in windy weather the passage is more difficult and unsafe; but at this time of the year no great danger was to be apprehended. The Gentleman's name who delineated the Road for me to Hoes Ferry is Thompson."

NELLY

IT WAS for a special reason that Nelly wanted to go back home. It was not that she was unhappy in her new home for it was beautiful there at the head of the deeply wooded valley with the Blue Ridge towering in the distance. The frame house, which had been built by her husband's father, was modest but comfortable, and there were slaves to do the heavy work. Still, she wanted to go home and her husband humoured his nineteen-year-old wife, and prepared for the journey.

To Nelly home was the low country—the flat lands where the air was damp and the fogs rolled in from the River.

Nelly probably traveled home in a carriage of some sort for the trail led through the virgin forest. The nights were doubtless spent at farmhouses along the way. As they neared Fredericksburg they probably met up with other travelers on horseback, and teamsters with wagons loaded with wheat and tobacco for export.

Fredericksburg was all "a-bustle" at that time with foreign ships lying at the wharves and wagons rumbling along the streets. What a welcome sight the Rappahannock must have been to Nelly! And there was the ferry which would carry her across to her homeland! It was a rope-hauled ferry, pulled back and forth across the River by the ferryman.

Once the River was crossed it was only a ten or twelve mile ride down through King George County to her childhood home on the banks of the Rappahannock. This was the plantation of Nelly's stepfather, John Moore. She had known him as a father as long as she could remember, for her own father, Francis Conway, had died when she was only a year old. Her mother, Rebecca Catlett Conway, had soon married John Moore. Many of Nelly's relatives lived in this region of the Northern Neck. What a happy home-coming it must have been for Nelly.

The chill winds of winter were still blowing across the Rappahannock, but the crocuses were in bloom, when Nelly's baby arrived, on March 16, 1751.

The Northern Neck relatives assembled for the christening. Nelly's cousins, Judith and Elizabeth Catlett, acted as godmothers, and Mary Catlett's husband, Jonathan Gibson, was godfather. The infant was named for his father, James Madison.

The Catletts and Conways and Madisons must have rejoiced at the birth of Nelly's first baby, but they had no reason to think that the birth of little "Jemmy" Madison would some day be a matter of national importance. And little did Nelly dream when she made the long journey home that by so doing the Northern Neck would fall heir to another famous son.

"Little Jemmy" grew up to be one of the foremost figures in the creation of the American nation. He became the fourth President of the United States, and he is remembered as "the Father of the Constitution."

James Madison's birthsite in King George County later became known as Port Conway.

MISS BETSY

IN THE SPRING of 1752 George Washington was riding down to Naylor's Hole, in Richmond County. He had his mind set on a certain young lady who lived there, but up to this time she had been uncooperative. George had written to her father, Colonel William Fauntleroy:

"I purpose . . . to wait on Miss Betsy, in hopes of a revocation of the former cruel sentence and see if I can meet with any alteration in my favor."

Betsy was just sixteen and she was probably having a good time at her home on the Rappahannock. It was lively there on the River, for the Rappahannock was the main highway for the tobacco trade and her father was interested in ships and trade, and he operated a ferry. When she tired of the River she could always go visiting in her father's imported riding chair, drawn by "two horses abreast." It was a smart "turn-out"; even the whip had her father's name on it.

As George rode through the blossoming forest, which Betsy's ancestor had bought from the Indians a century before, he must have had mingled emotions. There was the pleasure of the expectation of seeing Betsy again, mixed with the uncertainty of the outcome of his suit. Then too, he must have wondered if she would notice the scars on his face. While he had been in the Barbadoes, where he had accompanied his brother Lawrence in his fruitless search for health, George had contracted the smallpox which had left permanent scars on his face.

Tradition says that Betsy did notice the scars. Whatever the reason may have been—George's mission was unsuccessful.

For years historians have tried without success to settle the question—was Betsy Fauntleroy the "Lowland Beauty" to whom Washington made references in his correspondence, or did he have in mind another Northern Neck beauty named Lucy Grymes?

THE PROPRIETOR OF THE NORTHERN NECK

IT WAS an autumn day in the year 1753. A group of men lounged in the sunshine before a rudely constructed log tavern in a Virginia wilderness clearing. Their rough attire of buckskin and homespun and their knives and rifles proclaimed them to be hunters, trappers and settlers.

Suddenly they were aroused by a noise in the forest. The drooping tree boughs came to life and the tall grasses were pushed aside as an amazing spectacle for this frontier setting emerged. With a great rattling of wheels, creaking of leather and clumping of hooves, four shiny horses came forth drawing behind them an English chariot that would very well have graced the streets of London.

The liveried driver drew up before the hitching rack and the

A Story of the Historic Northern Neck of Virginia

footmen descended from behind and opened the door of the chariot. Out stepped a middle-aged man, so tall and so gigantic in frame, that he had difficulty in getting through the opening. He was richly clad in a coat of brown cloth decorated with embroidery and a waistcoat of yellow silk, ornamented with silver thread and flowers. His peruke was carefully powdered and his shirt ruffles were snow-white.

As he issued from the chariot he drew about him the folds of a red velvet cloak, and then bowing his head slightly to the admiring crowd, he entered the tavern.

This man was no stranger to these frontiersmen. Most of them had hunted with him, or eaten at his "broad board," or transacted business with him in his little stone office. But it was rarely that they saw him thus, in the trappings of an English gentleman. They had seen him stab his hunting-knife into a deer's throat, and hold up the brush of a fox at the end of the chase, but then his garments had been weather-beaten and on his head he had worn an otter-skin cap with a buck's tail stuck in it.

But this strange gentleman had no hunting trip in mind today. He soon came out of the tavern and the chariot was rumbling away down the forest road, for he was due to preside over a session of the justices' court at the frontier town of Winchester. And although the Shawnee Indians were still not too far distant, this gentleman evidently believed in carrying into the wilds of the New World something of the English idea of the propriety of full dress on occasions of ceremony.

And who was this man who could change so easily from backwoodsman to gentleman? None other than Thomas, sixth Lord Fairfax of Cameron, and sole proprietor of that vast tract of land known as the Northern Neck. This, his inheritance, embraced all lands lying between the headwaters of the Rappahannock and Potomac Rivers to the Chesapeake Bay, comprising more than five million acres.

Thomas, sixth Lord Fairfax had inherited, in 1719, the Northern Neck of Virginia, through his mother, Catherine, daughter of Thomas, Lord Culpeper, and wife of Lord Fairfax. It was through this marriage that the grant became known as the Fairfax Proprietary.

In 1673, Thomas, Lord Culpeper had bought out the other grantees and had become the sole proprietor of the original grant. He had cunningly had the terms of the patent changed to the "first heads of springs" of the two rivers, instead of "within the heads" of the two rivers, as originally stated in 1649. The change in these few words changed the size of the tract from one million to more than five million acres. This change in description apparently was not noticed in the colony at the time.

It was in this way that Culpeper's grandson, Thomas, sixth Lord Fairfax, through inheritance became sole proprietor of the Northern Neck.

Lord Fairfax was born in Leeds Castle, England, in 1693. He was educated at Oxford University and developed such a fondness for literature that he wrote a number of papers for the *Spectator*. But he was unlucky in affairs of the heart—he was jilted at the altar.

After a time the embittered Fairfax decided to take a voyage to Virginia to examine his inheritance. So well pleased was he with his domain that he decided to make it his home. Perhaps the free way of life and new hunting grounds appealed to him. He returned to England, arranged his affairs and voyaged back to his wild new home, in 1748.

Fairfax built a home in the Shenandoah Valley, called Greenway Court, and went there to live in 1751. Tradition says that he planted a white post—one mile distant—as a guide to his dwelling, and thus the town of White Post was later so named.

Lord Fairfax cultivated a large farm at Greenway Court. He had probably one hundred and fifty negro slaves, who lived in huts scattered about in the woods. There was very little cultivated ground around his house because he preferred to leave the land as a natural park. The grounds were encircled by a rude fence, which served also as a hitching rack.

Locust trees shaded the mansion. It was a long stone building with a slender chimney on each end and two belfries between on top of the roof. These bells were probably used to call the servants or as an alarm when Indians were near. There were four dormer-windows and a portico across the front. This building was used by the steward, it was said, while Fairfax lived and died in a single clapboard story-and-a-half house.

Nearby the main house stood a small limestone structure, where quit-rents were given and titles drawn of his lordship's domains. He lived almost wholly from his rents. We can imagine him there, with a court of deer-hounds at his feet. On the table lies a rudely drawn map of the frontier, some folded letters, an inkstand and an eagle's quill pen. Here he delivered the title deeds of nearly all of that portion of Virginia over which he had dominion.

Perhaps, too, it was here that he conversed with his young friend, George Washington, who surveyed part of the immense tract among the valleys of the Alleghany mountains for him. These were divided into lots to enable Fairfax to claim quit-rents and give titles.

In spite of the difference in their ages, Fairfax and Washington

A Story of the Historic Northern Neck of Virginia

had another interest in common—they were both passionately fond of hunting. Tradition says that sometimes they passed weeks together in the pleasures of the chase.

When fox-hunting Lord Fairfax made it a rule that "he who got the fox, cut off his tail, and held it up, should share in the jollification which was to follow, free of expense." An early historian says that "as soon as a fox was started, the young men of the company usually dashed after him with great impetuosity, while Fairfax leisurely waited behind with a favorite servant who was familiar with the water-courses, and of a quick ear, to discover the course of the fox. Following his directions, his lordship would start after the game, and, in most instances, secure the prize, and stick the tail of the fox in his hat in triumph."

It is probable that some of these "jollifications" that followed the hunt were held in a tavern in Winchester, for tradition says that he occasionally held "levees" there. (This building was later used as a stable.)

Sometimes Fairfax entertained in the great room at Greenway Court. This room, according to tradition, was a combination of crudity and refinement. Rough oak furniture, carven mahogany, silver plate, cheap crockery, leather-bound books, fishing nets, portraits, antlers and blunderbuses, all intermingled. But Fairfax was a generous host and the board groaned with ham, beef, fowl, game as well as mellow Jamaica rum. But Fairfax did not drink, and women were never invited to his parties.

When in the humor Fairfax sometimes gave away whole farms to his tenants, simply demanding for rent some trifle like a turkey for his Christmas dinner.

Fairfax lived the life of a bachelor and adopted the rough customs of his new land, but his life was not altogether happy in the New World. Quit-rents were not willingly paid and he was constantly occupied with lawsuits over boundaries. The Indian hostilities retarded the settlement of his domain and therefore lessened his revenue. He was considered eccentric and "a hoarder up of English gold."

In spite of his friendship with George Washington, Fairfax was a Tory to the end. When he heard that Cornwallis had surrendered he told his body servant, "Take me to bed, John, it is time for me to die." He died shortly after, on December 9, 1781.

He was buried at Winchester, under the old Episcopal church, which was on the public square. When this structure was later taken down the bones of Fairfax were removed to a tomb in the crypt of Christ Church in Winchester. At the time of his disinterment, it is said that a large mass of silver was found, which was the mounting of his coffin.

Around 1840 some excavating was done about the grounds at Greenway Court and a large quantity of joes and half-joes were found. These were what was termed cob-coin, of a square form, and dated about 1730. They were supposed to have been secreted there by Lord Fairfax.

Fairfax never married, therefore he left no child to inherit his vast estate. He devised a large portion of his property to a nephew in England. Later the estate passed through several hands and was finally sold.

A few years after the war of the Revolution an attempt was made by the colonists to confiscate the estate. At last a compromise took place between those who had bought it and the Virginia state government.

During and after the Revolution no quit-rents were paid, and in 1785 an act was passed by the Virginia Legislature which abolished the proprietary system in the Northern Neck. The people there were finally free of landlords, after one hundred and twenty-five years.

THE MARSHALLS

JOHN MARSHALL "of the forest" owned two hundred acres of land in Westmoreland County. "Of the forest" was a term used in the Northern Neck in referring to those whose homes were some distance from the water.

John "of the forest" acquired this land by deed, for five shillings, from William Marshall of King and Queen County. It is probable that this William was the elder brother of John "of the forest" and that they were both sons of Thomas "the carpenter," of Westmoreland. The latter's will was probated in the same county in 1704. (In this will there was mentioned "a heifer . . . . called White-Belly.")

This land of John "of the forest" was located on Appomattox Creek. It was low marshy land of such inferior quality that the former owners had not bothered with it. Originally it had been a part of twelve hundred acres which had been granted to "Jno. Washington & Thos. Pope, gents.—& by them lost for want of seating."

John "of the forest" married Elizabeth Markham, daughter of

the Sheriff of Westmoreland County. To John and Elizabeth were born ten children. They lived simply on their farm until John died in 1752.

Among the items left to Elizabeth by John was "one Gray mair named beauty and side saddle." He also left her the use of his land "during her widowhood and afterwards to fall to my son Thomas Marshall and his heirs forever."

Thomas was twenty-two years old at the time of his father's death. One year later his mother deeded half of the two hundred acres to him.

Thomas Marshall was fortunate in that he was powerful of stature and intelligent. He was of a serious but adventurous nature. He and his neighbor, George Washington, seem to have been friends from boyhood. For about three years Thomas had been Washington's companion when he helped him to survey the western part of the Fairfax domain.

Thomas Marshall left Westmoreland County not long after his father's death to seek his fortune in the frontier country toward the Blue Ridge.

In 1754 Thomas married a well born and well educated girl named Mary Randolph Keith. To this union were born fifteen children, the best known being John, who became the fourth Chief Justice of the United States Supreme Court.

THE LEEDSTOWN RESOLUTIONS

THE TOWN OF LEEDS on the banks of the Rappahannock River was a thriving center of trade and shipping in colonial days. Here the big ships lay at anchor while their holds were filled with tobacco for the London market. Here the returning ships unloaded the English luxuries that were so dear to the hearts of the Northern Neck planter-families.

Leeds had been incorporated in 1742. When ten or twelve years later the English visitor, George Fisher, spent a night at "Leids Town" he was well pleased with the fine furnishings he found in the ordinary. There were other ordinaries in the village, comfortable homes with gardens and Leeds Church.

George Washington often visited Leedstown. With his wife he dined there in 1759. He spent the night there in 1763. Many times he crossed the nearby ferry as he traveled between Mount Vernon and Williamsburg.

On a winter's day in 1766 there was unusual activity at Leeds. The excitement came about because Thomas Ludwell Lee had written to his brother Richard Henry Lee as follows: "We propose to be in Leedstown in the afternoon of the 27th inst., Feb. 1766, where we expect to meet those who will come from your way. This would be a fine opportunity to effect the scheme of an association, and I should be glad if you would think of a plan."

It is easy to visualize the arrival of the planters in their coaches and on horseback—to hear the rattle of wheels, the thud of hoofs, the creaking of saddle-leather and the excited voices speaking with a London accent.

The "plan" that Richard Henry Lee had thought of and prepared in manuscript form and had brought to Leedstown that day could probably have hanged him, and the one hundred and fourteen others who signed it, if it had fallen into the wrong hands. But the Northern Neck was a remote fortress and its inhabitants were bold when their freedom was threatened.

Among those who signed Lee's document were six Lees, five Washingtons, and Spence Monroe, father of President James Monroe. The text of The Leedstown Resolutions follows:

"Rouzed by Danger and alarmed at Attempts foreign & domestic to reduce the People of this Country to a State of abject and detestable slavery by destroying that free and happy constitution of Government under which they have hitherto lived,—We who subscribe this Paper, have Associated, & do bind ourselves to each other, to God, and to our Country, by the Firmest Tyes that Religion & Virtue can frame, most sacredly and punctually to stand by, and with our Lives & Fortunes to support, maintain and defend each other, in the Observation and Execution of these following Articles.

"First, we declare all due Allegiance and Obedience to our lawful Sovereign George the Third King of Great Britain. And we determine to the utmost of our Power to preserve the Laws, the Peace and good Order of this Colony as far as is consistent with the Preservation of our Constitutional Rights and Liberty.

"2.dly As we know it to be the Birthright Privilege of every British Subject (and of the People of Virginia as being such) founded on Reason, Law and Compact, That he cannot be legally tryed but by his Peers, and that he cannot be taxed but by Consent of a Parliament in which he is represented by Persons chosen by the People and who themselves pay a part of the Tax they impose on others—If therefore any Person or Persons shall attempt by any Action or Proceeding to deprive this Colony of those fundamental Rights we will immediately regard him or them as the most dangerous Enemy of the Community and we will go to any Extremity not only to prevent the Success of such Attempts but to Stigmatize and punish the Offender.

"3.dly As the Stamp Act does absolutely direct the Property of the People to be taken from them without their Consent express'd by their Representatives, and as in many cases it deprives the British American Subject of his Right to Trial by Jury; we do determine at every hazard and paying no Regard to Danger or to Death; we will exert every Faculty to prevent the Execution of the said Stamp Act in any instance whatsoever within this Colony—And every abandoned Wretch who shall be so lost to Virtue and publick Good, as wickedly to contribute to the introduction or fixture of the Stamp Act in this Colony, by using Stampt Paper, or by any other Means; we will with the utmost Expedition convince all such Profligates, that immediate danger and disgrace shall attend their prostitute Purpose.

"4.thly That the last Article may most surely and effectually be execut'd, we engage to each other, that whenever it shall be known to any of this Association that any Person is so conducting himself as to favor the Introduction of the Stamp Act, that immediate Notice shall be given to as many of the Association as possible, and that every Individual so inform'd shall with expedition repair to a place of meeting to be appointed as near the Scene of Action as may be.

"5.thly Each Associator shall do his true endeavor to obtain as many Signers to this Association as he possibly can.

"6.thly If any attempt shall be made upon the Liberty or Property of any Associator for any Action or Thing to be done in Consequence of this Agreement, we do most solemnly bind ourselves by the sacred Engagements above enter'd into, at the utmost risk of our Lives and Fortunes to restore such Associate to his Liberty, and to protect him in the enjoyment of his Property.

"In Testimony of the good Faith with which we resolve to execute this Association, we have this 27 day of February 1766 in Virginia put our hands & Seals hereto

Richard Henry Lee   Will Robinson   Lewis Willis   Thomas Lud. Lee   Samuel Washington   Charles Washington   Moore Fauntleroy   Francis Lightfoot Lee   Thomas Jones   Rodham Kenner   Spencer

Mottsom Ball   Richard Mitchell   Joseph Murdock   Rich'd Parker   Spence Monroe   John Watts   Robert Lovell   John Blagge   Charles Weeks   William Booth   Geo: Tuberville   Alvin Moxley   Wm. Flood   John Ballantine Jun.   William Lee   Thomas Chilton   Richard Buckner   Will Chilton   Joseph Peirce   John Williams   Jn. Blackwell   Winder S. Kenner   Wm. Bronaugh   Will Peirce   John Berryman Jn. Dickson   John Browne   Edward Sanford   Charles Chilton   Lau. Washington   W. Roane Jr.   William Sydnor   John Monroe   William Cocke   William Grayson   Wm. Brockenbrough   Sam Selden   Daniel McCarty   Jer Rush   Edwd. Ransdell   Townshend Dade   Laur. Washington   John Ashton   W. Brent   Francis Foushee   John Smith Jr.   Will Balle   Thomas Barnes   Jos. Blackwell   Reuben Meriwether   Edw. Mountjoy   Thomas Mountjoy   William Mountjoy   John Mountjoy   Gilbt. Campbell   Jos. Lane   Richard Lee   Daniel Tebbs   Fran. Thornton Jun.   Peter Rust Jun. John Lee Jun.   Fran Waring   John Upshaw   Merriwether Smith   Thomas Roane   James Edmondson   James Webb   John Edmondson   James Banks   Smith Young   Thomas Logan   Jo. Milliken   Rich Hodges   James Upshaw   James Booker   A. Montague   Richard Jeffries   John Suggett Jn.   L. Woodcock   Robert Wormeley Carter   John Beale Jun.   John Newton   Will B—le Jun.   Chs. Mortimer   John Edmondson   Charles Beale   Peter Grant   Thomson Mason   Jon. Beckwith   James Samford   John Belfield   W. Smith   John Aug. Washington   Thomas Belfield   Edgecomb Suggett   Henry Francks   John Bland Jun.   Jas. Emerson   John Richards   Thos. Jett   Thomas Douglas   Max. Robinson   John Orr   Ebenezer Fisher   Hancock Eustace."

Text and names have been copied from a photostatic copy of the original manuscript by Florienette Matter Knight, Organizing Regent, Leedstown Resolutions Chapter, N.S.D.A.R. The original manuscript, handwritten by Richard Henry Lee, is in the archives of the Virginia Historical Society, Richmond, Va.

FITHIAN

ON AN OCTOBER day in the year 1773 a man on horseback rode down through Westmoreland County until he came to the entrance of a plantation known as Nomini Hall. The avenue leading to the great house was bordered with poplar trees, through which the white stuccoed house appeared "romantic" and "truly elegant."

Philip Vickers Fithian, lately graduated from Princeton, had been seven days on the road since he had left New Jersey. He had ridden two hundred and sixty miles and crossed a number of ferries.

Fithian was not sure that he was doing the right thing in coming to Virginia. His friends had tried to persuade him not to go to that "wicked colony" where he would be sure to fall in with evil companions and become a drunkard or a gambler. If his parents had lived Fithian would probably have stayed in the North, but they had recently passed away, and the salary as a plantation tutor was good. With a last prayer to the Lord that he would be strong enough to stick to his upright way of life, Fithian set off on his journey to the Northern Neck of Virginia.

Nomini Hall was the seat of one of King Carter's grandsons, Robert Carter, III. His holdings, amounting to seventy thousand acres, were scattered over a number of counties. He owned more than five hundred slaves and employed numerous white overseers, clerks, stewards, craftsmen and artisans. Tobacco was still the main crop of the plantation, but its profits were now waning and Councillor Carter sought other money crops to supplement this chief product. Carter also manufactured supplies for the use of his plantations and for his neighbors' needs. He operated grain mills, textile factories, salt works and bakeries.

Nomini Hall was laid off in the usual formal English style, with four dependencies—one equally distant from each corner of the manor. These were the large dependencies—there were many others, probably as many as thirty. In the square thus formed by the four buildings there was a bowling green, and gardens interspersed with oyster-shell walks.

In one of the large dependencies, Fithian was established. Here he and the Carter boys slept upstairs over the schoolroom. The five Carter girls who were to be his pupils—"all dressed in white"—slept in the great house. Fithian liked his room in the schoolhouse—"a neat chamber, a large Fire, Books, & Candle & my Liberty to stay in this room or to sit at the great house." In the household he held a delicate position—equi-distant between the master and his eldest son.

There was never a dull moment at Nomini Hall. There was the music teacher—and the traveling dancing teacher who followed a plan of rotation between the plantations. He spent about a week at each place, which ended with a small informal dance. The big balls were splendid affairs, lasting for days and nights. There was a continual procession of chariots, drawn by four or six horses, with coachman, and postillions, and attended by horseback riders, moving back and forth between Nomini Hall and its neighboring plantations. The Carters often dined and danced with the Lees at

Stratford and Chantilly, the Washingtons at Bushfield, the Tubervilles at Hickory Hill, and with the Tayloes at Mount Airy, about twelve miles distant. Christenings, birthdays, house-warmings—anything served as an excuse for a celebration among these Northern Neckers! In no part of Virginia were there more great planters than in the Northern Neck.

Fithian observed everything and wrote it all down in his Journal. One of the first things that he noticed were the ladies with the white handkerchiefs: "Almost every Lady wears a red Cloak; and when they ride out they tye a white handkerchief over their Head and face, so that when I first came into Virginia, I was distress'd whenever I saw a Lady, for I thought she had the Tooth-Ache!"

Fithian walked often in the evenings in the garden with Mrs. Carter when she was giving a last look at the poultry or the growing things. He had a great admiration for the beauty and elegance of Mrs. Carter. With Councillor Carter he attended the county courts and the horse-races in Richmond County. Around the stables he watched the cock-fights. There was skating on the "Mill-pond," and when warm weather came, the "fish-feasts" and barbecues. The latter, he wrote, were just like the "fish-feasts" except that they had roast pig instead of fish.

Fithian did not approve of Sunday in Virginia—"A Sunday in Virginia don't seem to wear the same Dress as our Sundays to the Northward. By five o'clock on Saturday every face looks festive and cheerful. . . . It is a general custom on Sundays here, with Gentlemen to invite one another home to dine, after Church; and to consult about, determine their common business, either before or after Service. . . . It is not the custom for Gentlemen to go into Church til Service is beginning, when they enter in a Body, in the same manner as they came out; I have known the Clerk to come out and call them into prayers. . . . They stay also after the Service is over, usually as long, or longer, than the Parson was preaching."

Nomini Church stood on the banks of the River Nomini about six miles from the manor. The Carter family attended this church, traveling by both land and water. Councillor Carter had a boat built for the purpose "of carrying the young Ladies and others of the Family to Nominy Church. It is a light neat Battoe elegantly painted & is rowed with four Oars." On the way to church by boat, Fithian saw the river alive with people, in boats and canoes, fishing.

Whenever it was possible Fithian excused himself from the social gatherings and stayed in his room, writing in his Journal and working on his sermons, for he was to become a Presbyterian minister.

He was happiest there alone because he could not fit in with these strange Northern Neckers. He felt a little sorry for himself because he was a somber "meagre" figure in his dark clothes among these gay people. His greatest handicap was that he had never learned to dance and—"blow high, blow low, Virginians will dance or die!" He wrote to a friend in the North: "Here we either strain on Horseback, from home to Church, or from house to house if we go out at all—or we walk alone into a dark meadow, or tall wood. But I love solitude, and these lonely recesses suit exactly the feeling of my mind."

In spite of his disapproval Fithian grew fond of the Northern Neck and its people. When he returned from a visit home he wrote: "I am much more pleased with the Face of the Country since my return than I have ever been before— It is indeed delightsome! How natural, how agreeable, how majestic the place seems! Supp'd on Crabs & an elegant dish of Strawberries & Cream!"

On Christmas morning Fithian was awakened by the guns being fired around the house. Then the boy who made the fire came in with a "Christmas Box," for a tip, and the other servants followed with their "Boxes." Mrs. Carter sent him over some spermaceti candles—"large clear & very elegant." The holidays were a round of balls and parties, which Fithian excused himself from as much as possible. He was glad when they were over—"We had a large Pye cut to-day to signify the conclusion of the Holidays."

It was so cold in January that "a cart and three pair of oxen which every day bring in four loads of wood, Sundays excepted." In the manor and other houses there were twenty-eight "steady fires & most of them are very large." It grew so cold that the cart went for wood on Sunday also.

Mail was gotten infrequently from the post-office at Hobb's Hole, which was the name of present-day Tappahannock. Newspapers from the North and *The Virginia Gazette* brought accounts of the Tea Party in Boston, and other rumblings in the colonies. These "Golden Days" in Virginia were not to last much longer—war was in the making.

Fithian left Nomini Hall late in 1774. He could no longer stay away from his Northern "dream-girl," the "fair Laura" of his Journal. He was married to her in October, 1775. He enlisted in the Revolutionary forces in 1776 as a chaplain, but his "meagre" body could not stand the life of the army. He died shortly after the battle of White Plains.

But Fithian had not lived in vain—his Journal was a legacy to posterity.

THE SCHOOL IN THE WILDWOOD

IN COLONIAL DAYS a small school was conducted in the forest of Westmoreland County by a Scotch minister. His own sons were his pupils, and a few children who lived close enough to walk to school through the woodland lane which was cut for several straight miles through the woods and was known as the Parson's Road.

In 1755 the "Parson" had petitioned the Court of Westmoreland County to have a road from the "new Glebe opened to Round Hill Church." The petition was granted, for the Reverend Archibald Campbell was an influential man in the region.

Mr. Campbell came to Virginia from Scotland in October, 1741. The "new Glebe" was purchased, tradition says, from Thomas Marshall, "the surveyor," about 1753. The "Parson" moved to the "new Glebe" and lived there until his death in 1775. It was there that he conducted his school.

The "new Glebe" was situated on Mattox Creek, originally called Appamatox Creek after the Indians who had once lived there. This Glebe was located not far from the present village of Oak Grove.

The Reverend Archibald Campbell came from a distinguished and learned Scottish family—his nephew, Thomas Campbell, became one of Britain's greatest poets. The "Parson" himself was well equipped with "all the learning which the Scottish universities could give."

At the school in the forest it was all work and little play, for the "Parson" was a hard taskmaster. His pupils were said to have been "especially well grounded in mathematics and Latin . . . . and in their various subsequent careers they were noted for solidity of character." At least two of his pupils became historic figures.

JAMES AND JOHN

ON WINTER mornings it was still dark when the Monroe family breakfasted, but the "large living room" was cozy with its glowing hearth where pots and kettles bubbled and steamed on their cranes and trivets.

Around the breakfast table were seated Spence and Elizabeth

A Story of the Historic Northern Neck of Virginia 155

Monroe and their children who, according to age, were—Elizabeth, James, Spence, Andrew and Joseph Jones.

Breakfast at the Monroe home was not as formal as breakfast at the homes of their neighbors at Stratford and Nomini Hall. Spence Monroe was not a wealthy planter, although he was a gentleman and a small landowner. His home in Westmoreland County was situated between Monroe Bay and Mattox Creek, not far from present-day Colonial Beach. The Monroes had been living in the Northern Neck since about 1650.

The Monroes lived in a plain frame two-storied house "within a stone's throw of . . . . a virgin forest." The Potomac flowed not far away.

After breakfast James would start for school with his books under one arm and his gun slung over his shoulder. The Monroe table never lacked for game while James was around.

James was tall for his fifteen years, and built like an athlete. He well knew the forest and river.

Somewhere along the woodland road James was joined by another tall well-built youth, who was dressed in a pale-blue hunting-shirt and trousers, fringed with white, and a black hat decorated with a buck's tail. He also had a gun and books. There was the look of the mountains about this lad. John Marshall's home was in Fauquier County and he was only visiting in the Northern Neck. He had learned his classics from his father in their frontier cabin, but now Thomas Marshall had sent his son back to his people in Westmoreland for more schooling.

John was three years older than James. He was dark—skin, eyes and hair—with rosy cheeks and a round face. His eyes twinkled, for he was as merry and fun-loving as James was solemn and serious. The two tall boys must have made a fine-looking pair as they walked down the Parson's Road, with gun and books, on a bright winter's morning in the year 1773. As they come within sight of the Glebe we will leave them—in the firm hands of the Reverend Archibald Campbell.

Little did these boys dream of the adventures that lay ahead for them. For these two backwoods boys were destined to become makers of history: John Marshall, the great Chief Justice, who "found a Constitution on paper and made it power"; and James Monroe who became the fifth President of the United States and who formulated and declared the Monroe Doctrine.

CAPTAIN DOBBY

CAPTAINS OF THE SHIPS constantly lying at anchor in the rivers were often guests at Nomini Hall and the other Northern Neck plantations. Captain Dobby was a general favorite. Fithian described him in his Journal as "a Man of much Spirit and Humour: A great Mimick."

In the summer of 1774 Captain Dobby invited the Carters of Nomini and Fithian, the tutor, "on Board his Ship next Tuesday to Dine with him & wish them a pleasant Passage as the Ship is to Sail the day following." Fithian must have especially liked the Captain for he commented in his Journal: "If the Weather is not too burning hot I shall go, provided the Others go likewise."

On the appointed day, in August, Fithian and Ben Carter set out for the River. They had intended to breakfast at Colonel Tayloe's, twelve miles distant, "but the Servant who went with us was so slow in preparing that we breakfasted before we set out. We arrived at Colonel Tayloe's however half after nine."

Colonel John Tayloe was one of the wealthiest men in the Northern Neck. His manor house, Mount Airy, in Richmond County, was situated on an elevation, and overlooked the Rappahannock River, several miles distant. An interesting feature of the plantation was the deer park, located in a grove of oaks and cedars.

Fithian described Mount Airy as "an elegant Seat!—The House is about the Size of Mr. Carter's, built with stone, & finished curiously, & ornamented with various paintings, & rich Pictures. This Gentleman owns Yorick, who won the prize of 500 pounds last November, from Dr. Flood's Horse, Gift— In the Dining-Room, besides many other fine Pieces, are twenty four of the most celebrated among the English Race-Horses, Drawn masterly, & set in elegant gilt Frames. He has near the great House, two fine two Story stone Houses, the one is used as a Kitchen, & the other, for a nursery, & Lodging Rooms— He has also a large well-formed, beautiful Garden, as fine in every Respect as any I have seen in Virginia. In it stand four large beautiful Marble Statues."

Mount Airy was built after the style of an Italian villa. The main entrance was guarded by bronze dogs.

When Fithian and Ben arrived at Mount Airy they found "the young Ladies in the Hall playing the Harpsichord."

Joined by the Tayloes the party set out for the River. The

"Colonel and his Lady" and daughters traveled in "their Great Coach," while Fithian and Ben and the servants were on horseback.

The land from Mount Airy to the ferry, opposite Hobb's Hole (Tappahannock), was level and the road lay between fields of corn and flax. As they neared the River the fields changed to marshes "covered with thick high Reed."

The Rappahannock River was about two miles wide here and they could see ships lying at anchor on the other side near the town. They counted six ships "riding in the Harbour, and a number of Schooners & smaller Vessels."

The party waited for half an hour in the burning sun. At last they saw the long-boat coming, covered with an awning and rowed by four oarsmen. It was past noon when they reached the ship, where they were warmly welcomed by Captain Dobby.

The *Beaufort* was a "Stately Ship." For the comfort of his guests the Captain had arranged an awning from the "Stern . . . . to the Mizen-Mast," which kept off the sun but was open on the sides.

By three o'clock the guests had arrived, forty-five ladies and sixty gentlemen, and besides them the ship's crew, waiters and servants. Dinner was served and "we were not throng'd at all, & dined all at twice."

The guests were then entertained by a boat race—"A Boat was anchored down the River at a Mile Distance— Captain Dobby and Captain Benson steer'd the Boats in the Race— Captain Benson had 5 Oarsmen; Captain Dobby had 6— It was Ebb-Tide— The Betts were small—& chiefly given to the Negroes who rowed— Captain Benson won the first Race— Captain Purchace offered to bett ten Dollars that with the same Boat & same Hands, only having Liberty to put a small Weight in the Stern, he would beat Captain Benson— He was taken, & came out best only half the Boat's Length— About Sunset we left the Ship, & went all to Hobb's Hole, where a Ball was agreed on."

After the ball was over the guests spent the remainder of the night at Hobb's Hole. At half-past eight the next morning they were called to breakfast—"we all look'd dull, pale & haggard!"

After breakfast the party was entertained by the young ladies on the harpsichord. At eleven o'clock they all went down to the River, where the long-boat was waiting to take them back home to the Northern Neck.

PEDLARS

PROBABLY THE FIRST pedlars in the Northern Neck were the Indians of Cascarawaske, a merchant tribe that manufactured their products and sold them up and down the Potomac—Patow-meke—meaning "traveling traders," or pedlars.

During colonial days the itinerant pedlar traveled from plantation to plantation. He was welcome everywhere because he brought news and gossip as well as merchandise. Children were always watching out for the pedlar at certain seasons when he usually arrived.

He was not hard to identify for he bore on his back, by means of a harness of strong hempen webbing, two oblong trunks of thin metal, probably tin. He carried a stout staff to help him to walk with his burden and also for a weapon to ward off dogs and wild animals. He was usually called the "trunk pedlar."

His pack contained everything from dress materials and jewelry to "plumpers." The latter were thin, round, light balls used to put in the mouth and fill up hollow cheeks!

The "indigo-pedlars" had a specialized trade. Blue, in all shades, was the favorite color in colonial days, and indigo was used to dye this color. It was especially in demand for dyeing wool. Pedlars traveled all over the country selling indigo.

Pedlars continued to travel through the Northern Neck until the early part of the twentieth century.

SEVEN SATIN PETTICOATS

SETTLERS IN THE Northern Neck sometimes received boxes containing luxuries from relatives in England. These boxes were received even until a late date.

In one family there were seven sisters. In probably the last box they received from "home," as England was called for many years, there were seven satin petticoats, some pink and some blue. They were made of heavy satin and trimmed with lace.

Needless to say, these petticoats were treasured and passed on for several generations. When nothing was left of them except faded shreds, the tradition of the "seven satin petticoats" was then handed down from mother to daughter.

PHI BETA KAPPA

IN WILLIAMSBURG, VIRGINIA, on December 5, 1776, was founded the first scholastic Greek letter fraternity—Phi Beta Kappa. That a native of the Northern Neck had a part in this is shown by the minutes of that first meeting:

"On Thursday, the 5th of December in the year of our Lord God one thousand seven hundred and seventy-six and the first of the Commonwealth, a happy spirit and resolution of attaining the important ends of Society entering the minds of John Heath, Thomas Smith, Richard Booker, Armistead Smith, and John Jones, and afterwards seconded by others, prevailed, and was accordingly ratified."

". . . . Officers were elected—John Heath as President, Richard Booker as Treasurer, and Thomas Smith as Clerk, the society esteeming them as necessary persons for the functions of their several duties accordingly selected them."

These young gentlemen were students of William and Mary College. The Apollo Room of the Raleigh Tavern is believed to be the birthplace of the distinguished Phi Beta Kappa Society.

John Heath was a native of Northumberland County. Heathsville, the county seat, was named for his family.

John Heath owned an estate called Black Point, on the outskirts of Heathsville. Black Point was later known as Springfield.

LIGHT-HORSE HARRY

HE RODE INTO BATTLE FAST—with his sabre drawn and his three hundred screaming troopers following close behind. Under him was his own horse which he had ridden north from Virginia, one of those "fleet steeds" for which his home country was noted. From his tall leather helmet the horse-hair plumes streamed out behind and his jacket was a blur of green.

His white lambskin breeches and knee-high boots were perfection. His troopers were brilliant and shining—that was because Henry Lee would have his Virginians no other way. His detachment of cavalry stood out like a torch amid the ragged forces of Washington's army.

Henry Lee, lately graduated from Princeton, had been nominated by Patrick Henry in 1776, to command a cavalry company raised in

Virginia for service in the Continental Army, under the command of Colonel Bland. In 1777, Lee's Corps was placed under Washington's immediate control. It was the "flower of Washington's troop."

In Harry Lee's "flying detachment" there was one who was a neighbor of his back in Northern Virginia, John Marshall.

Light-Horse Harry Lee received his nickname because his outfit traveled light. He never had more than three hundred men and they were as lightly equipped as possible. Speed was necessary if they were to survive, for to them fell the hard and dangerous assignments.

It fell to them to spy on the enemy's movements, to harass them, to destroy them and capture their supplies. They hunted for food for Washington's hungry army. Their jobs were the lonesome ones, carried out in the still of the night, while Death stalked them—waiting for them to make just one sound, one slip, one mistake. But Light-Horse Harry and his men were like foxes, and Luck traveled with them.

General Washington was fond of Harry; he remembered him as a blond child who had come with his father and mother on neighborly visits to Mt. Vernon. He invited Harry to become one of his aides.

It was a tempting offer. Washington had been Harry's hero since childhood days and this was an opportunity to be near him. After a struggle with this great temptation, Harry won and sent his answer to General Washington: "I am wedded to my sword."

In 1779, Light-Horse Harry decided to do the impossible. He and his men would capture Paulus (Powles) Hook, a fort occupied by the British on a point of land on the west side of the Hudson, opposite the town of New York. The enemy had made the Hook an island by digging a deep ditch through which the river flowed. It was strongly guarded on all sides by British ships, troops or natural defenses.

For three weeks Harry's scouting expedition had been watching the enemy, moving among the ravines, hills and marshes, always in close touch with the British. In this detachment of Lee's was Captain John Marshall.

Lee laid his plans before General Washington, who approved, and made sure that there were lines of retreat.

On a hot day in August Light-Horse Harry and his men started on the adventure. It was rough going—a long march through marsh land that was doubtless swarming with mosquitoes. They had to make bridges in some places and at other places they waded or swam. They sank deep into the marshes.

On the night of August the eighteenth they crept among the hills and passed the main body of the British army, who were sleeping. At three o'clock in the morning they crossed the ditch. From then on it was a fast movement resulting in the capture of one hundred and fifty-nine prisoners, which was all except a few men in the blockhouse.

After the enemy's stores and supplies had been destroyed Light-Horse Harry and his men returned to Headquarters with their captives.

For this daring feat Lee received compliments from both Washington and Lafayette. But his glory was not to last long. Some of the older officers preferred charges against him for his conduct of the campaign. He was court-martialed, but exonerated from the charges, and Congress soon gave him a gold medal.

But the happiness of it all had fled from the heart of Henry Lee. He had fought four years with Washington in the North. Now he went South and joined General Greene for the remainder of the war. His fame continued to increase. Tradition says that he planned the final strategy at Yorktown.

At the surrender Light-Horse Harry stood in the line of officers as the British army marched out and Cornwallis surrendered his sword to General Washington. Lee was dressed in his usual brilliant perfection with his hair powdered and queued in the back, but in his heart he felt old and sad. At twenty-six he felt so old that he wanted to withdraw from the world and sink into obscurity.

After the war was over Light-Horse Harry turned his horse toward home. That was where he wanted to go—home to Leesylvania on the Potomac.

A BAND OF BROTHERS

KING CARTER once wrote: "Pray God send in the next generation . . . . a set of better-polished patriots."

An example of the kind of "polished patriots" that King Carter probably had in mind were the Lee brothers of Stratford: Thomas Ludwell, Richard Henry, Francis Lightfoot, William and Arthur. They were the sons of Thomas and Hannah Lee, and they were all born in the same southeast bedroom at Stratford.

Richard Henry and Francis Lightfoot were signers of the Declaration of Independence. All five brothers worked in various ways to win freedom from Great Britain for the colonies in America and to shape a government that would stand.

President John Adams described the Lee sons of Stratford as "that band of brothers, intrepid and unchangeable, who, like the Greeks at Thermopylae, stood in the gap, in defense of their country, from the first glimmering of the Revolution in the horizon, through all its rising light, to its perfect day."

THE DIVINE MATILDA

LIGHT-HORSE HARRY LEE soon tired of his isolation and decided one day to ride down to Stratford and call on the family of his cousin. It was a long ride, but Virginians of that day thought nothing of traveling long distances on horseback.

Thomas Lee had left Stratford to his oldest son, Philip Ludwell, who had lived there in great style. In his stables were a score or more of blooded horses, including the imported stallion Dotterel, which was said to be the "swiftest horse in all England (Eclipse excepted)." His imported coaches were the finest that could be had.

Philip had kept an open house, as Harry Lee well remembered, and he had entertained on a lavish scale. A whole ox could be roasted for guests in the kitchen fireplace. He had kept a band of musicians to whose airs his daughters, Matilda and Flora, with their companions danced in the Great Hall. But Philip Ludwell was now dead, Harry had heard, and Stratford had passed on to his oldest child, Matilda.

As Harry came up the oak and poplar lined road to Stratford, Matilda and Flora recognized him "as he rode past the grove of maples" and they "welcomed him with joy."

Flora was described by a contemporary as being haughty in manner, "very genteel and wears monstrous bustles." In describing Matilda the only word used by her contemporaries was "divine."

Harry was not prepared for this new Matilda. When he had last seen her she was at the awkward age of thirteen. Now she was nineteen and his first sight of her took his breath away.

There was tea-drinking in the garden with laughter and talk of the good old times before the war. Perhaps Matilda and Harry walked in the garden and "sat under a butiful shade tree" or climbed to one of the summer-houses on the roof from which they could see "Potomac's sea-like billows."

In less than a month Matilda was married to her cousin, Light-Horse Harry Lee. And what was Matilda like? There are no portraits or miniatures to tell us how she looked, no letters to unlock her personality. Only the word "divine" bequeathed by her contempories.

Matilda was expensive. Inventories tell us that her side-saddle cost 1,200 pounds of tobacco, and music lessons on the harpsichord cost 3,043 pounds of tobacco. "1 pc. fine Chintz in Pocket Money for Mis Matilda," whatever that meant, was 1,500 pounds, and another ninety pounds of tobacco went for dental care. Listed among her belongings were a cap, a pair of silk shoes and stays for her slender waist.

Matilda could afford to have expensive tastes. She had inherited Stratford and its six thousand acres of rich tobacco soil, with enough slaves to tend it, and other lands scattered all over northern Virginia.

Harry took Matilda to New York where for three years he represented Virginia in Congress. They were gay and happy years, but it was over all too soon.

When Matilda died, Harry wrote: "Something always happens to mar my happiness."

At the foot of the garden at Stratford, Harry built a vault for Thomas Lee's granddaughter, Matilda, who was called "divine."

Matilda was twenty-six years old when she died. She left three children, Philip Ludwell, Lucy Grymes and Henry.

MADAM WASHINGTON

AUGUSTINE WASHINGTON had left his wife, Mary: "the current crops on three plantations and the right of working Bridges Creek Quarter for five years, during which time she could establish a quarter on Deep Run."

Mary stayed on at Ferry Farm for twenty-nine years after her husband's death. It is possible that she spent part of this time on some of her adjoining property. Meanwhile her children had married—Betty Washington Lewis was living in Fredericksburg, and George was established at Mount Vernon, which he had inherited after Lawrence's death.

By 1772 George had persuaded his mother to move to a house which he owned in Fredericksburg where she would be close to Betty, at Kenmore.

When Mary Ball Washington moved to Fredericksburg, her property in the Northern Neck included: "43 Hoggs, Shoats and Pigs, 16 sheep, 24 head of cattle, 2 horses; and at the Quarters (her dower land of 400 acres, some miles down the river), 4 horses, 6 oxen, 8 cows and calves, 39 hogs." On the two farms there were ten slaves. The "Quarters" was bringing her an income of 30 pounds per year.

After Mary was installed in Fredericksburg, she had her coachman, Stephen, drive her almost every day to Ferry Farm. Mary's favorite carriage in her old age was a light open phaeton. She was respectfully greeted by everyone she passed on the streets of Fredericksburg.

In her later years Mary is said to have worn a mobcap and kerchief. A mobcap was a frilly white cap introduced from France. In summer she probably waved a fan made from the bronze feathers of wild turkeys.

During these years George Washington frequently visited his mother, and other relatives in the Northern Neck. In August, 1768, he "hauled the Sein for sheepsheads" off Hollis Marsh in Westmoreland County. In 1771, he dined at the Glebe in Cople Parish, and "returned to my brother's in the evening." George enjoyed the social life in Fredericksburg. He liked to play cards, and he liked to dance—the minuet and cotillions and country-dances. It was said that he liked beautiful women, punch, horses and hunting, and that he could be gay or dignified, whenever the occasion demanded. During Revolutionary days Washington and the Northern Neck patriots often gathered at the Rising Sun Tavern in Fredericksburg.

In 1784, while visiting Mount Vernon, Marquis de Lafayette rode to Fredericksburg to pay a visit to Madam Washington before he returned to France. When he returned to Mount Vernon after calling upon Mary Ball Washington he made this comment about her: "I have seen the only Roman Matron living at this day."

George Washington traveled to Fredericksburg in March, 1789, to tell his mother good-bye before leaving Mount Vernon to go to New York for his first inauguration. She did not live to see him again.

Mary Washington was buried in Fredericksburg, near Meditation Rock, a spot near her home where she often went to read her Bible, pray and meditate. It was her request that she be buried there. Many years later a monument to her was erected there.

The modest house where she spent her last years became a national shrine in 1890. A college in Fredericksburg was later named for Mary Washington.

"All that I am I owe to my honored Mother," is the tribute that the great George Washington paid to Mary Ball Washington.

AFTER THE REVOLUTION

THE NORTHERN NECK, like the rest of Tidewater Virginia, changed after the Revolution. War had taken its toll of manpower and money.

The tobacco lands had become exhausted, therefore the culture of tobacco had been almost abandoned. Wheat and corn were now the main crops.

The once thriving tobacco river ports fell into decay. Foreign ships no longer tied up at the plantation landings. The tobacco rolling-roads were no longer needed for their original use.

After the war the English clergy was withdrawn and the churches were unused and deserted for years. Some fell into ruins or were used for other purposes. The glebes became "bones of contention" between the Episcopal Church and the "people." In 1802 the General Assembly passed an act by which the glebes were sold for the benefit of the public.

After the Revolution other religious denominations gained a foothold in the Northern Neck.

People now turned away from anything British, even in architecture and dress. Before the Revolution boys and girls dressed precisely like their parents in miniature. After the war they wore a special dress of their own.

In 1789, there were still few conveniences of life in the Neck, or elsewhere in the country. All cloth was woven by hand. Most of the farm implements were made of wood. Wheat was cut with a scythe, raked with a wooden rake and beaten out with sticks or "trodden out" by oxen.

There were as yet no matches with which to make a fire. Flint and tinder box were used instead and live coals were kept as a basis for the next day's fire. Wood was the chief fuel and candles were used for light.

Bananas and oranges were rarely seen in the Northern Neck then, for sailboats were too slow to bring these fruits any distance in good condition. Communication was slow. By 1790 there were fifteen post-offices in Virginia. The postal service was crude. Mails were carried by post-riders and stages.

People of the Northern Neck lived comfortably but the great prosperity was gone, and although eventually it was recovered in part, the pattern of living was never on such a grand scale again as it was before the Revolution. The large estates were broken up by division or sale. New families took the places of the old. Many of the old names passed into oblivion. The old order of social aristocracy declined, but the people still clung to their old customs, traditions and family life.

MANTUA

"CHICACONY" was selected as a townsite by the Burgesses some time after John Mottrom and his friends had settled there. Mottrom had built a wharf and a warehouse at Coan and he had plans for a "Brew-House." If he had lived, the town might have matured. But Colonel Mottrom died and the plans for a town seem to have been abandoned. Plantation life did not encourage the growth of towns.

The Coan Hall property passed on to the descendants of John Mottrom. Coan Hall and the other early homes in the vicinity either burned or fell into ruins. Toward the close of the eighteenth century, when the Coan Hall property went out of the Mottrom family, there appears to have been few traces left of the once thriving settlement at Coan.

James Smith, a wealthy Baltimore merchant and shipowner, purchased a portion of the Coan Hall estate from a Mottrom heir and erected a brick mansion on a slope there, about 1785. He called his new home Mantua.

Mantua was built along the traditional lines of a Virginia house —a central hall, two rooms on each side and large end chimneys. From the outside it appeared to have three stories but there were really six floor levels. Later, identical wings were added on each side by Smith's sons. Still later, Smith's grandson added an imposing front portico. Before this addition coaches were driven, tradition says, right up to the front steps and ladies could step from coach to marble steps without soiling their dainty slippers. The conveyance could then continue around to the stables on the west side, or follow the driveway on to Coan Stage Road, which ran back of the plantation.

The marble steps, marble window-sills and paneled inside blinds were handsome details of Mantua which may have been the outcome of Smith's residence in Baltimore. Originally he was a native of County Derry, Ireland.

A Story of the Historic Northern Neck of Virginia 167

In the rear of the house there were five terraces, planted with flowers and, perhaps, vegetables and herbs. Brick slave quarters were ranged in a semi-circle beyond the terraces.

The second story front windows of Mantua overlooked both the Coan and the Potomac. Before government lighthouses and buoys marked the waterman's course in this section, he had only the stars, landmarks and a lighted window here and there to guide him. Mantua was a help to the watermen for they could always be sure of a lighted window there, a lamp purposely placed by members of the Smith family, and by day the towering poplar trees were familiar landmarks.

PART III

Nineteenth Century

A Story of the Historic Northern Neck of Virginia

ROBERT E. LEE

IN 1791, Light-Horse Harry Lee became Governor of Virginia. While he was in Richmond he had the opportunity to visit the plantations along the James River.

When Harry rolled up before Shirley in all the trappings of a Virginia governor, it is not surprising that the young daughter of the house saw in him her "heart's desire."

But Charles Carter did not see Harry through his daughter's rosy vision. He saw him as a widower who was seventeen years older than Ann, and as a soldier who had been disillusioned by war and had not adjusted to peace.

However, Harry won his suit and carried the happy Ann back with him to Stratford. Ann was a brunette of medium height and twenty years old. Little else is known about her except that she was good.

Ann's first impression of the Lee mansion must have been a gloomy one. Gayety had left Stratford with Matilda. The musicians had long since been gone, and the blooded horses. The windows once so brightly lighted were dark, and with no voices and laughter to fill the house, one could hear the wolves howling at night in the forest. This remote fortress in the fastness of the Northern Neck was different from anything that this great-granddaughter of King Carter had ever known. Shirley had been warm and happy.

Harry had no taste or ability as a farmer, and even if he had, Westmoreland County was now losing ground as a tobacco country. At first Ann may have traveled to Richmond with her husband and visited Shirley, for Harry was thrice elected to the governorship of Virginia. But as the years went by, Ann and her small children were more and more alone at Stratford. As his political career waned, Harry stayed away from home more and more, chasing various "will o' the wisps" which he believed would recoup his fortune.

Sometimes Ann stayed at Stratford as long as six months at a time without going anywhere to visit, or without seeing her social equals. Still, Ann wrote a friend that she was too busy to be bored. We can imagine her moving about the house, sometimes carrying a charcoal brazier with her into the living room, to warm her frail body or to give the illusion of warmth.

Into this sombre setting was born, on January 19, 1807, a new

Young Robert E. Lee learning to ride.

baby. He was christened: Robert Edward Lee. He was born in the southeast bedroom of Stratford, the same room in which the other great Lee men had been born.

The nursery was probably the coziest room at Stratford in those days. Ann's one known accomplishment was singing, so we can picture her there as she sang to the new baby while she rocked him in his wooden cradle, and watched the flames in the fireplace as they illuminated the guardian cherubs on the iron fireback. Perhaps those days with her children were not unhappy. She taught her boys to be "honorable and correct" and to "practice the most inflexible virtue."

Meanwhile, Harry's last wild speculations had ended in his complete financial ruin. Ann and the children were now living on a trust fund left to them by her father, Charles Carter, when he died in 1806.

One day, when Robert was not yet four years old, a carriage stood in front of Stratford, waiting to take the family for their last ride down the driveway. Stratford had been left to Matilda's son, Henry, and he had now come of age and was ready to take over the estate. Harry and his family traveled to Alexandria where they moved into a smaller house.

A legend says that when everything was ready for departure little Robert could not be found. He was finally discovered in the nursery saying good-bye to the two cherubs on the fireback.

After this Harry had still greater misfortunes. His body was broken and maimed for life. In 1813, when Robert was six years old, his father left Virginia, bound for the British West Indies, seeking health and a new grip on life. He spent the next five years wandering about among the islands. In 1818, he sailed for home but became so ill that he was put off at one of the islands. There he found the family of his old friend, General Greene. He was tenderly cared for by them during his final illness. He died there and was buried in their family burying ground on Cumberland Island, off the coast of Georgia.

NOTE: In 1913 the body of General Henry (Light-Horse Harry) Lee was brought from Cumberland Island and placed in the Chapel at Lexington, Virginia, beside that of his famous son, Robert E. Lee.

SMITH POINT LIGHT

FOR MANY YEARS the watermen of the Chesapeake "steered by the stars," by trees, and by a lighted window here and there.

One of the earlier government lighthouses on Chesapeake Bay was the Smith Point Light located at the mouth of the Potomac on Smith Point, Northumberland County.

There seem to be no available records concerning the erection of this lighthouse. In an 1804 issue of *Blunt's American Coast Pilot* reference is made to a lighthouse having been "erected lately on Smith Point." This establishes the date of its erection as prior to 1804.

In the 1833 issue of the same book there is a small drawing of the lighthouse at Smith Point which shows a tower with a house close by. These structures appeared to be situated on the tip end of a point with a gently sloping hill, or bank, in the rear. The picture shows a lighthouse with the same general appearance as the first government lighthouse at Cape Henry at the entrance to the Chesapeake, built in 1791. The Smith Point tower, however, was round instead of octagonal.

According to older natives of the region who remembered the original lighthouse at Smith Point, it was a round tower built of sandstone blocks, approximately sixty or seventy feet high. A spiral inside stairway with stone steps led up to the lantern at the top.

The sandstone blocks for the tower at Cape Henry had been brought from abroad as ballast in ships. The same thing may have been true of the sandstone blocks of which Smith Point lighthouse was built.

The light at Cape Henry first consisted of oil lamps burning, in turn, whale oil, colza (cabbage) oil, lard oil, and finally kerosene after the discovery of petroleum in Pennsylvania in 1859. The same type of lamps and fuel were doubtless used at Smith Point.

The keeper's house at Smith Point, according to tradition, was located thirty or forty yards back of the tower. It was a brick story-and-a-half house with outside chimneys on each end and an ell in the back. There were fireplaces in every room and a dark underground room which was referred to in later years as the "dungeon."

When this early lighthouse was built there were still a few pirates lurking about the Bay.

THE RAIDERS

FRIGHTENING RUMOURS must have flown up and down the Northern Neck in the early part of the year of 1813.

In June, 1812, Congress had declared war against Great Britain. The Virginia militia had been called out to drill, and to prepare to defend Washington if necessary. The sound of drum and fife was heard once more in the countryside. Brass buttons were polished and firelocks were put in good shooting condition.

Now, in February of 1813, Admiral George Cockburn of the British Navy had entered the Chesapeake with a flotilla of two brigs, several tenders and a force of land troops.

Along the grapevine ran the news that Admiral Cockburn was directing his efforts principally against the citizens. The farmhouses and plantations along the waterfront were being plundered and burned and the cattle were being driven away or slaughtered. While the planters were away with the militia some of their families had taken refuge with their tenants who lived in the forest.

Naval battles were taking place in the rivers. In April, the U. S. S. *Dolphin* was captured in the Rappahannock by the British ship *St. Domingo*. In July a battle was fought in the Yeocomico, a tributary of the Potomac. The U. S. S. *Asp*, a three-gun sloop, was at that time overpowered by five British barges.

Troops were stationed at Windmill Point, at the mouth of the Rappahannock, in November, 1813. Here, April 23, 1814, the British made a landing and pillaged a vessel. They were driven off by militia stationed across the creek. It was perhaps on this same trip that the raiders visited Corotoman.

The crew went ashore and made themselves at home in the old house built by John Carter, while the officers took over the home built later by his son, King Carter. The well-stocked wine cellar and an abundance of fine Rappahannock oysters furnished the ingredients, tradition says, for an all-night party.

In August, 1814, reinforcements consisting of many vessels of war and a large number of troops arrived in the Chesapeake from Europe. Of this force several frigates and bomb vessels were ordered to ascend the Potomac.

At this time the shores of the Potomac were ravaged and a number of fine and ancient homes were burned. Washington city was captured and burned, and President Madison and his wife Dolly were forced to seek refuge in Virginia.

Skirmish between the Virginia Militia and the British during the War of 1812 at Farnham Church.

In October, 1814, a force of British troops came up the Coan River and marched to Heathsville. This force with some mounted troops continued their march up through the Neck, pillaging, burning and destroying as they went. At North Farnham Church, in Richmond County, a skirmish was fought between the raiders and the Virginia militia, leaving bullet holes in the walls of the church to mark the battle.

In September, 1814, the British were on their way to bombard the city of Baltimore. The Sunday before at their camp on Tangier Island, in the Chesapeake Bay, they had been warned of their coming defeat by Joshua Thomas, the Methodist "Parson of the Islands."

At Fort McHenry the "Parson's" prophecy came true, and at the same time an immortal song was born—"The Star-Spangled Banner."

STEAMBOATS

THE *CHESAPEAKE* was the first steamboat on Chesapeake Bay. She made her first run in 1813. The next steamer to make her debut was the *Washington*, on the Potomac, in 1815. The next year the *Virginia* started running from Norfolk to Richmond.

From then on until the Civil War the steamboat business expanded. All the bay and river boats had both freight and passenger services to Baltimore, Washington or Norfolk. These services were interrupted by the war.

During the Civil War, according to several unpublished letters of that period, the steamboats *George C. Peabody* and *North Point* collided in the Potomac on the night of August 13, 1862. Of the three or four hundred persons on board the two boats only one hundred were saved.

After the Civil War the steamboat services were restored.

When the first steamboat ran up the Rappahannock, Bewdley was used as a landing place. This Lancaster County home belonged to the Ball family, relatives of George Washington's mother. When passengers awaited the arrival of the boat at Bewdley, a white flag was raised as a signal by day, and at night a light was placed in one of the many dormer-windows.

HANNAH AND THE FALLING STARS

IT WAS HANNAH'S custom to get up before daybreak. She was a sixteen-year-old Negro girl of Northumberland County. On this particular morning she was to get the scare of her life. She started to go to the well for a bucket of fresh water but when she stepped outside she dropped her bucket and ran to her mistress screaming: "The stars are all falling down!" Needless to say the whole plantation was aroused to watch the strangest phenomenon they had ever beheld.

Hannah was not the only person who was scared or bewildered that morning. Throughout the eastern part of North America people were exclaiming: "it is snowing fire," "the end of the world has come," "the sky is on fire," "the Judgment Day is here!"

What Hannah and the others had witnessed was the Leonid shower of November 12-13, 1833, which lasted from midnight until day. People of that time were generally uninformed about meteoric showers. It was a topic of comment and speculation for many generations.

Hannah lived many years to tell of the time when she saw "the stars fall." She outlived most of her children and those who were living at the time of her death were too feeble to attend her funeral. She was buried in a quiet spot among the pines on the banks of the Great Wicomico River. Her tombstone bears this inscription: "Hannah Crocket, 1817-1933, Age 116 yrs."

DEAR TO HIS HEART . . .

NEAR THE beginning of the Civil War, General Robert E. Lee's daughter visited Stratford. The great manor no longer belonged to the Lee family. She wrote to her father who was in the South at that time, and described her visit to his childhood home. He answered her as follows:

"I am much pleased at your description of Stratford and your visit. It is endeared to me by many recollections and it has always been a great desire of my life to be able to purchase it. Now that we have no other home, and the one we so loved (Arlington) has been so foully polluted, the desire is stronger with me than ever. The horse-chestnut you mention in the garden was planted by my mother. I am sorry the vault is so dilapidated. You did not mention the spring, one of the objects of my earliest recollections."

On Christmas Day, 1861, General Lee wrote his wife: "In the absence of a home I wish I could purchase Stratford. That is the only other place that I could go to, now accessible, that would inspire me with feelings of pleasure and local love. You and the girls could remain there in quiet. It is a poor place, but we could make enough bread and bacon for our support and the girls could weave us clothes."

General Robert E. Lee's desire was never fulfilled.

THE BLOCKADE

FROM TIME to time various writers have stated that the isolated Northern Neck of Virginia was "out of bounds" or "bypassed" in the Civil War. Despite these statements, which so lightly dismiss the Neck during the war years, natives of that region did not spend that time in the carefree, unmolested state thus implied.

All able-bodied men of the Neck were away on the battlefields. Anxiety for them, and for the South, hung like a pall over the remaining population. More tangible worries beset them also.

Although the bordering waters of the Potomac, Rappahannock and Chesapeake were rich with food, when the Virginians tried to take the oysters, crabs and fish, a tug from the Federal flotilla which patrolled these waters would come "steaming out to hasten them home, with sometimes a six-pound shot sent after them for emphasis."

The women, girls, old men and boys raised what they could, but many fields, once lush with corn, tobacco, sugar cane and other crops, now lay barren save for sedge and pine seedling. Many of the men had ridden away to war on the horses. The people at home gave as much as they could of what they could raise to the men at the front.

The Federal gunboats shelled homes and landed soldiers who carried off everything they could find. Many are the tales that lingered on in the Neck about the geese that were struck down by swords, the bowls of milk that were lifted to mouths and gulped down, the firkins of butter that were carried away by soldiers who thrust their arms elbow deep in the butter and carried it off that way, the cattle that were slaughtered before the hungry eyes of the natives, the churches that were profaned—the list could go on and on. And there were some instances when the invaders were kind, or fair.

The resourceful women of the Neck invented substitutes for lost luxuries. Tea was brewed from sassafras, wheat, sage or mullein; coffee was concocted from sweet potatoes and other things. Sorghum and honey served for sugar. They got out the discarded spinning-wheels and looms and revived those skills. They carded, spun and wove the wool from their sheep. Polk berries and walnut hulls were used as dyes, and a special mixture of plants produced a shade that would pass as Confederate gray. The latter was used to dye garments made of the homespun so that there was always a new suit ready for the soldier when he came home on furlough. Thorns were used for pins, and seeds such as persimmon had holes bored in them and were used for buttons.

In spite of these and other ingenious substitutes the supplies of food and clothing had been very nearly exhausted by 1862. Thus, the natives of the Northern Neck were driven to running the blockade.

At that time Hampton Roads was blockaded by Union naval forces, and the rivers were patrolled by them. Maryland, just across the Potomac from the Neck, was divided territory. Leonardtown, in southern Maryland, was a trading center for the blockade runners from the Neck.

On the Virginia side of the Potomac, Kinsale in Westmoreland County, situated on an estuary called Yeocomico River, was one point of departure and arrival. This village had become quite cosmopolitan, for the country people were not the only ones who ran the blockade. Strangers from the North and South—merchants, speculators, adventurers, Northern draft dodgers, Southern sympathizers from the North, pro-Unionists trying to reach the North, even ladies, usually married women traveling with their husbands—all rubbed elbows in Kinsale. And there was at least one blockade-runner among them who dodged the tugs on the Potomac and blistered his hands on the muffled oars for no more serious reason than romance.

A steady stream of canoes from Maryland sneaked through to the Neck bringing quinine and other drugs, food, and Southern sympathizers. They landed anywhere in the Northern Neck.

The rivers were probably dark, for by the latter part of April, 1861, practically all lights in the lighthouses and lightships had been extinguished, removed or destroyed, from the Chesapeake to the Rio Grande by the Southerners.

THE HOME GUARD

THOUGH NO major battles were fought in Northumberland County during the Civil War, it was the scene of a number of skirmishes which were never recorded in history.

The geographical position of this county in the tip end of the Neck and surrounded on three sides by water isolated it from the main stream of the war, but made it vulnerable to enemy naval raiders. Also, small groups of Union cavalry rode through the Neck from time to time looking for deserters from their own army and for Confederate soldiers who might be at home on furlough. Homes were looted.

A Federal flotilla was stationed across the Potomac at Piney Point, Maryland, and although this river was not formally blockaded during the war, it was patrolled, and the smaller rivers were patrolled from time to time. Many of the homes adjacent to the shoreline were shelled by these boats. The crew often landed and raided farms and houses.

For the purpose of keeping these raiders away and defending the women and children, a home guard was organized. (They were probably organized in all the counties of the Neck.) Since the ablebodied men of Northumberland were away on the battlefields, this group was composed of teen-aged boys and old men.

Except traditionally, very little has been known about this organization. A notarized statement written by a former member of the Northumberland Home Guard, sheds some light on their activities. It is as follows:

"I'm going to try and write something in regard to the Home Guard to which I belonged but hardly know what to write. I was only a boy then, and as to giving dates, I couldn't tell you what month or even the year we organized but we didn't organize untill those Yankee raids began to take place. The Gun Boats would come in the rivers and land soldiers, go to the farm Houses and carry off anything they wanted, so we organized to try and keep off those raids and defend the Women and children while the menfolks were in the War. Our Company, I suppose was what you might call an independent company, don't think the Confederate Government ever furnished us with anything except Guns and ammunition. I think they permitted us to organize.

"Yankee" foragers during the Civil War.

"We had several skirmishes with the raiders, one in the vicinity of Lotsburg where we captured a Horse and perhaps killed the rider. His fellow soldiers got Him away but we got the Horse. After getting their wounded or dead comrad aboard ship they left. On another occasion at Glebe Point on the Great Wicomico River, we opened fire on a Gun Boat that was going up the river. She stoped immediately and turned around and went on down the River. We kept up our fire untill she was out of Gunshot. They gave us a severe shelling of shrapnell but shot too high, didn't kill anyone. I heard one Horse was killed. And at another time on Raisons Creek we captured a little Picket Boat No. 2. She carried one brass cannon and a crew of seven men. One man was shot in the leg. The Captain of the Boat gave up His Sword and revolver to our Captain. We sent the Prisoners to Richmond and Burned the Boat."

(Signed)   Bertrand B. Haynie

Apr 7—1927

Further data are added concerning this organization by Rev. C. T. Thrift, who spent his boyhood at Wicomico Church, Northumberland County. He writes:

"Many Yankee gunboats came in the Great Wicomico River from time to time. Marauding parties landed and did much pillaging. Poultry and pigs and other things were taken. The women and children were frightened not a little.

"One such boat came in and anchored on the Wicomico side between Rowe's landing and Blackwell's Wharf. A band of pillagers landed and took what they wanted and then returned to their boat. Young . . . . had hidden himself while the band was at the home where he lived. He waited until they had left the shore. Then he took an old rifle and crept down to the water's edge, hiding in the bushes. The captain greeted his marauders upon their return and stood leaning against the deckhouse sunning himself.

"Young . . . . raised his rifle aimed carefully and fired. The bullet struck the captain in the forehead, killing him instantly. Panic ensued on board, for they had no idea where the shot came from nor did they have any idea how large a force might be attacking. There was no time to be lost for they needed to go and they could not stand on the order of their going.

"So they unfastened the end of the anchor chain at the capstan and fled, leaving the chain and the anchor in the mud of the river bottom. He said (many years later) that he supposed this was still where it was left. He had thought of going there to search for it but he had never done so."

Young . . . ., tradition says, was a member of the Northumberland Home Guard.

THE MYSTERY OF HORSE POND

WHEN THE YANKEE gunboats patrolled the waters surrounding the Northern Neck during the Civil War they found the entrance to Little Wicomico River—where the Potomac and Chesapeake meet. They entered through its natural channel which was open then and quite deep.

Men went ashore to hunt for provisions—vegetables from the gardens, eggs, milk and freshly made butter. Even preserves and jellies from the shelves of the good housewives of Little Wicomico. They searched for men who might be at home, too.

One day near the beginning of the war, a small sailing vessel, probably twenty-two feet in length, and with several persons on board, came into Little Wicomico. She sailed in through the channel with the stone tower lighthouse on Smith Point to her right and Tranquility Farm to her left. She passed through Rock Hole, by tiny Bamboozle Island and around Gough's Point. It was straight sailing then with Ellyson Creek to the right and Sharps Creek to the left.

When the boat passed the tract of land between Sharps Creek and Horse Pond those on board were too far away to note the face of a woman pressed to a window pane of the house on the left bank of the River.

The woman, Sardelia, watched the boat with interest for it was a strange boat, and no doubt with a little uneasiness since those were dark times. Any unfamiliar boat was cause for alarm.

To Sardelia's surprise the boat dropped anchor just beyond her house and abreast of a strip of woodland near the pond where the horses drank. She saw the persons on board go ashore and enter the woods. After a short while they came out, boarded their boat, headed out of the River and sailed out of sight.

Sardelia called her little girl, Florence, and together they hurried through their barn-yard and into the woods. They found the place where the men had come ashore, their footprints on the sand, broken bushes and bruised foliage in the woods, but they could find no clue to the mysterious mission. Sardelia finally gave up her search and sat down under the big water oak tree there in the woods to ponder what she had seen.

Nearly four years later, after the close of the war, Sardelia again saw almost an exact re-enactment of the same scene she had witnessed before. The same boat came into the River, stopped at the same place and the persons on board went ashore and disappeared into the woods. After a short while they boarded their boat and sailed away—for the last time, so far as Sardelia ever knew.

Sardelia again hastened to the woods. This time her search was not in vain. About forty feet back from the shore amidst the trees she found a newly dug hole. It had been hastily and loosely refilled with earth.

This called for more than one period of meditation under the water oak tree. Who were they? Why did they select this particular spot to bury whatever they had buried? (The island at the mouth of the River would have been a perfect setting for buried treasure.) Why did they come into an inhabited area—almost in the barn-yard? Were they evading Federal gunboats? Or, perhaps they were from the North themselves. Did they come from one of the islands in the Chesapeake? And what did they bury?

Tales of buried treasure circulated around Little Wicomico for a long time, although many who lived close by never knew how it all started. The woods became haunted, too, especially the big water oak. But the haunts must not have been too bad because Uncle Zeke, a respected colored man, lived peacefully for many years in his little house in the woods by Horse Pond.

SCHOONER IN A MILL-POND

ON NOVEMBER 18, 1863, Abraham Lincoln passed through Baltimore on his way to dedicate a battlefield cemetery at Gettysburg.

At least one Virginian happened to be in the city on that same day also. Captain Jehu, who hailed from the lower Northern Neck, was in Baltimore on business. His schooner, *Pioneer*, lay at a city dock, unloaded of her cargo of wood and ready for the return trip home, but the Captain was having difficulty in getting his money for the wood.

Nerves were tense in Baltimore on that day. Maryland was

officially a neutral state but her loyalties were divided. Matters were very bad with the Confederate army near the end of 1863, and Captain Jehu was a Virginian. He finally settled for part of a load of lime in payment for the wood and sailed back down the Chesapeake as fast as the wind would carry him.

When he arrived home he found that matters were even worse there. Word had spread that the Yankees were burning boats. Watermen were carrying their boats to the heads of the rivers in a desperate attempt to save them—perhaps they would be overlooked there, or the waters would be too shallow for gunboats.

Captain Jehu unloaded the lime and sailed the *Pioneer*, in company with a number of other boats, far up the Great Wicomico River to a place called Betts' Landing. The other boats were left by their owners to take their chances there on the mud flats where the water was only two or three feet deep, but Captain Jehu was not satisfied. He loved the *Pioneer*; she was like a part of him, and besides that, if the war ever got over, he had to make a living for his wife and children. In desperation he thought of an idea that he might have laughed at in ordinary times.

Captain Jehu sailed the *Pioneer* on to Public Landing at the very head of the River. He waited there until the tide was at its full height, then cautiously he floated the seventy-five-foot schooner through the almost hidden entrance to a mill-pond.

Once the schooner was well inside the pond Captain Jehu took down the sails and bundled them up and carried them ashore and hid them in a nearby barn.

He then did something that any waterman would hate to do— he bored a hole in the bottom of his boat.

Captain Jehu went ashore again and started walking toward Burgess Store, which was quite a distance. He had heard that men were being recruited there for the Confederate army. He was in his late thirties and he had a wife and several small children depending on him, but men were desperately needed to fight and the time had come when he was needed even more on the battlefield than at home. He joined the army that day.

While in the Confederate army, Captain Jehu was taken prisoner by the enemy and carried to Point Lookout, Maryland. There in a log pen he had plenty of time to look up at the stars by which he had steered so many times and to wonder what it was all about anyhow. He had not heard from his family for so long—he didn't even know if they were still living. His thoughts probably wandered to his early life.

He had been cast out of his home by a cruel stepmother when he was twelve years old, and had found refuge on a schooner that freighted lumber from the river heads of the Northern Neck to Baltimore and Philadelphia. He was too young to do much but he had helped with the cooking. This was done in a fireplace which was in the cabin and was the only source of heat on the "wood lugger." The fireplace was made of brick and the chimney protruded through the top of the cabin.

Those were hard days too. No doubt he thought of the proud day when he finally owned his own schooner, the *Pioneer*. And how was she faring now? Was she still sinking into the mire of the mill-pond or was she just another charred skeleton?

At last an eternity at Point Lookout came to an end. The prisoners were herded on board an old tub of a steamer and carried to Richmond where they were to be exchanged for Federal prisoners in Libby Prison.

When Captain Jehu arrived at Libby Prison he was too weak to get in line for mess. A big Irishman took pity on him, covered him with a blanket where he lay on the floor and brought him his own rations. The food tasted good after the maggoty fat back he had been living on at Point Lookout, but the steaming coffee was the thing that revived him.

Meanwhile, back in the Northern Neck, Captain Jehu's family was having a hard time. His wife, who "never weighed more than a hundred pounds in her life," raised what she could to feed her children. She grew cotton and spun and wove it and made clothes for them. In the winter, and winters were very cold in the Neck then, she went into the woods and cut enough cordwood to keep them warm. In the words of one of her sons, "She got along any way she could."

One day, some time after the close of the war, Captain Jehu arrived home, having walked all the way from Newport News. His wife didn't recognize him and one of his small sons ran away and hid in the woods all day thinking that he was a Yankee. He wore Yankee breeches and jacket with nothing underneath. Years later one of Captain Jehu's sons described the return of his soldier-father: "An awful-looking object came walking home. He was hairy as a monkey, lousy, barefoot, and had lost interest in everything."

The happiness of being at home again and the necessity of making a living must have aroused Captain Jehu's interest before very long. The first thing he did was to go up the Great Wicomico River to look for his boat. When he reached Betts' Landing he found a graveyard of blackened ribs sticking out of the water. The Yankees had done a thorough job there.

It must have been with great trepidation that he once more entered the mill-pond. But there—hidden among the cattails and deep in the mud—lay the *Pioneer*.

At low tide he shoveled the mud out of his boat, plugged up the hole and bailed her out. He then floated her out of the pond on high tide and carried her down the River to a place called Deep Landing, where he cleaned her up and got ready for the sea once more. (He found the sails safe in the barn, where muskrats had nested in the folds.)

After the *Pioneer* was put in shape again Captain Jehu freighted lumber in her for twenty years.

WAR BONNETS

SHOPPING TRIPS to Baltimore were curtailed by the Civil War. Even if it had been possible to slip through the Federal patrol, Confederate money was of little value.

Women who still wanted bonnets for themselves and for their daughters were forced to be resourceful. The most practical substitute they could find for straw was the corn-shuck. They picked the shucks in the early fall while they were still green and put them aside to work on during the lonely winter evenings beside the fireplace.

By that time the shucks were dry and stiff but the women soaked them in water until they were pliable. Long strips were plaited and sewed around and around together to form crown and brim. The finished product was trimmed with a feather plucked from the barn-yard rooster, or with some natural material, such as dried grasses, gum balls, sea shells or small pine cones.

One corn-shuck hat, made for a "Confederate bride" of the Neck, was trimmed with flowers made of small white feathers. Each flower was centered with a bit of gold from a raveled Confederate epaulette.

AMANDA AND THE YANKEES

ON AN APRIL DAY in 1864 a young couple on horseback traveled down a muddy Northern Neck road. Once they paused by the wayside to drink from a spring that bubbled conveniently near, and toward evening they drew rein under a giant mulberry tree at the head of a lane where gate-posts with acorn finials marked the entrance. From this vantage spot a cabin roof showed here and there at the edge of the woods, and open fields enclosed by zig-zag chestnut rail fences could be pointed out and called by name—Upper Field, Lower Field, Middle Field, Back Field and Shelly Bank.

The house at the end of the lane could be glimpsed through its grove of locusts, paper mulberry and towering ailanthus. It was a typical early Tidewater Virginia house—story-and-a-half, without dormers. Three or four brick outside chimneys and a small entrance porch were the outstanding features. It was flanked on the right by a barn, cornhouse and tobacco house, and on the left by a smokehouse, off kitchen, laundry house and small sheds.

In the background water gleamed where Cockerell's Creek meandered into one of its many coves, and finally trickled up on either side to form marshes, lush with wild flags and the foliage of wild lilies and mallows.

The couple were bride and groom and this was the bride's first view of her future home, Pleasant Grove. The groom had little time to familiarize his new wife with his ancestral acres as he was a Confederate soldier and the honeymoon must end when his furlough ended, which was soon.

When the bridegroom went back to join Lee's dwindling forces, the bride took up her new duties as mistress of Pleasant Grove. She was alone except for the servants. How many stayed on after the war started, tradition does not say. Amanda was well versed in the art of housekeeping, thanks to the rigid early training of her mother. There was plenty to do. The groom was an orphan and an only child and he had been living in solitary freedom for some time before the war. She was too busy at first to be lonely.

The central passage, paneled to chair rail height and plastered above, was as dark as night when all the doors were closed. If she opened the heavy front door she could look out and see the little porch with its built-in benches on each side that looked something like short church pews. The yard was enclosed with a horizontal plank fence and the gateposts had small acorns to match the larger ones on the Outer Gate. They were always called the Outer and Inner Gates.

The rooms of the house, like the fields, were named. Besides the doors to the parlor and dining-room which opened from the passage, there was a small door which opened to reveal a narrow twisted stairway which led up to the Big Room and the Little Room.

The shed addition on the rear was two steps lower than the main house. There Amanda found the Chamber Room, the Middle Room and the Back Room. All walls were of white-washed plaster and the floors and woodwork were of heart pine. (The house was built of heart pine and put together with hand-made nails. The cornhouse was fastened together with wooden pegs.)

Amanda had fun exploring the old house and bringing it back to life once more. One day she was dusting the clock on the dining-room mantel when she discovered that it hid the opening to a secret metal box built in the chimney. A hiding place for valuables! A lot of good that did her. Confederate notes were of little value and the tobacco which she used in place of money couldn't be hidden there.

Amanda finally chose the Chamber Room as her bedroom, because it was usually full of sunlight, had a cozy fireplace and a view of the creek and garden. At the back of the house there was a combination garden of flowers, herbs, vegetables and fruit trees, laid out in the English manner. A walk down the center led to the Creek. Trees grew on both sides of the Creek and Amanda's view ended where the Creek disappeared around a point. She wondered what was on the other side and if the water was deep enough for a Yankee gunboat.

One afternoon Amanda was taking a nap in the Back Room when she was suddenly and violently awakened by a great noise. The whole house seemed to be shaking. Her eardrums felt like they would burst. After the noise had subsided and the house became still and she had gotten her wits together again she ventured outside. The frightened negroes pointed to a jagged hole in the underpinning under the Back Room and a fragment of cannon ball lying nearby.

After the gunboat's rude salutation, Amanda was not surprised when one day she looked up the lane and saw a number of Federal soldiers on horseback turning in at the Outer Gate. She went out on the porch and waited for them.

Many years later Hannah, one of the servants, described the incident. Through the cracks in the cornhouse where she was hiding Hannah saw the soldiers dismount. Two of them went to the porch where "Missus" was waiting. They talked some, then "Missus" went in the house and the men who had talked with her sat down on the porch. The other soldiers sprawled on the grass under the trees. Pretty soon she heard "Missus" call so she "snuck" out of thhe cornhouse.

"Hannah," said "Missus," "they are going to stay to dinner so we must hurry and cook a good meal. Kill some chickens, put those ducks that are already dressed in the oven and get a ham out of the meat house."

Hannah remonstrated. "Stay to dinner, all dem men and dem wearing blue coats, too!" But "Missus" was determined. "They are hungry, Hannah, and I invited them. Besides, if they get a good dinner maybe they'll go away and not burn the house or take the tobacco."

Such a dinner! Baked duck, chicken, fried ham, batter bread and hot biscuits—more things than Hannah could remember—and little glasses of wine to "top off wid." After dinner the soldiers went out in the yard again. A fat old goose came wandering around and one of the men took out his sword and was about to cut off its head, but "de boss" who had talked most with "missus" told him to put up his sword.

The officer no doubt felt mellow and relaxed after the good meal. After resting awhile they all rode away in high good humour, waving warm good-byes.

Thus the goose was saved. When a tired Confederate soldier came walking home from Appomattox after the war had ended he found everything intact as he had left it.

THE HORSEHAIR RING

WHEN IN THE beginning of May, 1864, General Lee permitted General Grant to cross the Rapidan without molestation in order to lure him into the Wilderness, where it would be impossible for the Federals to use their artillery, he intended to destroy the Federal Army in the depths of that "bewildering thicket" by a surprise attack where Grant would be forced to fight at a great disadvantage.

The woods were very thick—so dense that a regimental commander could not see the whole of his line at the same time, and in many instances the only guides were the points of the compass.

The battle was raging on May 6. In a bulletin sent to the Secretary of War at the close of that day, General Lee stated: "Our loss in killed is not large, but we have many wounded, most of them slightly, artillery being little used on either side."

General Grant's army had suffered severely, and he had become convinced that it was useless to try to drive Lee from his position.

He decided to move his army southward to Spotsylvania Court House and get between Lee and Richmond.

During the afternoon of May 7, Grant sent his trains off in the direction of Spotsylvania Court House, which was only fifteen miles distant, and ordered the army to prepare to follow at nightfall.

Among Grant's wounded men there was by some mistake a wounded Confederate soldier. Perhaps the color of his home-made uniform, dyed with a brew of herbs and vegetables concocted by his wife was not too accurate a shade of Confederate gray, especially when obscured by the blood and filth of the long battle. Whatever the reason may have been, he was carried along by the enemy with their own wounded men.

Near Spotsylvania Court House a home was commandeered by the Federals for their wounded, but when the Confederate's uniform was recognized, he was left lying in the yard.

The lady of the house saw him there. She dared not take him inside, but she made a pallet on the ground for him, and stayed by him, and comforted him as best she could.

The soldier was still conscious. He told her of his wife, her name and where she lived, of his children, and of a ring in his pocket. He told her that when he was holding the horses one day while a battle was in progress, he had plucked some hairs from the mane of a horse and fashioned a ring as a gift for his wife. It was a crude thing, he said, entirely lacking in beauty, but he had woven his love into it. He hoped that in some way it could be conveyed to her.

The woman promised the dying man that his wish would be carried out, having faith that in some way she could fulfill her promise.

Satisfied by her promise, the soldier died quietly there on the pallet, toward evening of May 7, 1864.

The woman covered his body and left him there until nightfall. Under cover of darkness she returned with a woman servant, and together they laboriously dug a grave for him there in her yard. Before laying him to rest she searched his pockets and found the ring and two Confederate notes for fifty cents each, both issued April 6, 1863. Two Confederate notes and a ring made of horsehair—the total possessions on his person.

The ring, as the soldier had said, was lacking in beauty, but it was skillfully made. He had fastened together a circle of horsehair about the size of a slender woman's finger, then he had covered it by weaving a few strands of the hair around it, making a sort of buttonhole stitch on both edges.

After the war had ended the woman managed in some way to fulfill her promise. She wrote the soldier's widow a letter telling her the details of her husband's death and enclosed the contents of his pockets. Whether the postal system had been restored in the region where the letter traveled, or whether it was conveyed by hand, is not known, but it did finally reach its destination.

As soon as it was possible, relatives of the bereaved family, an old man and a small boy, made a long, weary and sad journey by ox-cart from their home in the lower Northern Neck, through Fredericksburg to Spotsylvania Court House, a distance of more than a hundred miles, for the purpose of transporting the remains of their kinsman back to his homeland. When this mission was accomplished, the remains of the young Confederate sergeant were laid to rest in the family burial ground, near Burgess Store, in Northumberland County.

For many years the soldier's widow and the loyal Southern lady corresponded. Although they never did meet, their spirits were bound together by that common denominator—war.

MIRACLE AT KETCHUM'S CAMP

TOWARD THE CLOSE of the Civil War the fortunes of the lower Northern Neck like those of the entire South were low. This section was then so isolated that news from the battlefields was long in coming, and usually bad when it did arrive. Food was meager and monotonous and, despite the ingenious efforts of the women, could only be stretched so far.

As another war Christmas approached there was little heart to make merry, but for the sake of the children the older people felt that an appearance of festivity was necessary. A fowl of some sort was killed and dressed and hung in the cold smokehouse in readiness for its last minute stuffing. The tree had been selected but would not be cut until late Christmas Eve. Some chose a holly, because it needed less trimming and the berries held up for quite a while in the poorly heated rooms, but cedar was still the favorite. The little ones were stringing long garlands of holly berries and popcorn and making ornaments from whatever they could find.

On the night of December the twenty-third, the small spark of

Christmas spirit that had been kindled was dampened by a terrific storm that raged over the Chesapeake, dashing huge breakers against the beach and shaking and rattling the houses along its shoreline, like some monster bent on destruction. By morning the wind and waves had subsided leaving a chill gray atmosphere that warned of a snow-storm in the making.

It is the natural thing for people who live close to the water to scan the horizon the last thing before retiring and the first thing upon arising, so on this bleak Christmas Eve it was not long after dawn when residents along that section of the Bay between Smith Point and Taskmakers Creek had observed two dark objects drifting toward shore near a spot later known as Ketchum's Camp. In those uncertain days anything unusual was viewed with great alarm. Not long before this, one of the houses along this same stretch of beach had been fired upon by an enemy gunboat and saved only because two daughters of the house had waved a sheet on a pole and implored the officers who came ashore to cease firing.

Now, as the alarm went out members of the Home Guard swiftly assembled with their miscellaneous firearms ready for action. These fiery lads were sometimes overzealous in their defense tactics so on this day they were restrained by their elders until the objects drifted in so close that all could see that they were nothing but clumsy unmanned boats of the scow type.

The boys and a few very old men who were there hastened out in small boats to the stranded vessels. As they pulled back the tarpaulin coverings they could scarcely believe their eyes when they saw that both boats were loaded with provisions. After much discussion, they concluded that these must be Federal supply boats which had broken loose during the storm while being towed up the Bay. Of course, the idea that they were putting one over on the Yankees appealed to the Home Guard even more than the food. They hastily and joyfully began the task of transporting the windfall to shore. By midafternoon the beach was lined with people who had learned the good news through the grapevine.

A nondescript crowd they were, but representative of the countryside at that time. Very old men, children and boys were there but the majority were women of all ages. The clothes of every one were knitted and homespun, their main virtue being warmth. They had come on foot, on horseback, in carriages and wagons. Their faces were alight with the thought of real coffee and tea on Christmas morning after months of nauseous brews made from sweet potatoes, wheat or sage, sweetened with sorghum. Real white loaf sugar!

Their eyes glistened with delight—or maybe, tears. Bacon, too, and flour and molasses! Plenty for all. They did not doubt that this was a miracle.

The children jumped and screamed in ecstatic anticipation of the wonderful Christmas to come. Snow began to fall but now it was not the dreaded stuff that makes the woes of the poor greater, but, instead, it was the beautiful, dream-making substance that belongs to Christmas. It fell softly on the loaded vehicles and on the heads of those who knelt with one accord on the lonely sand beach and gave thanks to God.

Note: This spot which was called Ketchum's Camp soon after the Civil War, because a sawmill camp was located there, has in recent years been known as Chesapeake Estates, a summer cottage area.

DESPERATE PASSAGE

IT WAS APRIL of the year 1865, and Lee had already surrendered his army at Appomattox.

On the night of April 22nd a row-boat moved cautiously across the Potomac in the direction of the Virginia shore. This was the second time, it is believed, that the two men in the boat had tried to make the river crossing from Maryland to Virginia. The night before they had failed because it had been too dark and the tide had been too strong. The past eight days had doubtless seemed like an eternity to them.

Now they could see the Virginia shore and the dim outline of a landing but the thin youth at the oars did not head for the public wharf. He rowed on until he came to a smaller landing which belonged to a private home. They landed there, at Upper Machodoc Creek near what later became Dahlgren, in King George County.

The younger man helped his passenger out of the boat and together they approached the house on the bank of the creek, knocked on the door and asked for lodging for the night. The mistress of the house could doubtless see that the dark handsome man in the muddy Confederate uniform was badly in need of rest. Tradition says that she took them in for the night.

The next morning the two men left the Quesenberry home. The older man was limping badly and seemed to be in much pain. That day they traveled slowly on foot over back roads.

Toward dusk they came to a home set in a grove of beautiful

trees. It was Cleydael, the residence of Doctor R. H. Stuart. Tradition says that the men knocked on the back door and asked for food and aid.

Whether Doctor Stuart rendered surgical aid to the man in the tattered uniform is still a controversial subject in that region. They did receive food and were waited on by Junius and Patsy Dixon, servants at Cleydael. Tradition says that the older man left a note to Doctor Stuart in which he enclosed a five-dollar bill and grudgingly thanked him for "what we did get."

Stories vary as to where the two men spent the night of April 23rd.

At some time or other they rested in the yard of St. Paul's Church, it is said. One account says that they spent the night at the house of a man named Rollins near Office Hall. Another story says that they found shelter for the night in the cabin of William Lucas, a Negro, and that the next day the man who was burning with fever, ordered Lucas's son to take him and his companion to the Rappahannock ferry at Port Conway.

All accounts seem to agree that the men came to the Rappahannock in daylight on April 24th, and that they were in a spring wagon driven by a Negro man.

It seems that the ferryman was fishing and wouldn't come ashore for only two fares. At this point three Confederate soldiers who, it has been said, were veterans of Mosby's Raiders and were on their way home, rode up on horseback.

The haggard man got out of the wagon and limped over to the soldiers, the story goes, and told them who he was and asked them to help him. Tradition says that the young veterans moved off and held a conference together and when they had reached a decision they told him that they were not in sympathy with what he had done, but since he had thrown himself on their mercy they would help him.

One story says that the Confederate veterans then leveled their rifles at the ferryman and ordered him to come ashore at once and get them or he would have his head blown off. The ferryman came ashore and the two men and at least one of the veterans got on the ferry.

It was in this way that John Wilkes Booth, who had shot and killed Abraham Lincoln in Washington on the night of April 14th, and his faithful companion, Herold, finally completed their journey across the Northern Neck, from the Potomac to the Rappahannock.

In their devious flight across the Neck they had traveled perhaps twenty miles.

The painful journey was in vain, however, for it was only a matter of hours before Federal soldiers would track down the assassin and his companion and find them in a barn on Garrett's farm.

AFTER THE WAR

THE OLD ORDER of things finally died in the Northern Neck with the surrender of 1865. But, though the splendor was gone, the people continued to cling to the old ways—the traditions, customs, family life and ties of kinship.

With the younger generation—the war children—there began a new type of manhood. Knowing nothing except privations, they grew up with hard bodies and practical minds, and though thrust into manhood while they were still adolescent, they shouldered their responsibilities.

Those who lived near the water turned to it because it was now more fruitful than the land. Its harvests could be reaped more quickly, and they could be reaped by one man working alone, or by several men working together.

Bundled up in home-made garments and warmed by caps, mufflers, socks and mittens knitted by their mothers and grandmothers, these boys sallied forth at dawn in the bitterest weather to tong oysters. Winters were much colder then. They worked until nightfall, often in open boats, stopping only long enough to refresh themselves with a hearty lunch, which was usually packed in a tin bucket, and usually included pork, biscuits and sorghum molasses. This was washed down with cold coffee drunk from a stone jug.

The girls too had changed and they now belonged to this new regime. During the winter evenings they helped the older women to knit fish nets. They used home-made wooden needles for this, and sometimes they fastened one end of the net to wooden pegs driven in the wall. (Years later people were to wonder why those pegs were found in some homes of the lower Neck.) The women helped the men to fashion sails for their boats by sewing together pieces of canvas.

With the nets and small sailing vessels the men caught fish in what were known as pound nets. These were staked out on weir poles.

The seafood and whatever other marketable farm produce they could assemble was conveyed up the Bay to the nearest and best cash market, which was Baltimore, one hundred miles from the end of the Neck. They brought back from this city clothing, sugar, molasses, kerosene and hardware, among other things. This contact with a large cosmopolitan city greatly influenced the lives and natures of the natives of the Northern Neck. Those who could manage it sent their children there to be educated. Other children were educated by older relatives, or by anyone who would teach them. Some received very little education during this period.

Children had few toys and those they had were almost as crude as those of the pioneer children—toys made of corn-cobs and pieces of wood. Children were glad to have an old coffee pot to pull on a string. There was no money for toys.

Farther inland men turned to the forests where they cut cordwood and railroad ties. These were carried to the heads of the rivers and loaded on vessels bound for Baltimore, Philadelphia or Norfolk.

Men then did any sort of work where they could make an honest dollar and still stay in the Northern Neck. It was rugged but they managed to survive.

As things began to ease up, they picked up some of the old sports again—horse-racing, fox-hunting and jousting. The men were intensely interested in politics.

Court Day was one of the biggest events for the men in those days. These were colorful occasions, with the hundreds of people gathered together, horses tied to the rails and ox-carts, stallions and hucksters all milling about the green. This was an opportunity for making a little cash. There was a man at Heathsville, at one time, who made a specialty of "cent cakes" on Court Days. These were of especial interest to little boys who came with their fathers. The cakes were big round and flat and had one raisin in the center of each. Negro women cooked oyster stews in the open and served them on tables improvised from dry-goods boxes and covered with clean sheets. Bars were in full swing, brass knucks, pistols and knives glinted here and there. There were many fights, or tests of prowess. It was often late at night when the revelers, or perhaps their horses, found the way home over rough country roads.

The women had less exciting pleasures, such as quilting parties, "spending the day" with a neighbor, and church socials.

The colonial pattern of living and way of speech lingered on until the beginning of the twentieth century. Tradition tells of a wedding feast as late as 1872 where roast suckling pig with an apple in its mouth, conical sugar loaves and butter sculptured in the form of Solomon's Temple were featured. The flavor of seventeenth century England still lingered in the Northern Neck at that time.

The marriages between the families of the Neck were endless and thus the Anglo-Saxon strain remained pure in the region.

SPEECH

THE EARLY population in the Northern Neck were mostly from London and the surrounding counties where the classic English language of Shakespeare was spoken.

There is evidence that the speech of the people of the Northern Neck had from early days little of the provincial or dialectal about it.

Until the early part of the twentieth century such Shakespearean expressions as, "wrack upon ruin" and "all mommicked up," were commonly used in the Neck. The now archaic word mommick meant to mutilate. The play of the double noun was also frequently heard until a late date—men-folks, women-folks, baby-child, man-child, boy-man, and so on.

Many of the indentured servants came to the Northern Neck from Warwickshire and their manner of speech was added to the region, for instance: off sporting, or frolicking, meant, having a good time; traipsing about, meant, off walking about; make the fire, meant, kindle the fire, and peart, meant, lively.

The constant reading of the Bible also helped to keep the speech pure and simple.

SHOPPING TRIPS

AFTER THE WAR the shopping trips to Baltimore were resumed, but with a difference. There were few men in the Neck now and the women had changed. Hardened by sorrow and privations they were now able to face realities. There were many widows.

They gathered their children together, and all the produce they could assemble, and traveled to town on the sailing vessel of some older relative or neighbor who might be taking a cargo of oysters or cordwood to market.

When they arrived in Baltimore, usually in the very early morning, the sleepy children must be aroused and dressed. Pantalettes,* so painstakingly laundered before leaving home, were now dirty and wrinkled. With the bedraggled children, coops of quacking ducks and hissing geese, crates of eggs and firkins of lard and butter, the brave women finally landed on the dock and made their way up Light Street to the commission merchants, who would buy their produce. After disposing of their business they went to the stores to shop for necessities to carry home to the Northern Neck.

*Pantalettes were generally worn about 1830-50. The fact that they were still being worn by children of the Northern Neck is probably due to the isolated location of this peninsula.

MENHADEN

IN THEIR VOYAGE of discovery in the Chesapeake Captain John Smith and his companions found schools of fish agitating the surface of the water. The written accounts of these men state that the fish were so thick that they attempted to dip them up in a frying-pan but it proved to be "not a good instrument to catch fish with."

These fish are believed to have been menhaden, known to naturalists as brevoortia. This ordinary looking fish was destined to change the course of history in the lower Northern Neck.

The Indian names for this species, munnawhatteaug (corrupted to menhaden), and pauhagen (pogy), literally means fertilizer— "fish that enriches the earth." The Indians were accustomed to employ this species, with others of the herring tribe, in enriching their cornfields. They showed the white men how to make their corn grow by putting two dead fish in each hill of corn.

The following passage written by Thomas Morton in 1632 shows the use of fish as fertilizer in Virginia at that time: "There is a fish at the spring of the yeare that passe up the rivers to spawn in the ponds, & are taken in such multitudes that the inhabitants fertilize their grounds with them."

The menhaden was called alewife by the Virginia colonists because of its resemblance to the allied species known by that name in England. Alewife was corrupted to old-wife and ell-wife. It has been said that the half-grown menhaden were called bug-fish by Virginia negroes in early days because they believed them to have been produced from insects. This superstition probably arose from the fact that a parasitic crustacean, known to watermen as "a fish louse," was often found clinging to the roof of the menhaden's mouth.

The menhaden had many other popular names, among them: porgie, bony-fish, poggie, mossbunker, greentail, bunker, yellowtail, white-fish, fat back, and another Indian name, chebog. "Mossbunker" is a relic of the Dutch Colony at New Amsterdam. It was in use there as early as 1661, probably a corruption of their Dutch word, *marsbancker*.

It is said that the Indians did not like to eat menhaden because of their oily content. Many years later it was learned that this fish was also rich in minerals. Early settlers ate them, salted them for winter use, and fed them to the stock.

Catesby wrote, 1731-1742, concerning a fish called a "Fatback: It is an excellent Sweet Fish, and so excessive fat that Butter is never used in frying. At certain Seasons and Places there are infinite Numbers of these Fish caught, and are much esteemed by the Inhabitants for their Delicacy."

Menhaden were used to some extent as a food by watermen for many years but it does not appear probable that they were ever extensively used for food except in seasons of scarcity. They were used for many years to feed stock.

Menhaden were used at an early date as a fertilizer all along the Atlantic coast. In 1792 a paper published in New York gave directions concerning the use of fish as a fertilizer: "Experiments made by using the fish called menhaden or mossbankers as a manure have succeeded beyond all expectation. In dunging corn in the holes, put two in a hill on any kind of soil where corn will grow, and you will have a good crop. Put them on a piece of poor loamy land and by their putrefaction they so enrich the land that you may mow about two tons per acre." About eight or ten thousand fish to the acre was considered about the right amount.

Farmers also spread the fish "head to tail" in a plowed furrow and covered them with earth. They also mixed the fish with earth in a compost.

It seems that the possibilities of making use of the fish oil were not considered at this time. Whale oil was still being used. It was not until about 1850 that the value of menhaden oil was recognized.

The following statement of Eben B. Phillips, a Boston oil merchant, dated 1874, throws some light on the beginning of the use of menhaden oil: "In about 1850 I was in the oil business in Boston. An elderly lady by the name of Bartlett, from Bluehill, Maine, came to my store with a sample of oil which she had skimmed from a kettle in boiling menhaden for her hens. She told me the fish were abundant all summer near the shore. I told her I would give her $11 per barrel for all she would produce. Her husband and sons made 13 barrels the first year. The fish then were caught in gill-nets. The following year they made 100 barrels. From that time and from that circumstance has grown a business as extensive as I have represented."

Mr. Phillips then furnished nets, and large kettles, which they set up out-of-doors in brick frames, for trying out the fish. It was thought that much oil was thrown away with the refuse fish or scrap, and the idea of pressing this scrap was suggested. At first this was accomplished by pressing it in a common iron kettle with a heavy cover and a long beam for a lever. Later it was weighted down by heavy rocks, in barrels and tubs perforated with auger holes. Mr. Phillips then fitted out some fifty parties on the coast of Maine with presses of the model known as the screw and lever press.

Others claim to have manufactured menhaden oil at about the same time. "At that time," according to another statement from Rhode Island, "there were some few whalemen's try-pots used by other parties in boiling the fish in water and making a very imperfect oil and scrap."

Tradition says that at first some of the oil merchants mixed the menhaden oil with whale oil, or sold it outright as whale oil. It was used for tanning hides, currying, in paint, in soap, for "smearing sheep" and for other things.

After the value of menhaden oil was recognized many makeshift menhaden fish factories were established along the coast of Maine and elsewhere on the northern coast. It was much easier for the whaling men to go offshore a few miles, return with a boat-load of fish and spend the night at home.

By the end of the Civil War the menhaden catch along the coast of Maine was beginning to drop off.

In 1866 a party of New Englanders visiting the Chesapeake found menhaden in almost incredible quantities—"they were so thick that for 25 miles along the shore there was a solid flip-flap of the northward swimming fish." One member of the party is said to have jumped into the water and with a dip-net thrown bushels of fish upon the beach.

In December, 1866, the floating fish-factory, *Ranger* of 1,500 tons, hailing from Greenport, N. Y., came to Virginia. She was equipped to cook fish and extract oil on board. Tradition says that on these first floating factories the scrap was thrown overboard. The *Ranger* remained in Virginia only about eleven days during that year but returned each of the two succeeding years.

In the late summer of 1867, Elijah W. Reed, of Sedgwick, Maine, loaded his kettles and presses on two small sailing vessels, the *Two Brothers* and the *A. F. Powers*, and sailed for Virginia. He landed first at Back River, then moved up the Chesapeake and operated his kettles and presses on the Bay shore between the Little Wicomico and the Great Wicomico Rivers. The spot was in Northumberland County and was later known as Ketchum's Camp.

That winter the New Englander moved into Cockrell's Creek, in the same county. It was a sheltered harbor near the mouth of the Bay with deep water running close to the shore. He built there, at Point Pleasant, the first menhaden plant on the Chesapeake Bay.

From 1868 factories were built from time to time by local people, and others, on points in Cockrell's Creek, and at other points on various inlets of the Chesapeake, and on Tangier Island.

These early factories were known as "kettle-factories." The kettles were brought down the Bay from Baltimore. The menhaden products, oil and green scrap in bulk, were carried back to the same city by sailing vessels. The scrap, or guano, was sold both in the city market and locally for fertilizer.

These first Virginia fish factories were crude affairs consisting of five or six iron kettles, each with a capacity of one hundred or more gallons. They were established on a brick firebox with a chimney in the center of the unit and openings at both ends for firing. This was protected by a rough frame shelter with a slab-pine roof. This was a typical factory, though the number of kettles varied.

Cordwood was used for fuel. Scows with sails were sent to the heads of the rivers where wood was brought down from "the forest" and loaded on them.

At the temporary Ketchum's Camp factory the fish were pulled up on the shore in haul seines. After that they were caught in purse seines operated from sailing vessels.

It had been found, as previously explained, that by cooking the fish much more oil could be extracted. The fish were boiled and then dipped out with dip-nets and put in what was called a press. Burlap was then placed over the mass of fish, and then boards on top of that. The boards were then pulled down tight with a screw-jack.

After the oil and water had been pressed out, the residue of fish was spread out on the wharf in the sun to dry. To hasten this process the mass was turned over and over by men with pitchforks. Acid was sprayed on the "green scrap" to kill the maggots. It usually took about a week to change the menhaden from the raw state into oil and guano.

The following government report is probably the first of the menhaden industry of the Chesapeake and its tributaries. It is dated 1869.

Men employed on vessels fishing.....................12
Vessels employed 4
Men employed making guano......................... 9
Fish taken 3,000,000
Oil made ....200 bbls.
Guano made ....300 tons

In 1873 Reed's factory on Point Pleasant burned. The next year he built another factory on another point on Cockrell's Creek on a spot where a windmill for grinding corn had been previously located. This location was known as Windmill Point. Later the village of Reedville grew up on this small peninsula.

By 1874 the manufacture of menhaden oil and guano had become identified as one of the important industries of this country. The annual yield of the menhaden oil now exceeded the whale oil (from American fisheries) by about 200,000 gallons.

By 1878 the menhaden industry of the Chesapeake area had grown considerably according to the government report of that year:

Men employed on vessels fishing.....................286
Vessels employed fishing............................ 78
Men employed on shore..............................201
Fish taken 118,309,200
Gallons of oil made.............................234,168
Tons of guano..................................10,832

The next advancement in the industry came when steam cooking superseded the use of the kettles. The first steam factory in Virginia was built by Elijah Reed in 1879. The first fishing steamer used in the business in the Chesapeake, *Starry Banner*, was purchased by him in Rhode Island. This steamer's capacity was one hundred and fifty thousand fish.

The menhaden fishing industry continued to grow and to advance with the times. It brought prosperity to the lower Northern Neck. Reedville became an important menhaden fishing center and fishing port.

Eventually menhaden became the biggest fishery in America.

THE OLD STONE PILE

ABOUT 1868 the tower lighthouse on Smith Point was condemned by the government as unfit for use. At that time a new lighthouse of the screw pile type was built two and one-half miles offshore from Smith Point.

After the tower was condemned the keeper's house on the government reservation was rented to various tenants. In summer the Point became a social center for the neighborhood. Carriages, road-carts, and perhaps even ox-carts tied up at Tranquility, the nearest farmhouse, on a Sunday afternoon, and their occupants strolled up the beach with their picnic baskets.

The breakwater some distance out in the water from Smith Point was a favorite fishing spot, but the high point of any trip there in those days was a climb to the top of the condemned tower. The long, full skirts of the ladies of that era were hard to maneuver up the narrow spiral stairway.

The tower finally became too dangerous to enter. During an easterly storm in the spring of 1889 it crumbled in the night, so gently that the people living in the keeper's house didn't hear it fall.

The sandstone blocks lay there for many years and later generations knew them as "the old stone pile." Each year the sea took its toll of the Point until the land between the tower and the water, where "ten rows of corn" had once grown, finally disappeared completely. And then "the old stone pile" was swallowed by the persistent sea.

The keeper's house gradually deteriorated and then it too was claimed by the sea. For many years after, people of the region came at low tide and loaded their ox-carts and wagons with the stones and bricks. The stones were used for foundations of buildings and the bricks were used to line wells. Only the burial ground was left at Smith Point. There on the bank, "under the wide and starry sky," rest some of the early keepers of the light.

KEEPERS OF THE LIGHT

WHEN THE NEW lighthouse was built two-and-one-half miles offshore from Smith Point in 1868, it was manned by only two men. Shore leave or need for provisions meant a trip for one man in a small open sail boat, weather permitting, and a lonely watch for the man left behind.

If a keeper became ill he had to make out as best he could with a chest of medicine and a doctor's book. He had to be his own cook and housekeeper. Due to lack of refrigeration the lighthouse diet became monotonous, although seafood was a help. Kerosene for the lamps and firewood was brought by a lighthouse tender. The lonely keepers of the light often kept pets. Canaries and parrots made good companions, but dogs sickened and died.

The lighthouse keeper had to be a machinist, carpenter and painter, in order to keep the lighthouse in working order. Stamina was perhaps the quality most needed in a keeper of those days. The bell had to be wound up like a clock every half hour and kept ringing during storm and fog. There were instances when the keeper sometimes stayed awake for eight days and eight nights. But he kept the bell ringing, and without the aid of alcoholic drink.

A lighthouse keeper had to be a waterman, and that meant a man who had been born and bred in the region. Many lives were saved by these early lighthouse keepers. Winters were colder then. In those days the Bay often froze over like a millpond.

The winter of 1895 was a cold winter. The Bay was frozen, and, to make matters worse, in February there was a blizzard that went howling through the region of Smith Point. Both keepers were on duty that night when part of the ice started moving. They felt it hit the lighthouse and they loaded whatever they could find on a boat and somehow they got out alive. Before they started away the lighthouse had gone to pieces. They took turns pushing the boat over the ice toward land. That was a long two-and-a-half miles, but they made it.

They were welcomed by people on shore who waited, with lanterns, to serve them hot coffee and food. They had seen the light go out and had been anxiously waiting, as there was nothing that they could do to help. The lighthouse keepers were taken into warm homes that night. Later they found that the ice had carried the remains of the lighthouse six miles away from its foundation.

Years later one of the keepers who had been on Smith Point lighthouse that night said: "Things like that happened all the time then."

A light-ship was stationed at Smith Point until another lighthouse could be built. The new lighthouse was built on a cylindrical pier of metal. The tower was square and made of brick, with an octagonal dwelling. It was completed in 1897.

THE HEADLESS DOG

IN THOSE DAYS between the end of the Civil War and the turn of the century, life in the Northern Neck still followed the old Southern pattern, but in a diminished way. War had destroyed all glamour and pared the design down to its skeleton. The planter had become a farmer, the mistress of the plantation a farmer's wife. An independent way of life remained, however. Each farm was a self-sustaining unit, though besides the occasional day hands there were usually only a colored girl who helped with the housework, laundry and dairy and a colored boy who tended the stock, did the chores and worked in the fields. The Boy and Girl, as they were always called, were regarded with affection, especially by the children.

"Evening-time," when work was over for the day, was something to be looked forward to by the children. They gobbled their suppers with a listening ear toward the soft murmur of voices in the kitchen, for they were anxious to hear the latest news about the Headless Dog, who prowled the by-roads, bottoms and graveyards of the Neck after dark.

As soon as permission was granted the youngsters to leave the supper table they would make a dash for the kitchen where the Boy and Girl sat at the big pine table lingering over their dessert. When pressed for the latest news of the Headless Dog they pretended an indifference and ignorance that was maddening. The children then began a breaking down process, made up of threats and cajolery, which they had cunningly developed from experience over a period of time.

Finally, the Boy would remember that he did "just catch a glimpse" of the Dog the night before when returning from the store. As he reached the bottom it seemed that the Dog appeared for an instant and faded before his eyes.

Bottoms, which were low places where creeks or ponds "made up" near the roads, seemed to be favorite haunts of the Headless Dog. This was possibly due to the mists which arose from the marshy places and made his appearances and disappearances quite easy, as well as dramatic.

Sometimes, when the Boy borrowed the horse and road-cart for a Sunday's visit to his people "up in the forest," he encountered the Dog near a graveyard. The sudden halt of the horse and the pointing of his ears were signals of the Dog's proximity. If you wished to see him, the certain way was to look at the space between the horse's ears, like sighting through a camera. You could always find him in that spot—"a great big dog with no haid a-tall." Further details as to the Dog's appearance were left to the imagination. When the horse lowered his ears and began to move cautiously forward, you knew that the Dog was continuing his journey to some other graveyard or bottom and it was safe to proceed.

The Boy's meetings with the Dog were much more exciting than the Girl's, maybe because she did not travel very much at night. Sometimes she would see him at the "edge of dark," usually just before or shortly after the death of some local person. Her stories were always gruesomely connected with death.

While these tales were spinning out in the kitchen where the fire burned low in the iron range, the children, who had heard them a hundred times before, huddled closer and closer together. Their eyes shone round and bright, and, if the flame of the lamp flickered, they jumped and drew away from dark corners. When the Girl had washed and dried the last dish and set the morning rolls to rise behind the stove, the Boy took his hat from its peg and prepared to depart for his nightly visit to the store.

Hours later the children, snug in their beds, were aroused by music. In that delicious stage between sleep and waking they lay half-dreaming and unaware that they were listening to some unwritten bars of a blues melody that were being created and lost to posterity on the still night air. They only knew that the perfect notes were being produced by the Boy on his jew's-harp and accompanied by the yeast powder bottles, mouth organs and guitars of his companions, the Nehemiahs, Daniels and Zechariahs of the neighboring farms. (Bible names were popular then.)

The children knew, too, that their friends were wending their leisurely way home from the store where the nightly session was over. Their interest was not in music, but in the hope that the Boy had met with adventure in that marshy, ferny and woodsy-smelling place known as the bottom.

The lower section of the Neck was evidently a favored land at that time. Besides being a hideout for the Headless Dog, a white mule and a Headless Man, it also furnished a routine route for another interesting Dog. This Dog had a head. Furthermore, the head was punctuated by glaring red eyes. According to good authority, he was as big as a calf, brown in color except about the mouth which was patched with gray. His neck was encircled with a chain which dragged on the ground and rattled as he moved. He was a methodical animal and traveled always at night, and only between Cockrell's Neck and Heathsville, and only before or after the death of some local person. Instead of appearing suddenly and fading out like the Headless Dog, he had a disconcerting habit of trailing moving vehicles.

After motor vehicles became numerous the Headless Dog was seen no more, but the Cockrell's Neck Dog was still seen occasionally for some time after that. His systematic ways probably kept him going longer. Some said that he was not brown but black, and if you struck at him with a whip it went clear through him.

PART IV

Conclusion

THE ANCIENT MANSION SEATS

VISITORS TO THE Northern Neck often ask the question: "Where are the old houses?"

Most of the remaining ancient seats are off the beaten path due to the fact that when they were built the rivers, creeks and bays were the highways.

Many of the old houses burned, either accidentally or during the wars. Others fell into decay during the years of depression following the Civil War, and after traffic by boat was discontinued.

Some of the early homes were remodeled beyond recognition, or torn down to give way for new buildings. Some were bought by persons of wealth and faithfully restored by them. A few of the old seats are still owned and lived in by descendants of the original planters who built them.

Portions of some of the old mansions of the Northern Neck found their way into museums. An instance of this is a room from Marmion, a Fitzhugh home of King George County. The Marmion Room in the American Wing of the Metropolitan Museum of Art, New York City, is described in the museum literature as follows: "Of all the rooms we have gathered together, possibly the most extraordinary and impressive is the one from Marmion."

Stratford Hall in Westmoreland County had been lost to the Lee family in 1820. Many years later, in 1929, the Robert E. Lee Memorial Foundation, Incorporated, was organized to acquire, restore, furnish and preserve the Stratford plantation. After a great deal of dedicated effort by a great many people this goal was finally achieved. Under the painstaking guidance of the ladies of the Foundation Thomas Lee's mansion was restored to its original splendor. The garden was restored by the Garden Club of Virginia.

Stratford Hall and plantation is now a restored working colonial plantation open to the public. The restored mill grinds meal. Virginia cured hams hang in the smoke-house, and jellies and preserves are made by old recipes.

Thoroughbreds stand again in the stables. The fields are worked by modern machinery, but the 1,164-acre estate is run as nearly as possible as it was in the days of Thomas Lee.

Stratford Hall is pronounced "of prime architectural importance" by the American Institute of Architects.

George Washington referred to his birthplace as "the Popes Creek home" or the "ancient mansion seat in Westmoreland County."

The name Wakefield seems to have been given the plantation about 1773 by the Washington heir who lived there at that time. The name is said to have been suggested by Goldsmith's "Vicar of Wakefield."

The original house at Popes Creek was destroyed by fire. It is believed to have burned on Christmas Day, 1779.

Thirty-six years passed before the birthsite of George Washington was marked and then it was only by a simple stone which bore an inscription.

In 1881 Congress authorized the construction of a monument to mark the birthsite, but fifteen years passed before the granite shaft was erected.

A group of patriotic women were not satisfied. They dreamed of the plantation as it was when George Washington was born, and they planned to bring it alive again. In 1923, under the leadership of Mrs. Josephine Wheelright Rust, they organized the Wakefield National Memorial Association. Their goal was to restore the Wakefield plantation and make it a shrine for all people.

The Association acquired land which adjoined Government property, and Mr. John D. Rockefeller, Jr., purchased additional acreage of the old Wakefield plantation and transferred it to the Federal Government.

An act of Congress granted the Association authority to erect a building on the birthsite "as nearly as may be practicable, of the house in which George Washington was born."

By act of Congress, January 23, 1930, the 394.47 acres owned by the Federal Government was designated as George Washington Birthplace National Monument to be administered by the National Park Service of the United States Department of the Interior.

The dream of the patriotic women came true when the new Memorial Mansion was erected in 1930-31. It was immediately opened to the public.

Reliable information concerning the appearance of the original house could not be found, therefore the house that was erected represents a typical Virginia plantation house of the eighteenth century.

In the old-fashioned garden established near the Memorial Mansion there is a sundial bearing this inscription:

> "A place of rose and thyme and scented earth—
> A place the world forgot,
> But here a matchless flower came to birth,
> Time paused and blessed the spot."

Wakefield plantation is a memorial to the many people who had a part in saving it and bringing it to life again, as well as a monument to George Washington.

APPENDIX

NORTHERN NECK BURGESSES (JAMESTOWN ASSEMBLIES)

Assembly of October, 1644
Northumberland County..........Capt. Fr. Poythers, Jo. Trussell

Burgesses of the Assembly, convened November 20, 1645
Northumberland County.........................John Matrum

Assembly of 1651
Northumberland County...........................Richard Lee

Members of Assembly, convened April 26, 1652
Northumberland County..........John Mottram, George Fletcher
Lancaster County ....Francis Willis

Members of Assembly, November, 1652
Lancaster County..............Capt. H'y Fleet, Wm. Underwood

Assembly convened July 5, 1653
Lancaster County...........Capt. M. Fantleroy, William Hackett
Northumberland County......Lt. Col. Fletcher, Walter Broadhurst

Assembly convened November 20, 1654
Lancaster County....................John Carter, James Bagnall
Northumberland County..........................John Trussell
Westmoreland County.............John Holland, Alex. Baynham

Burgesses, March 13, 1657-8
Lancaster County......Col. John Carter (a member of the Council)
Northumberland County..Peter Montague, John Hanie, Peter Knight

Burgesses, March, 1658-9
Lancaster County................Col. John Carter, Henry Corbin
Northumberland County.........................Geo. Coleclough

Assembly of March, 1659-60
Lancaster County.....Col. John Carter, John Curtis, Henry Corbin
Northumberland County.....................Capt. Peter Ashton
Westmoreland County.......................Capt. Tho's Foulke

Burgesses in Assembly, September, 1663

Northumberland County.........................Wm. Presley
Westmoreland County.......................Col. Gerard Fowke
Lancaster County...............................Raleigh Frances

Assembly convened October, 1666

Lancaster County..............................Raleigh Traverse
Westmoreland County....Col. Nich. Spencer, Col. John Washington
Northumberland County....................Mr. William Presley

May 4, 1683

Nich. Spencer and Jos. Bridger were Councillors at this time.

(Compiled from old manuscripts and documents. This list is probably incomplete.)

COUNTIES

The formation of the counties of the Northern Neck took place as follows:

Northumberland, 1648; Lancaster, 1651; Westmoreland, 1653; Stafford, 1664; Richmond, 1692; King George, 1721.

The names of these counties reflect the English origin of the first white settlers.

NATIVE SONS (Northern Neck of Virginia)

George Washington, First President of the United States; "First in war, first in peace, and first in the hearts of his countrymen." (These famous words were written by General Henry (Light-Horse Harry) Lee.

James Madison, Fourth President of the United States, and Father of the Constitution.

James Monroe, Fifth President of the United States, and author of the Monroe Doctrine.

Signers of the Declaration of Independence: Richard Henry Lee, and Francis Lightfoot Lee.

General Robert Edward Lee: Leader of the Confederate forces in the Civil War.

Hall of Fame for Great Americans: George Washington, James Madison, James Monroe, Robert Edward Lee.

SOURCES

PART I—SEVENTEENTH CENTURY

INDIANS AND EARLY EXPLORERS
Virginia, Its History and Antiquities, published about 1840.
Travels and Works of Capt. John Smith, edited by Arber.
The Life of Capt. John Smith, by W. Gilmore Simms, 1846.
History of Virginia, by Mary Tucker Magill, 1888.
History of Virginia, by R. B. Smithey, 1898.
A History of the United States, by Franklin L. Riley, 1910.

CAPTAIN JOHN SMITH
Travels and Works of Capt. John Smith, edited by Arber.
The Life of Capt. John Smith, by W. Gilmore Simms, 1846.
Arrival of the First Permanent English Settlers Jamestown, by G. B. Coale, 1950.

POWHATAN'S EMPIRE
Bureau of American Ethnology, Smithsonian Institution, Washington, D. C.
Virginia, Its History and Antiquities, 1840.
Beverley's *History of Virginia*.
Virginia, Virginia Writer's Project, 1940.

CAPTAIN SMITH VISITS THE NECK
Travels and Works of Capt. John Smith, edited by Arber.
The Life of Capt. John Smith, by W. Gilmore Simms, 1846.
Virginia, Its History and Antiquities, published about 1840.

"A PLAINE WILDERNES"
Travels and Works of Capt. John Smith, edited by Arber.
Virginia, Its History and Antiquities, published about 1840.

"WILD BEASTES"
Travels and Works of Capt. John Smith, edited by Arber.
Clayton's *Virginia*, p. 37, Force's *Historical Tracts*, Vol. III.
Writings of Ralph Hamor, William Strachey and other early writers.

"BIRDS TO VS UNKNOWNE"
Travels and Works of Capt. John Smith, edited by Arber.
The Cradle of the Republic, by Lyon G. Tyler.
Economic History of Virginia in the 17th Century, by P. A. Bruce, Vol. I.
Writings of: William Strachey, Thomas Hariot, Ralph Hamor, Robert Beverley, and other early writers.

THE NOMINIES
Virginia, Virginia Writers' Project, 1940.
Bureau of American Enthnology, Smithsonian Institution, Washington.
Travels and Works of Capt. John Smith, edited by Arber.
Economic History of Virginia in the 17th Century, by P. A. Bruce, Vol. I.
Our Republic, Riley, Chandler, Hamilton, 1910.
History of Virginia, Magill, 1888.
Life of Capt. John Smith, by W. Gilmore Simms, published 1846.
Indians in Seventeenth-Century Virginia, by Ben C. McCary, 1957.

THE DISCOVERERS

Life of Capt. John Smith, by W. Gilmore Simms, published 1846.
Travels and Works of Capt. John Smith, edited by Arber.
Virginia, Its History and Antiquities, published about 1840.
History of Virginia, by R. B. Smithey, published 1898.

THE RIVER OF SWANS

Travels and Works of Capt. John Smith, edited by Arber.
Writings of Dr. Walter Russell and Anas Todkill.
Life of Capt. John Smith, by W. Gilmore Simms, published 1846.
Tidewater Virginia, by Paul Wilstach, published 1929.

MOTHER OF WATERS

Travels and Works of Capt. John Smith, edited by Arber.
Writings of Dr. Walter Russell and Anas Todkill.
Life of Capt. John Smith, by W. Gilmore Simms, published 1846.
Economic History of Virginia in the 17th Century, by Bruce, Vol. I.
Tobacco Coast, by A. P. Middleton, Ph. D.
Chesapeake Bay, by M. V. Brewington.
"The Chesapeake's Million Years," by Harold A. Williams, in *Baltimore Sunday Magazine*, October 18, 1953.
Tidewater Virginia, by Paul Wilstach.
The Bay, by Gilbert Klingel.

QUICK-RISING-WATER

Travels and Works of Capt. John Smith, edited by Arber.
Life of Capt. John Smith, by W. Gilmore Simms, published 1846.
Virginia, Virginia Writers' Project, published 1940.
Tidewater Virginia, by Paul Wilstach.

HENRY AND POCAHONTAS
HENRY AND KING PATOWMEKE
HENRY'S RELATION
BETRAYED

Henry Spelman's, *Relation of Virginia*, a manuscript first published in London, in 1872.
Virginia Carolorum, by Edward D. Neill, pp. 52-53.
Life of Capt. John Smith, by W. Gilmore Simms, published 1846.
History of Virginia, by Mary Tucker Magill, published 1888.
Travels and Works of Capt. John Smith, edited by Arber.
Tidewater Virginia, by Paul Wilstach, published 1929.
Virginia, Its History and Antiquities, published about 1840.
Virginia, Virginia Writers' Project, published 1940.
"The Virginia Indian Trade to 1673," by A. J. Morrison. *William & Mary College Quarterly*, 2nd Series, vi.
The Genesis of the United States, by Alexander Brown, Vol. 2, pp. 1020-1021.
Howes' Abridgment.
Observations of William Simmons, Doctor of Divinity, 1609.
Writings of William Box, 1610.
Narratives of Early Virginia, by Lyon G. Tyler.
Indians in Seventeenth-Century Virginia, by Ben C. McCary, 1957.

KIDNAPPED

Smith's Generall Historie, Book IV.
State Historical Markers of Virginia, Sixth Edition, 1948, p. 16.

A Story of the Historic Northern Neck of Virginia

Life of Capt. John Smith, by W. Gilmore Simms, published 1846.
History of Virginia, by Mary Tucker Magill, published 1888.

THE INDIAN TRADER (*also* FLEET'S POINT)

Virginia Carolorum, by Edward D. Neill, p. 238.
Cavaliers and Pioneers, by Nell M. Nugent.
"The Money of Colonial Virginia." *Virginia Magazine of History and Biography,* Vol. 51, pp. 36-54, January, 1943, by Mrs. Philip W. Hiden.
The Story of Virginia's First Century, by Mary Newton Stanard.
Tidewater Virginia, by Paul Wilstach.
Chesapeake Bay, by M. V. Brewington.
Smith's Generall Historie, Book IV.
Henry Fleet's *Relation.*
"The Virginia Indian Trade to 1673," by A. J. Morrison. *William & Mary College Quarterly,* 2nd Series, vi.

A PETITION

Virginia Carolorum, by Edward D. Neill, p. 289.

FROM NORTH OF THE POTOMAC

Jamestown and St. Mary's, Buried Cities of Romance, by H. C. Forman, 1938.
"The Virginia Indian Trade to 1673," by A. J. Morrison. *William & Mary College Quarterly,* 2nd Series, vi.
Narratives of Early Virginia, by Lyon G. Tyler.
History of Virginia, by R. B. Smithey, 1898.
Our Republic, by Riley, Chandler & Hamilton, 1910.
"Roving Maryland's Cavalier Country," by William A. Kinney. *The National Geographic Magazine,* April, 1954.
"History of Northumberland County," by Lillian Anderson Hatton Metcalfe. *Northern Neck Historical Magazine,* December, 1951.
"Maryland Influence in the Northern Neck," by Henry Wright Newman. *Northern Neck of Virginia Historical Magazine,* December, 1954.

THE FIRST SETTLER

"Mottrom," *William and Mary Quarterly,* Vol. 17, p. 53. Archives of Maryland, Vol. IV, p. 269.
York County Records (Shallop).
Economic History of Virginia in the 17th Century, Vol. I, by P. A. Bruce.
Historic Dress in America, 1607-1800, by Elizabeth McClellan.
Tobacco Coast, by Arthur Pierce Middleton, Ph.D., published 1953.
Chesapeake Bay, by M. V. Brewington, published 1953.
Historic Northern Neck of Virginia, by H. Ragland Eubank, published 1934.
State Historical Markers of Virginia, Sixth Edition, 1948, p. 180.
"A Little Tour of Northumberland County," by Thomas Lomax Hunter, (published in the *Richmond Times-Dispatch,* date unknown).
"Northumberland, Mother County," by Thomas Lomax Hunter, (published in the *Richmond Times-Dispatch,* date unknown).
"History of Northumberland County," (From 1648 to War of Revolution), by Lillian Anderson Hatton Metcalfe. *Northern Neck Historical Magazine,* Vol. I, December, 1951.
History of Northumberland County, by Miss Lucy Brown Beale. (Pageant)
"Old Northumberland," by Elwood Street. (An article in the *Richmond Times-Dispatch,* April 19, 1942.)
Virginia Magazine, X, (402).
Northumberland County Records.
Tidewater Virginia, by Paul Wilstach, published 1929.

COAN HALL

Jamestown and St. Mary's, Buried Cities of Romance, Henry C. Forman, p. 33, 1938.
The Holy Bible, Genesis 2: 8-10, 19.
"Log Cabin or Frame," by Janet Foster Newton. *Antiques Magazine*, Nov. 1944.
1953, Williamsburg Antiques Forum, Theme: "European Influence on American Craftsmanship"; "Architecture Up to the Time of the Revolution." Speaker, Dr. Richard H. Howland, Chairman of the Art Department of Johns Hopkins University.
The Log Cabin Myth, by Harold R. Shurtleff.
The Homes of Our Ancestors, by R. T. H. Halsey and Elizabeth Tower, 1937.
A Treasury of Early American Homes, by Richard Pratt, published 1946.
"Notes on Imported Brick," by Charles E. Peterson. *Antiques Mag.*, July, 1952.
Glassmaking at Jamestown, by J. C. Harrington, published 1952.
"Roving Maryland's Cavalier Country," by William A. Kinney. *The National Geographic Magazine*, April, 1954.
Cradle of the Republic, by Lyon G. Tyler.
Economic History of Virginia in the 17th Century, by Philip A. Bruce.
Social Life of Virginia in the 17th Century, by Philip A. Bruce.
Home Life in Colonial Days, by Alice M. Earle.
"The Buttolph-Williams House," (In Wethersfield, Connecticut) by Frederic Palmer. *Antiques Magazine*, September, 1951.
"Hurstville," by Jennie Harding Cornelius, in *Northumberland Echo*, Heathsville, Va.
"Green Spring," by Leonora A. Wood, in *Richmond Times-Dispatch*, March 27, 1955.
Westmoreland County Records, 1661-1662.
"A Visit to Historic Old Marmion," by Joseph A. Billingsley, Jr., in *Richmond Times-Dispatch*, August 6, 1939.

NEIGHBORS

Maryland Archives (Vol. V: 204).
The Homes of Our Ancestors, by R. T. H. Halsey and Elizabeth Tower, 1937.
Historic Northern Neck of Virginia, by H. Ragland Eubank, 1934.
Home Life in Colonial Days, by Alice M. Earle.
Economic History of Virginia in the 17th Century, by Philip A. Bruce.

THE "KIDS"

Virginia Carolorum, by Edward D. Neill.
George Washington, Vol. I, by Dr. Douglas Southall Freeman.
Diary of John Harrower, (A journal by an indentured servant-teacher.)
"Spirits," from a treatise published in 1657, by Lionel Gatford, B. D., p. 278.
Economic History of Virginia in the 17th Century, by Philip A. Bruce.

INDIAN SERVANTS

Economic History of Virginia in the 17th Century, by Philip A. Bruce.
William Presley, by Miss Lucy Brown Beale.

MONEY

"The Money of Colonial Virginia," by Mrs. Philip W. Hiden. *Virginia Magazine of History and Biography*.
Northumberland County Records.
Old Virginia and Her Neighbors, by John Fiske, Vol. I.
Tobacco Coast, by A. P. Middleton, 1953.
James Madison, by Brant, p. 413.

A Story of the Historic Northern Neck of Virginia 223

A PARADISE DISCOVERED

Statutes at Large: Being a Collection of All the Laws of Virginia, edited by William Waller Hening. Richmond, 1809. 1619-60.
Jamestown and St. Mary's: Buried Cities of Romance, by Henry Chandlee Forman, Baltimore, 1938. (The Johns Hopkins Press.)

A VISIT TO JAMESTOWN

Jamestown and St. Mary's: Buried Cities of Romance, by Henry Chandlee Forman, Baltimore, 1938. (The Johns Hopkins Press.)
The Oldest Legislative Assembly in America and Its First Statehouse, by Charles E. Hatch, Jr. Washington: 1943.
The Cradle of the Republic, Jamestown and James River, by Lyon G. Tyler, Richmond, Va., 1906. The Hermitage Press, Inc.
Minutes of the Council and General Court of Virginia, 1622-1632, 1670-1676, edited by H. R. McIlwaine, Richmond, 1924, pp. 497-498.
Journals of the House of Burgesses of Virginia, 1619-1658-59, edited by H. R. McIlwaine, Richmond, 1915, p. 36.
Works of Capt. John Smith, edited by Arber.
Social Life of Virginia in the 17th Century, by Philip A. Bruce.
Historic Dress in America, 1607-1800, by Elizabeth McClellan.

FRANCES

Historic Northern Neck of Virginia, by H. Ragland Eubank, 1934.
"Old Northumberland," by Elwood Street. (An article in the *Richmond Times-Dispatch*, April 19, 1942.)
Northumberland County Record Book, 1652-1665, p. 47. ("cow calfe")
Historic Dress in America, 1607-1800, by Elizabeth McClellan.
Social Life of Virginia in the 17th Century, by Philip A. Bruce.
Economic History of Virginia in the 17th Century, by Philip A. Bruce.
Home Life in Colonial Days, by Alice M. Earle.
Child Life in Colonial Days, by Alice M. Earle.
The Homes of Our Ancestors, by R. T. H. Halsey and Elizabeth Tower, 1937.

FOREVER LOST

Hening's *Statutes at Large, 1619-60*.
Northern Neck Historical Magazine, December 1951, p. 6.

URSULA

William and Mary Quarterly, Vol. 17, p. 53. (Archives of Md., Vol. IV, p. 269.)
Social Life of Virginia in the 17th Century, by P. A. Bruce.
Home Life in Colonial Days, by Alice M. Earle.
Archives of Maryland, IV, 66.
Northumberland County Records, 1655-56, 1657-58.
Maryland Archives, Vol. V: 204.
Homes of Our Ancestors, by Halsey and Tower, 1937.
Records of Lancaster Co., Orig. Vol., 1690-1709, p. 21. (Ref. to leather coverlet.)
Records of Lancaster Co., Orig. Vol., 1674-1687, p. 77. (Wardrobe of F. Pritchard.)

THE YARD

George Washington, Vol. I, by D. S. Freeman.
Patrician and Plebeian in Virginia, by T. J. Wertenbaker.
Home Life in Colonial Days, by Alice M. Earle.
Beverley's *History of the Present State of Virginia*.

KITTAMAQUND

Genealogy of the Brent Family, compiled by W. B. Chilton, Washington, D. C.

Virginia Magazine of History & Biography, V. 12, July, 1904-April, 1905.
(Relatio Itineris, *Father Andrew White, S. J.*, pp. 74, 76 & 82.)
Maryland Historical Magazine, Vol. III, p. 30.
Landmarks of Old Prince William, p. 43.
Maryland Council Proceedings, Vol. 3, p. 403.
"Maryland Influence in the Northern Neck," by Harry Wright Newman, in *Northern Neck of Virginia Historical Magazine*, 1954.

THE GIFT

The First Patent of the Proprietary.
George Washington, V. I, by D. S. Freeman.
A History of the Valley of Virginia, by Samuel Kercheval, 1833.
Historic Dress in America, 1607-1800, by Elizabeth McClellan.
History of England, by Charlotte M. Yonge, 1879.
Our Republic, by Riley, Chandler & Hamilton, 1910.

THE CAVALIERS

Smithey's *History of Virginia*, 1915.
Tobacco Coast, by A. P. Middleton, 1953; pp. 8, 15, 16.
Cavaliers and Pioneers, V. I, by N. M. Nugent, published 1934.
The Story of Virginia's First Century, by Mary N. Stanard, 1928.
Old Virginia and Her Neighbours, by John Fiske, 1897, V. I. & V. II.
Patrician and Plebeian in Virginia, by Thos. J. Wertenbaker, 1910.
Social Life of Virginia in the 17th Century, by P. A. Bruce, 1927.
Virginia, Its History and Antiquities, published about 1840.
A History of the Valley of Virginia, by Samuel Kercheval, 1833.
"Cavaliers of the Northern Neck in the 17th Century," by Dr. J. E. Monohan, in *Northern Neck of Virginia Historical Magazine*, 1953.
Virginia, A History of the People, by John Esten Cooke, 1883, p. 227.
Historic Dress in America, 1607-1800, by Elizabeth McClellan.
George Washington, V. I, by D. S. Freeman.
William and Mary Quarterly, V. 17, p. 196.
"Perfect Description of Virginia," Force's *Tracts* II, No. viii.
Hammond's, *Leah and Rachel*.

"CHARLIE-OVER-THE-WATER"

Life of General R. E. Lee, by J. D. McCabe, Jr., 1866.
The Lees of Virginia, by Burton J. Hendrick, 1935. ("Introductio ad Latinam Blasoniam," by John Gibbon, 1629-1718. Lee's trip to Brussels.)
Stratford Hall and the Lees, by F. W. Alexander, 1912.
Old Virginia and Her Neighbours, John Fiske, 1897.
Virginia Carolorum, by E. D. Neill, 1886.
George Washington, V. I, by D. S. Freeman, pp. 452-453.

THE LEGACY

Old Virginia and Her Neighbours, V. II, p. 19, by John Fiske, 1897.
Stratford Hall and the Lees, by F. W. Alexander, 1912.
The Lees of Virginia, by Hendrick (B. J.).
Life of General R. E. Lee, by J. D. McCabe, Jr., 1866.
Historic Northern Neck of Virginia, by H. Ragland Eubank.

THE INDIAN DEED

Barons of the Potomack and the Rappahannock, by M. D. Conway.
Tidewater Virginia, by Paul Wilstach, p. 247.
Historic Northern Neck of Virginia, by H. Ragland Eubank, # 148.

A Story of the Historic Northern Neck of Virginia 225

A SUMMONS TO JAMESTOWN

Archives of Maryland, V. IV, 269.
The Oldest Legislative Assembly in America and Its First Statehouse, by Charles E. Hatch, Jr., Washington: 1943.
Historic Northern Neck of Virginia, by H. Ragland Eubank, 1934. (Northumberland County, Record Book, 1652-1665.)
Virginia Carolorum, by E. D. Neill, 1886.
Virginia and Its Antiquities, about 1840.
Magill's *History of Virginia*, 1888, p. 80.
"The Treaty of Jamestown, 1652," by W. H. Gaines, Jr., in *Virginia Cavalcade*, Spring, 1952.

THE OATH

"The Treaty of Jamestown, 1652," by W. H. Gaines, Jr., in *Virginia Cavalcade*, Spring, 1952.
"History of Northumberland County," by Lillian Anderson Hatton Metcalfe, *Northern Neck Historical Magazine*, December, 1951. (Northumberland Order Book, 1650-53.)
Virginia's First Century, by M. N. Stanard.

THE CHALLENGE

"Courthouses of Lancaster County, 1656-1950," Abstracted and Compiled from County Court Records by Elizabeth Combs Peirce, in *Northern Neck Historical Society Magazine*, December, 1951.
Social Life of Virginia in the 17th Century, by P. A. Bruce, pp. 250-252.
Virginia Magazine of History and Biography, V. II, p. 96.
Patrician and Plebeian, by T. J. Wertenbaker.
Lancaster County Records, V, 1652-56, p. 64.

TRADE

Cradle of the Republic, by Lyon G. Tyler.
Old Virginia and Her Neighbours, by John Fiske.
Economic History of the 17th Century, by P. A. Bruce.
Lancaster County Records, Original volume, 1654-1702.
Lancaster County Records, 1652-57.
Orders of Wm. Fitzhugh.
Records of Lancaster County, Original volume, 1682-1687.
Virginia Carolorum, by E. D. Neill, 1886.
Virginia and Its Antiquities, p. 67.

JOHN CARTER

Virginia's First Century, by M. N. Stanard.
The Chesapeake Bay Country, by Sampson Earle.
Robert Carter of Nomini Hall, by Louis Morton, 1945.
Journals of the House of Burgesses of Virginia, edited by H. R. McIlwaine (1619-1658/59, p. 94).
Economic History of Virginia, by P. A. Bruce, V. II, p. 124.
"Old Virginia Bottles," by Walter J. Sparks, in *Richmond Times-Dispatch Sunday Magazine*, 1938.

FLEET'S POINT (*see* chapter, The Indian Trader)

GEORGE MASON

The Life of George Mason, by Kate M. Rowland (1725-1792).
Westmoreland Court House Records, 1664.
Virginia Carolorum, by E. D. Neill, 1886, p. 344. From a MS. owned by the Virginia Historical Society.

Hening's *Statutes*, Vol. II (storehouse).
Hening's *Statutes*, Vol. III (boats).
Copy of an old paper of 1793, by Geo. Mason, of Lexington.
Westmoreland Court House and Virginia Land Registry Office (patent).
Hening's *Statutes*, Vol. II, 1661-2 (Indian trouble).

MARY CALVERT

Northumberland County Records, 1655.
"History of Northumberland County," by Lillian Anderson Hatton Metcalfe, in *Northern Neck Historical Magazine*, December 1951.
The Story of Virginia's First Century, by Mary Newton Stanard.
Social Life of Virginia in the 17th Century, by P. A. Bruce, 1927.

HE LIVED BRAVELY

William and Mary Quarterly, vol. 17, p. 53.
Social Life of Virginia in the 17th Century, by P. A. Bruce.
Surry County Records, vol. 1645-72, p. 246.
Lower Norfolk County Records, vol. 1686-95, f. p. 171.
York County Records, vol. 1675-84, p. 87.
Westmoreland County Records, vol. 1655-77, p. 186.
Virginia Historical and Genealogical Magazine, vol. X, p. 402.
Historic Northern Neck of Virginia, by H. Ragland Eubank, 1934.
Northumberland County Records, 1655-56.
George Washington, by D. S. Freeman (V. I, p. 4).

WITCHCRAFT

Northumberland County Records, 1656.
A History of the Valley of Virginia, by Samuel Kercheval, 1833, pp. 280-283.
William and Mary College Quarterly, vol. I, p. 127.

SEAHORSE OF LONDON

Virginia Carolorum (1625-85), by E. D. Neill, 1886.
George Washington, Vol. I, by D. S. Freeman.
1 Westmoreland Deeds and Wills, 88.
Westmoreland County Records.
Historic Northern Neck of Virginia, by H. Ragland Eubank.

"TENN MULBERRY TREES"

The Story of Virginia's First Century, by Mary Newton Stanard.
The Oldest Legislative Assembly in America and Its First Statehouse, by Charles E. Hatch, Jr., Washington: 1943.
Plants of Colonial Days, by Raymond L. Taylor, pub. 1952, Williamsburg, Va.
Child Life in Colonial Days, by Alice M. Earle.

ROADS

Old Virginia and Her Neighbours, Vol. II, by John Fiske.
The Mother of Washington and Her Times, by Sara Pryor.
George Washington, Vol. I, by D. S. Freeman.
Roads and Vehicles, William and Mary Quarterly, vol. III, pp. 37-43.
The Journal of Philip Vickers Fithian.
Cavaliers and Pioneers, by Nell M. Nugent, 1934.

MARKETS

Records, original volume 1652-1657, p. 214.
Cradle of the Republic, by Lyon G. Tyler.
Virginia Carolorum, by Edward D. Neill, 1886.

THE OLD DOMINION
Smithey's *History of Virginia*, published 1898.
Young Folks History of England, by Charlotte M. Yonge, published 1879.
The Story of Virginia's First Century, by Mary Newton Stanard.
Magill's *History of Virginia*, published 1888.

THE PROPRIETARY
George Washington, V. I, by D. S. Freeman.
Economic History of Virginia in the 17th Century, by P. A. Bruce.
A History of the Valley of Virginia, by Samuel Kercheval, published 1833.

A FIRST LADY OF JAMESTOWN
The Story of Virginia's First Century, by Mary Newton Stanard, p. 252.
Virginia Magazine, V. II, p. 33.
New England Hist. and Gen. Reg., Vol. XLV, p. 67.
Virginia Magazine, Vol. V, p. 257 (Anne Mottrom).
Historic Northern Neck of Virginia, by H. Ragland Eubank.
George Washington, Vol. I, by D. S. Freeman.
A collection of magazine and newspaper articles on early wedding customs.
Historic Dress in America, by Elizabeth McClellan.
"Cavaliers of the Northern Neck in the 17th Century," by Dr. John E. Monohan, in *Northern Neck of Virginia Historical Magazine*, December, 1953.
Home Life in Colonial Days, by Alice M. Earle.
Westmoreland County Records, Vol. 1665-77, folio p. 79 (Madam Spencer).
"Old Northumberland," by Elwood Street, in the *Richmond Times-Dispatch*, April 19, 1942.

PROCESSIONING
Home Life in Colonial Days, by Alice M. Earle.
George Washington, V. I, by Dr. Douglas S. Freeman.
Barons of the Potomac and the Rappahannock, by M. D. Conway.
James Madison, V. I, by Irving Brant, p. 44.

"THE BANQUETTING HOUSE"
9 Westmoreland Deeds and Wills, 344-45, March 30, 1670.
Historic Northern Neck of Virginia, by H. Ragland Eubank, Nos. 103, 106, 110, 112.
"The First Country Club in America," by Arnold Jones, in *Richmond Times-Dispatch*, 1953.
"A Mayflower Relic in Virginia," by Wm. M. E. Rachal, *Virginia Cavalcade*, Autumn, 1952.
Virginia Carolorum, by Edward D. Neill.
Maryland Archives, IV, 109, March 21, 1639.
Buried Cities, Jamestown and St. Mary's, by Henry Chandlee Forman.
The Lees of Virginia, by B. J. Hendrick.
"Revolutionary Suffragists," by Elizabeth Dabney Coleman, in *Virginia Cavalcade*, Autumn, 1953.

THE LAND AGENT
Westmoreland Orders, 1676-89, p. 529.
"Land Agents in Virginia," by G. H. S. King, in *Northern Neck of Virginia Historical Magazine*, December, 1954.
George Washington, Vol. I, D. S. Freeman, p. 458.
Economic History of Virginia in the 17th Century, by P. A. Bruce.

HANNA AND THE HORSESHOE
Northumberland County Records, 1671.

228 THE STRONGHOLD

William and Mary College Quarterly, Vol. 17, pp. 247-48.
A History of the Valley of Virginia, by Samuel Kercheval, 1833, pp. 280-83.
Historic Dress in America, 1607-1800, by Elizabeth McClellan.

MUSTER

Virginia County Records, 1689.
Virginia Historical Magazine, 1904-06, p. 191.
Minutes of the House of Burgesses, Sept. 30, 1696, B. T. Va., L 11.
Social Life of Virginia in the 17th Century, by P. A. Bruce.
Pirates and Buccaneers of the Atlantic Coast, by E. R. Snow.
Pirates of Colonial Virginia, by Lloyd H. Williams.

THE STORE

Virginia and Her Neighbours, Vol. II, p. 213, by John Fiske.
Virginia Carolorum, by Edward D. Neill, 1886.
Historic Dress in America, by Elizabeth McClellan.

THE WOLF-DRIVE

Northumberland County Records, Orders, September 16, 1691.
Clayton's *Virginia*.
Social Life of Virginia in the 17th Century, by P. A. Bruce.
Force's *Historical Tracts*, Vol. III.
Works of Capt. John Smith, edited by Arber, p. 60.
Beverley's *History of Virginia*.
Lancaster Court Records: 1677.
Northumberland County Record Book, 1666-78, p. 107.
The Chesapeake Bay Country, by Sampson Earle (McDonald Lee).

THE INDIANS AND ROBERT HEN

A History of the Valley of Virginia, by Samuel Kercheval, pp. 18-34.
The Story of Virginia's First Century, by Mary N. Stanard.
George Washington, Vol. I, by D. S. Freeman.
Virginia Carolorum, by Edward D. Neill, pp. 347-49.
Virginia and Her Neighbours, Vol. II, by John Fiske.
Spencer ii, 61, 80, 89, 111.
Descendants of Coll: Giles Brent, by Chester Horton Brent, 1946.
Force's *Tracts*, Vol. I, tract viii.
The Life of George Mason, by Kate M. Rowland.

THE ROYAL CAVALCADE and THE KING OF THE NORTHERN NECK

Robert Carter of Nomini Hall, by Louis Morton, Williamsburg, 1945.
Historic Northern Neck of Virginia, by H. Ragland Eubank.
The Chesapeake Bay Country, by Sampson Earle.
"Colonel Robert (King) Carter," by Samuel Bemiss, in *Northern Neck of Virginia Historical Magazine*, 1953.
"The Fruits of His Labor," by Samuel Bemiss, in *Virginia Cavalcade*, 1953.
Old Churches and Families of Virginia, by Meade, V. II, p. 116.
George Washington, V. I, by D. S. Freeman.
King Carter, the Man, by James Wharton.

KITH AND KIN

Robert Carter of Nomini Hall, by Louis Morton.
Historic Northern Neck of Virginia, by H. Ragland Eubank.
King Carter, the Man, by James Wharton.
Tidewater Virginia, by Paul Wilstach.
Baron of the Potomac and the Rappahannock, by M. D. Conway.

A Story of the Historic Northern Neck of Virginia   229

THE FIELDINGS
Virginia Historical Magazine, V. 12, pp. 98, 101, 215.
Robert Carter of Nomini Hall, by Louis Morton, p. 64.

PIRATES
"Pursuits of a Pirate," by Wm. H. Gaines, Jr., *Virginia Cavalcade*, Autumn, 1952.
"Treasure Trove," in *News from Home*, Autumn, 1955.
Pirates of Colonial Virginia, by Lloyd Haynes Williams, published 1937.
Tobacco Coast, by Arthur Pierce Middleton, Ph.D., 1953.
Chesapeake Bay, by M. V. Brewington, 1953, p. 198.
Virginia Carolorum, by Edward D. Neill.
The Mother of Washington and Her Times, by Sara Pryor.
Old Virginia and Her Neighbours, V. II, by John Fiske, p. 338.
Pirates and Buccaneers of the Atlantic Coast, by Edward Rowe Snow.
Records of Middlesex County, original volume, 1679-1694, p. 472.

CHRISTMAS AT COLONEL FITZHUGH'S
Description de la Virginie & Marilan dans L'Amérique, by Durand Du Dauphine.

INDIAN VISITORS
Description de la Virginie & Marilan dans L'Amérique, by Durand Du Dauphine.

HORSE RACING
The Social Life of Virginia in the 17th Century, by P. A. Bruce.
Minutes of House of Burgesses, Sept. 30, 1696. B. T., Va., Vol. LII.
Virginia Magazine of History and Biography, Vol. VIII, p. 130.
Northumberland County Records, Orders, January 17, 1693-4.
Northumberland County Records, Orders, August 22, 1695.
Westmoreland County Records, Vol. 1665-77, folio p. 211.
Westmoreland County Orders, January 11, 1687-8.
Westmoreland County Records, Orders, April 7, 1693.
Northumberland Orders of August 22, 1695.

MANUFACTURE
Home Life in Colonial Days, by Alice M. Earle.
Lancaster County Records, 1654-1702; 1674-78; 1690-1709.
Letters of Wm. Fitzhugh.
Virginia Carolorum, by Edward D. Neill.
Hening's *Statutes*, 1, 336, 337.

THE POTOMAC RANGERS
Hening's *Statutes*, Vol. II.
The Life of George Mason, Vol. I, by K. M. Rowland.
Virginia Calendar Papers, Vol. I, pp. 44, 60.
Ibid., p. xlvi.
James Madison, Vol. I, by Irving Brant, pp. 408-09.

PART II—*EIGHTEENTH CENTURY*

MURDERS IN STAFFORD
The Life of George Mason, by Kate M. Rowland.
Ibid., p. 69.
Letters of Col. George Mason, II.

FREE SCHOOLS

Cradle of the Republic, by Lyon G. Tyler.
History of Virginia, by Robert Beverley, 1703.
William and Mary College Quarterly, Vol. 17, pp. 244-247.
William and Mary College Quarterly, Vol. xvii, p. 188.
Social Life of Virginia in the 17th Century, by P. A. Bruce.
A History of Education in Virginia, by C. J. Heatwole.
William and Mary College Quarterly, Vol. XIII, Series 1, p. 158. (Landon Carter)

THE HOME IN THE FOREST

George Washington, V. I, by D. S. Freeman.
10 R. Lancaster Wills and Inventories, 88.
"Mary Ball Washington and Her Family," by Robert O. Norris, Jr., in *Northern Neck of Virginia Historical Magazine*, December, 1953.
Historic Northern Neck, by H. Ragland Eubank, Nos. 159, 161, 162.
Virginia Carolorum, by Edward D. Neill.

CHERRY POINT

George Washington, Vol. I, by D. S. Freeman.
"Mary Ball Washington and Her Family," by Robert O. Norris, Jr., in *Northern Neck of Virginia Historical Magazine*, December, 1953.
The Mother of Washington and Her Times, by Sara Pryor.
Historic Northern Neck, by H. Ragland Eubank.
"Will of Mary Hewes," found in Archives of Northumberland County, by Rev. G. W. Beale, published in *Virginia Historical Magazine.*
19 Northumberland Orders, 42.
Northumberland County Order Book, No. 6, p. 17.

SANDY POINT

George Washington, Vol. I, by D. S. Freeman.
"Mary Ball Washington and Her Family," by Robert O. Norris, Jr., in *Northern Neck of Virginia Historical Magazine*, December, 1953.
Historic Northern Neck, by H. Ragland Eubank, Nos. 115, 117, 121.
Will of Mary Hewes, (19 Northumberland Orders, 42).
Yeocomico Church, Virginia, W. P. A., 1946.
The Mother of Washington and Her Times, by Mrs. Roger A. Pryor, 1903.
Virginians at Home, by Edmund S. Morgan, 1952.
Westmoreland Deeds and Wills, 72. (Will of Samuel Bonum.)

AUGUSTINE

George Washington, Vol. I, by D. S. Freeman.
Historic Northern Neck, by H. Ragland Eubank.
Hening's *Statutes*, Vol. I, p. 160. (Fees)
"Mary Ball Washington and Her Family," by Robert O. Norris, Jr., in *Northern Neck of Virginia Historical Magazine*, December, 1953.
Wakefield, The Birthplace of Washington, by Paul Hudson, Museum Specialist National Park Service.
"Colonel George Eskridge," by Lucy Brown Beale, in *Northern Neck of Virginia Historical Magazine*, December, 1953.

POPES CREEK

19 Northumberland Orders, 42. (The will of Mary Hewes.)
George Washington, Vol. I, by D. S. Freeman.
Wakefield, The Birthplace of Washington, by Paul Hudson, Museum Specialist National Park Service.
Historic Northern Neck, by H. Ragland Eubank.

A Story of the Historic Northern Neck of Virginia   231

THE WAR PATH
James Madison, Vol. I, by Irving Brant.
The Life of George Mason (1725-1792), by Kate M. Rowland.
Colonial History of New York, Vol. V, pp. 655-677.
Virginia Historical Magazine, 1904-06.
James Mooney, *The Siouan Tribes of the East*, Smithsonian Institution: 1894.
Archeologic Investigation in James and Potomac Valleys, by Gerad Fowke, Smithsonian Institution: 1894.
George Washington, Vol. I, by D. S. Freeman.
Byrd Manuscripts, Vol. II, p. 262.

FALMOUTH
The Life of George Mason (1725-1792), by Kate M. Rowland.
Address of Rev. Phillip Slaughter before Virginia Historical Society, 1850.
In Tidewater Virginia, by Dora Chinn Jett, 1924.
A letter written by a Scotch girl while on a visit to Falmouth, published in *The Herald*, Fredericksburg, June 3, 1854.

BURNT HOUSE FIELD
Historic Northern Neck, by H. Ragland Eubank.
The Lees of Virginia, by B. J. Hendrick.
"President Thomas Lee of Virginia," by Wm. M. E. Rachal, in *Virginia Cavalcade*, Summer, 1953.
"Stratford Hall," by Henry F. and Katharine Pringle, *Holiday Magazine*, January, 1953.
"Carry Me Back to Old Virginia," Department of Conservation and Development of Virginia.

STRATFORD HALL
Stratford Hall and the Lees, by F. W. Alexander.
Historic Northern Neck, by H. Ragland Eubank.
"Stratford Hall," by Henry F. and Katharine Pringle, *Holiday Magazine*, January, 1953.
"President Thomas Lee of Virginia," by Wm. M. E. Rachal, in *Virginia Cavalcade*, Summer, 1953.
The Lees of Virginia, by Burton J. Hendrick.
A poem which described the early Stratford, by Carter Lee, brother of General R. E. Lee.
Virginia, W. P. A., 1946.
"The Summerhouse," a talk by Marcus Whiffen, Williamsburg Antiques Forum, February, 1956.

GEORGE WASHINGTON
George Washington, Vol. I, by Dr. Douglas S. Freeman.
"Wakefield, The Birthplace of Washington," by Paul Hudson, published in *The Commonwealth*, February, 1954.
Historic Northern Neck, by H. Ragland Eubank.

EPSEWASSON
George Washington, Vol. I, by Dr. Douglas S. Freeman.
Barons of the Potomac and the Rappahannock, by M. D. Conway.
Historic Northern Neck, by H. Ragland Eubank.

FERRY FARM
George Washington, Vol. I, by Dr. Douglas S. Freeman.
Historic Northern Neck, by H. Ragland Eubank.

Barons of the Potomac and the Rappahannock, by M. D. Conway.
King George Inventories, 1721-44, pp. 285-91.

FREDERICKSBURG

Act of establishing town of Fredericksburg.
Diary of Col. Wm. Byrd of Westover, 1732.
George Washington, Vol. I, by Dr. Douglas S. Freeman.
Barons of the Potomac and the Rappahannock, by M. M. Conway.
Tidewater Virginia, by Paul Wilstach.

SCHOOL DAYS

George Washington, Vol. I, by Dr. Douglas S. Freeman.
The Private Life of George Washington, by F. R. Bellamy.
Barons of the Potomac and the Rappahannock, by M. D. Conway.
Historic Northern Neck, by H. Ragland Eubank.
Wakefield, by Paul Hudson.

THE INDIANS

Old Virginia and Her Neighbours, Vol. II, by John Fiske.
Indians in Seventeenth-Century Virginia, by Ben C. McCary, 1957.
The Chesapeake Bay Country, by Sampson Earle.
Beverley's *History of Virginia*.

THE POW-WOW

"President Thomas Lee of Virginia," by Wm. M. E. Rachal, *Virginia Cavalcade*, Summer, 1953.
The Lees of Virginia, by Burton J. Hendrick.
A pamphlet: "A Treaty held at the town of Lancaster, Penn., with the Indians of the Six Nations, in June, 1744, Philadelphia; printed and sold by Benjamin Franklin at the New Printing Office near the Market, 1744."
A pamphlet describing the conference at Lancaster, published by William Parks, in Williamsburg, Va.
Virginia Magazine of History, XIII, 5.
James Madison, Vol. I, by Irving Brant, p. 46.

MOUNT VERNON

"To the Walls of Cartagena," by Wm. H. Gaines, Jr., *Virginia Cavalcade*, Winter, 1955.
George Washington, Vol. I, by Dr. Douglas S. Freeman.
Barons of the Potomac and the Rappahannock, by M. D. Conway.
The Private Life of George Washington, by F. R. Bellamy.

WASHINGTON WASHED HERE—

Spotsylvania Orders, 1749-55, p. 141.
George Washington, Vol. I, by Dr. Douglas S. Freeman.

THE ORDINARY

"Narrative of George Fisher (1750-55), His Voyage from London to Virginia," *William and Mary Quarterly*.

NELLY

Historic Northern Neck, by H. Ragland Eubank.
James Madison, by Irving Brant, 1941.
"James Madison, Father of the Constitution," by Wm. M. E. Rachal, *Virginia Cavalcade*, Winter, 1951.
"The Evening of Their Glory," by Wm. H. Gaines, Jr., *Virginia Cavalcade*, Summer, 1953.

MISS BETSY

George Washington, Vol. I, by D. S. Freeman.
Historic Northern Neck, by H. Ragland Eubank.
Virginia, W. P. A., 1946.
Barons of the Potomac and the Rappahannock, by M. D. Conway.

THE PROPRIETOR OF THE NORTHERN NECK

Virginia, Its History and Antiquities, circa 1840; pp. 235-36, 275.
A History of the Valley of Virginia, by Samuel Kercheval, 1833.
Smithey's *History of Virginia*, 1915; pp. 72-79.
Magill's *History of Virginia*, 1888.
Fairfax, by J. Esten Cooke, 1868.
Virginia, W. P. A., 1946.
State Historical Markers of Virginia, 1948.
George Washington, Vol. I, by D. S. Freeman.

THE MARSHALLS

The Life of John Marshall, by A. J. Beveridge.
Records of Westmoreland County, Deeds and Wills, viii, 1, 276.
Records of Westmoreland County, Deeds and Wills, xi, 419.
Will of John "of the forest," made April 1, 1752, probated May 26, 1752, and recorded June 22, 1752; Records of Westmoreland County, Deeds and Wills, xi, 419.
Autobiography, John Marshall.
Binney, in Dillon, iii, 287-88. (Description of J. Marshall.)
Will of Thomas Marshall, "carpenter," probated May 31, 1704; Records of Westmoreland County, Deeds and Wills, iii, 232, *et seq.*

THE LEEDSTOWN RESOLUTIONS

Fithian's *Journal*, pp. 84, 248, 258.
Historic Northern Neck of Virginia, by H. Ragland Eubank, No. 75.

FITHIAN

The Journal of Philip Vickers Fithian, 1773-74, edited by Hunter Dickinson Farish, Williamsburg, Va., 1945.

THE SCHOOL IN THE WILDWOOD

Historic Northern Neck, by H. Ragland Eubank, Nos. 31, 59.
Historical Atlas of Westmoreland County, Virginia, by David W. Eaton, p. 44.
The Life of John Marshall, by A. J. Beveridge.
Old Churches, Ministers, and Families of Virginia, by Bishop Meade, Vol. II, pp. 159-161.
James Monroe, by W. P. Cresson.
Manuscript by Rose Gouveneur Hoes, in James Monroe Law Office, Fredericksburg, Virginia.

JAMES AND JOHN

James Monroe's Childhood and Youth, by Rose Gouveneur Hoes.
James Monroe, by W. P. Cresson, 1946, Chapel Hill.
The Life of John Marshall, by Albert J. Beveridge.
Historic Northern Neck, by H. Ragland Eubank, Nos. 31, 58, 63.
Meade's *Old Churches, etc.*, V. 2, pp. 159-161.
Historical Atlas of Westmoreland County, Virginia, by D. W. Eaton, p. 44.
Binney, in Dillon, iii, pp. 287-288.

CAPTAIN DOBBY

Fithian's *Journal*.

234   THE STRONGHOLD

Historic Northern Neck, by H. Ragland Eubank.

PEDLARS
Life of Capt. John Smith, by W. Gilmore Simms, 1846.
Historic Dress in America, by Elizabeth McClellan.
Home Life in Colonial Days, by Alice M. Earle.

SEVEN SATIN PETTICOATS
Olivia Frances Jett Williams (1874-1940).

PHI BETA KAPPA
Encyclopedia of Virginia Biography, under the editorial supervision of Lyon Gardiner Tyler, LL.D., Vol. II, 1915.
The History of Phi Beta Kappa, by Oscar M. Voorhees, D.D., LL.D., 1945. (The Founding of the Society, 1776.)
"Records of Phi Beta Kappa Society of William and Mary College," printed in *William and Mary College Quarterly*, IV, 236.

LIGHT-HORSE HARRY
"Speech Delivered at Spring Celebration at Stratford," by Blake Tyler Newton, May 6, 1951. *Northern Neck Historical Magazine*, December, 1952.
The Life and Campaigns of General Robert E. Lee, by James D. McCabe, Jr., published 1866.
The Lees of Virginia, by Burton J. Hendrick.
John Marshall, by Albert J. Beveridge, p. 138.

A BAND OF BROTHERS
The Lees of Virginia, by Burton J. Hendrick.
Historic Northern Neck, by H. Ragland Eubank.
"The Six Brothers of Stratford Hall," by Rev. Edmund J. Lee, D.D., in *Northern Neck Historical Magazine*, December, 1952.

THE DIVINE MATILDA
Virginia, W. P. A., 1946.
The Lees of Virginia, by Burton J. Hendrick.
Stratford Hall and the Lees Connected With Its History, by F. W. Alexander.
"Stratford Hall," by Henry F. and Katharine Pringle, *Holiday*, January, 1953.
Historic Northern Neck, by H. Ragland Eubank.
Fithian's *Journal*.
Journal of a Young Lady of Virginia, 1782, published in Baltimore, 1788, by Lucinda Lee (daughter of Thomas Ludwell Lee).

MADAM WASHINGTON
George Washington, Vol. I, by D. S. Freeman.
Historic Northern Neck, by H. Ragland Eubank.
The Mother of Washington and Her Times, by Sara Pryor.
"Betty Lewis," by Elizabeth Dabney Coleman, *Virginia Cavalcade*, Winter, 1952.

AFTER THE REVOLUTION
"After the Revolution," by Arthur H. Jennings, *Richmond Times-Dispatch*.
Virginians at Home, by Edmund S. Morgan, 1952, p. 3.
Tobacco Coast, by Arthur Pierce Middleton, Ph.D., 1953, p. 42.
Historic Dress in America, by Elizabeth McClellan.
Virginia Methodism, by W. W. Sweet.
"The Colonial Glebes," by Emily Blayton Major, in *Richmond Times-Dispatch*.
Our Republic, by Riley Chandler Hamilton, 1910.

MANTUA

"Old 'Mantua'," by Lucy Brown Beale, from notes of Dr. George William Beale, published in the *Northern Neck Historical Magazine*, 1951.

Mr. and Mrs. Wayne Chatfield-Taylor, Mantua, Northumberland County, Virginia, 1952.

The late Miss Sallie H. Barron, Warsaw, Virginia, 1952.

PART III — *NINETEENTH CENTURY*

ROBERT E. LEE

The Lees of Virginia, by Burton J. Hendrick.

The Life of General Robert E. Lee, by James D. McCabe, Jr., published 1866.

"Stratford Hall," by Henry F. and Katharine Pringle, *Holiday Magazine*, January, 1953.

"W & L's 'Maybe Portrait'," by Sally Leverty, *Richmond Times-Dispatch*, Sunday Features, June 7, 1953.

SMITH POINT LIGHT

Blunt's *American Coast Pilot*, 1804 and 1833 issues, (courtesy of Robert H. Burgess, The Mariners' Museum, Newport News, Va.).

U. S. Coast Guard, Public Information Division, Washington, D. C. (Historically Famous Lighthouses.)

Capt. Clem F. Haynie, Reedville, Va.

Capt. Henry Haynie, Reedville, Va.

Miss Maggie Gough, Sunny Bank, Va.

THE RAIDERS

"Memoirs of Judge Samuel Downing," published in *Northern Neck Historical Magazine*, 1951.

Historic Northern Neck, by H. Ragland Eubank.

"Old Virginia Bottles," by Walter J. Sparks, published in *Richmond Times-Dispatch Sunday Magazine*, 1938.

Virginia Methodism, by W. W. Sweet.

Chesapeake Bay, by M. V. Brewington, 1953.

Virginia, W. P. A., 1946.

Hale's *United States*, 1844.

"The Chesapeake's Million Years," by Harold A. Williams, published in *The Baltimore Sun*, October 18, 1953.

STEAMBOATS

Civil War letters (unpublished).

The Chesapeake Bay Country, by Sampson Earle.

Chesapeake Bay, by M. V. Brewington, 1953.

HANNAH AND THE FALLING STARS

As told to the writer in 1932, by:

Hannah Crockett (1817-1933). A native of Northumberland County, Virginia.

Virginia Cavalcade, Winter, 1955.

The Diary of Governor John Floyd, of Virginia, 1833. (Virginia State Library.)

Northern Neck News, Warsaw, Va., February, 1931.

THE BLOCKADE

Unpublished Civil War letters (private collection).

"Annals of the War," by Col. Joseph Mayo, Hague, Va., published in *Philadelphia Public Ledger*, 1880.

Dr. Douglas S. Freeman, (correspondence).
S. Florence Covington Jett (1854-1926).
Historically Famous Lighthouses, published by U. S. Coast Guard.
Chesapeake Bay, by M. V. Brewington, 1953.

THE HOME GUARD

A notarized statement written in 1927 by a former member of the Northumberland Home Guard, Bertrand B. Haynie, Reedville, Va., addressed to the Virginia Pension Office in Richmond, and later transferred to the Archives of the Virginia State Library, Richmond. (This document was brought to the attention of the writer by Miss Eva Jett, Reedville, Va.)

"Rev. C. T. Thrift," Durham, N. C., in the Voice of the People, *Richmond Times-Dispatch*, April 5, 1952.

Incidents related to the writer by Hon. Theodore Augustus Jett (1850-1920), a member of the Northumberland Home Guard.

THE MYSTERY OF HORSE POND

As related to the writer by Hon. C. O. Hammack, Sunny Bank, Va., a grandson of Sardelia Evans.

SCHOONER IN A MILL-POND

As told to the writer in 1953 by two of Capt. Jehu's sons: Capt. Henry Haynie and Capt. Clem F. Haynie, both of Reedville, Va.

WAR BONNETS

S. Florence Covington Jett (1854-1926), a native of Northumberland County.
Estelle Betts Haynie, Reedville, Va., 1955, a native of Northumberland County.

AMANDA AND THE YANKEES

Olivia Frances Jett Williams (1874-1940).
Hannah Crocket (1817-1933). Interviewed by writer in 1932.
Bible records, letters, documents, etc.

THE HORSEHAIR RING

Olivia Frances Jett Williams (1874-1940).
Confederate Army records, Bible records, letters, obituaries, etc.
Tangible Proof: the Horsehair Ring and Confederate Note.

MIRACLE AT KETCHUM'S CAMP

S. Florence Covington Jett (1854-1926).
Hon. Theodore Augustus Jett (1850-1920), a member of the Northumberland Home Guard.

DESPERATE PASSAGE

"Rappahannock Ferry," by Turner Rose, published in *Washington Post*, March 13, 1938.
Historic Northern Neck, by H. Ragland Eubank.
"On the Trail of an Assassin," by Benjamin Herman, published in *Beltimore Sun Sunday Magazine*, 1954.
"America's Greatest Unsolved Murder," by Joseph Millard, published in *True Magazine*, February, 1953.
Virginia, W. P. A., 1946.
The Chesapeake Bay Country, by Sampson Earle, pp. 96-97.

AFTER THE WAR

Hon. J. J. McDonald, in *Northumberland Echo*, 1923.
S. Roland Hall, in *Northumberland Echo*, September 28, 1934.

A Story of the Historic Northern Neck of Virginia

Hon. Theodore Augustus Jett (1850-1920).
S. Florence Covington Jett (1854-1926).

SPEECH

Warwickshire Dialect, by Appleton Morgan.
The Cradle of the Republic, by Lyon G. Tyler.
Writings of Rev. Hugh Jones, A. M., 1722.

SHOPPING TRIPS

S. Florence Covington Jett (1854-1926), a native of Northumberland County, Va.

MENHADEN

Works of Capt. John Smith, edited by Arber.
Economic History of Virginia in the 17th Century, by P. A. Bruce.
The Menhaden Industry of the Atlantic Coast, by Rob Leon Greer, Bureau of Fisheries Document No. 811, Washington Government Printing Offce, 1917.
An Account of the Reed Family, written by the late George N. Reed, Reedville, Virginia.
American Fisheries: A History of The Menhaden, by G. Brown Goode and W. O. Atwater. New York, Orange Judd Company, 245 Broadway. Pub. 1880. (The fifth annual report of the Commissioner of Fisheries.)
Capt. Henry Haynie, Reedville, Va.
W. Harold Haynie, Reedville, Va.

THE OLD STONE PILE

Miss Maggie Gough, Mrs. Ruth Dodson, Capt. Clem Haynie and Capt. Henry Haynie, all natives of Northumberland County, Va.
1939 issue of the *Light List of the South Atlantic Coast*, (courtesy of Robert Burgess, Mariners' Museum).

KEEPERS OF THE LIGHT

Light List of the South Atlantic Coast, 1939 issue.
Capt. J. R. Moore of the Wicomico River Light, 1952.
Miss Maggie Gough, Sunny Bank, Va., and Mrs. Ruth Dodson, Edwardsville, Va.

THE HEADLESS DOG

From many traditional accounts.

WAKEFIELD · GEORGE WASHINGTON'S BIRTHPLACE

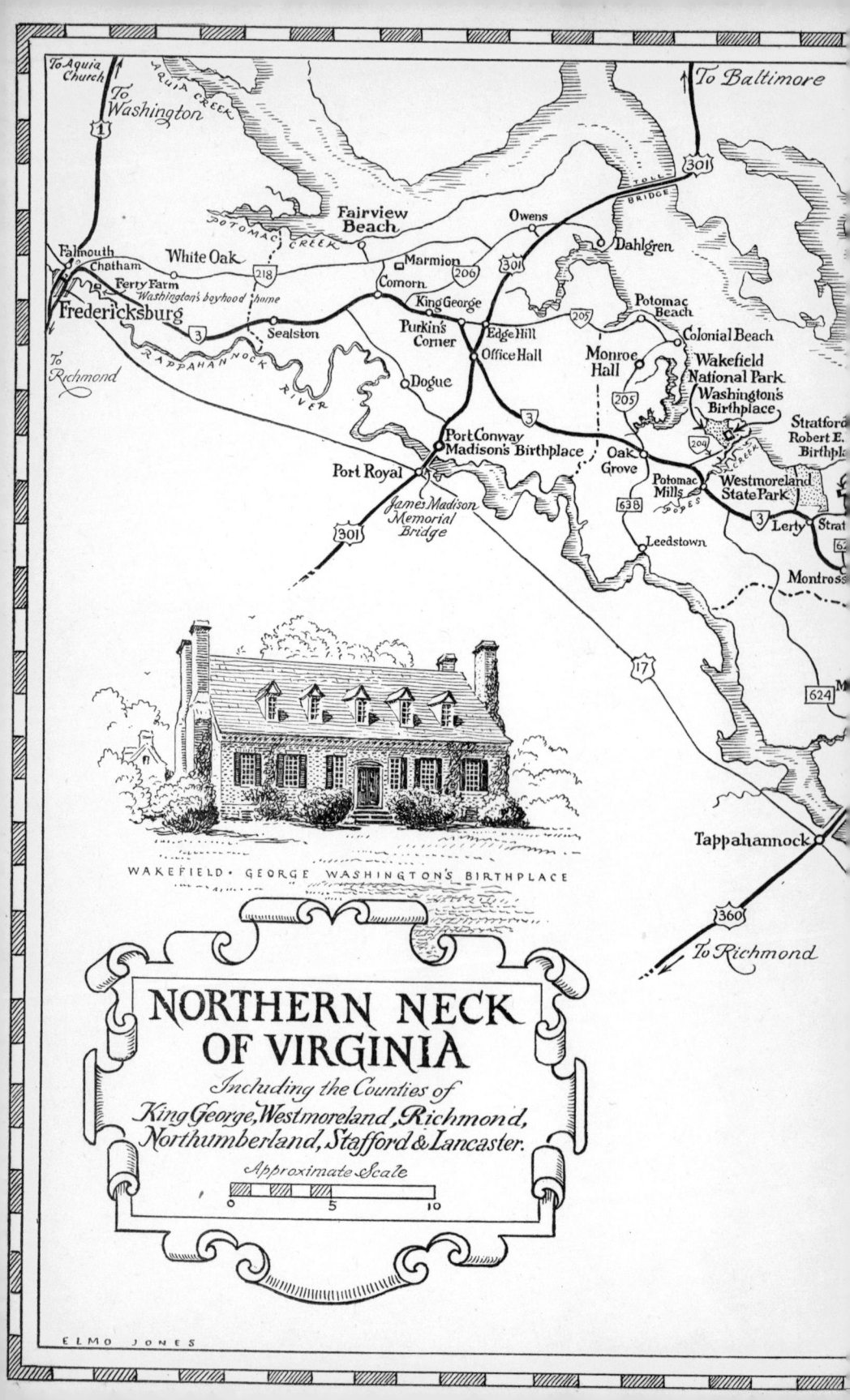

NORTHERN NECK OF VIRGINIA

Including the Counties of King George, Westmoreland, Richmond, Northumberland, Stafford & Lancaster.

Approximate Scale